Michel de Ghelderode

SEVEN PLAYS

With an Introduction by

GEORGE HAUGER

VOLUME 1

A MERMAID DRAMABOOK

HILL AND WANG · NEW YORK

A DIVISION OF FARRAR, STRAUS AND GIROUX

CONTENTS

INTRODUCTION

PERFORMANCES of Michel de Ghelderode's plays—in particular, of *Chronicles of Hell*—in Paris during 1949 caused considerable uproar. To the enthusiasm of some and to the anger of others was added the confusion of most, arising from an almost complete ignorance concerning the man who had written these plays. Since facts were not available, it was found necessary to invent them, and wild and fantastic stories about the author were heard. It was held that he was a very young man. It was maintained that he was a very old man—so old, according to some, as to have been a contemporary of Shakespeare's. He was declared to be an unfrocked priest. He was accused of lycanthropy. Speculation was boundless—and, for the most part, far from the truth. Nevertheless, one should not be too hard on the speculators. The scant information about Ghelderode that is available in print may not be extravagantly mistaken, but it is frequently inaccurate. Two of these not infrequent errors will serve as illustration. They occur in works one would have expected to be wholly reliable. In the renowned *Larousse du XXᵉ Siècle* (Supplément, 1953), we are told that Ghelderode became known by the publication of numerous stories "written simultaneously in French and Dutch." In fact, Ghelderode writes, and has always written, in French, although some of his works have been translated into Dutch; indeed, some of his plays had their first performances in that language. In *Belgian Literature* (Antwerp, 1958), Roger Bodart, a literary advisor to the Ministry of Public Education, writes, "The second play of de Ghelderode was *Saint Francis of Assisi* . . ." whereas this present volume of translations contains *Three Actors and Their Drama*, which is one of nine plays written between Ghelderode's first essay in theatre and *Saint Francis*.

A few facts about this apparently elusive playwright will not come amiss to the reader. "Few" is used deliberately, for the most important information relevant to

vii

Ghelderode's life and art will be found in the selections from *The Ostend Interviews;* furthermore, Ghelderode is concerned that his works, and not himself, shall be the object of people's attention. He wishes his writings to be judged for what they themselves are, and considers that works of art must be deficient to the extent that they need biographical justification.

Michel de Ghelderode was born in Brussels in 1898. He began writing stories in his late teens, and also at this time he haunted the Brussels marionette theatres, writing down and saving from oblivion the texts of the plays performed by the little wooden actors. His own first play was written in 1918. For a group that, every Thursday, enjoyed a lecture followed by a play, "the one more or less justifying the other," Ghelderode was to arrange an occasion dedicated to Edgar Allan Poe. But Poe wrote no plays—*Politian* hardly qualifies—so Ghelderode supplied *Death Looks In at the Window,* a play in the manner of Poe. If, previous to this occasion, he had been sensitive to the spirit of the theatre, Ghelderode now became inoculated with it. He writes, "The nail in the scenery that had made a tear in my jacket had likewise scratched my flesh." He continued to write stories and prose pieces, but could not escape a preoccupation with the theatre. In 1927 began his association with the Flemish Popular Theatre who created *Saint Francis, Barabbas,* and *Pantagleize.* In 1930, the death of the twenty-six-year-old actor Renaat Verheyen, who had played the principal roles in these plays, gave rise to Ghelderode's *The Actor Makes His Exit,* and the playwright withdrew from immediate and active collaboration in the theatre. After all, there were many things he wanted to write other than plays. But he found, as he says, that "the theatre is a trap," and although he had already written several plays that were so far unperformed, he continued to write for the theatre. He was convinced that the experience of working with the Flemish Popular Theatre had enabled him to write eminently playable works, and he was not mistaken; yet, playable as these works were, there was no rush to perform them, and their author was not concerned to pester, to convince, or even to approach theatre managers and directors. Ghelderode has said, "I am a man . . . who does not trouble about the fate of my works," and frequently in correspondence and in conversation he declares, "There is time!"—a somewhat surprising comment from one who has known illness for many years and who wrote plays true to his artistic conscience for over thirty years without enjoying what the world at large calls "recognition."

The increasing acknowledgment of Ghelderode as a playwright of genius began during the nineteen forties with the work of Catherine Toth in France. As already mentioned, he reaped the dubious reward of a *succès de scandale* in Paris with *Chronicles of Hell*. Today, the plays of this solitary by choice, whose everyday life is bounded by the walls of a room full of works of art, bric-à-brac and memories, but whose spirit is familiar with the far reaches of the universe and with man's essential nature, have been broadcast, televized, and seen in theatres from Sweden to Italy, from Poland to the United States. And Ghelderode has much more work planned, more stories, critical works, and memoirs, as well as plays—the sustained patient work of an artist who says, "As a matter of fact, I don't regard myself as either a dramatist or a storyteller, but as a poet who has used the forms of the story and the theatre." Michel de Ghelderode died in Brussels in April 1962.

Selections from

THE OSTEND INTERVIEWS

(*Entretiens d'Ostende*)

Translated by GEORGE HAUGER

The volume entitled The Ostend Interviews *derives from interviews with Ghelderode which were recorded at Ostend in August, 1951, and broadcast by Radiodiffusion Télévision Françaises in 1951–1952.*

In the present selections, the questions that Ghelderode was asked have been omitted, and the order of his comments is that in which they appear in the volume.

If I have a legend, I have had no part in it. It has been made for me. I have not contributed to it; but I shall not stoop to contradict it. The matter leaves me indifferent. The world has need of fables.

What am I?

I am going to tell you, and it is very simple.

I am a man who writes in a room—all alone—and who does not trouble about the fate of his works, who does not allow himself to be bothered by the row, the admiration, or the anger that his works may some day provoke. In short, a man who asks nothing from men except friendliness, a little tolerant understanding.

Even the theatrical representation of the world of my mind goes on apart from me. It goes on in a place where there are too many people, and on a physical plane, in the midst of an often aggressive crowd; and that makes me uncomfortable, even frightens me a little. That is why I am hardly ever seen in theatres—not from diffidence, or because of a pose, but by the fact of incompatibility, and because from the outset I chose solitude, the hard road.

Of course, dealings with men, social contacts, are necessary and valuable to us. If one denied oneself these, one would become arid, inhuman, incomprehensible: one would be analphabetic. Nevertheless, like the act of love, the work of art must be accomplished, not in darkness, but behind closed doors, in secret, away from witnesses and their curiosities, whether these be genuine or idle, away from confessions and confidences, gossip and interviews.

3

I must derive my taste for the supernatural from my mother. She was a timid soul who had remained close to nature, a primitive soul adept at the perception of the mysteries of nature, but also of certain extraphysical phenomena, and she was attracted by past ages and by the arts in their popular forms—images, for example. She was rich in proverbs, in forgotten songs, in haunted stories.

She had been at first brought up very freely in the country. Afterward she grew up in a convent at Louvain, and there she was taught the lives of the saints, there she was the witness of little miracles. She knew liturgical chant, spoke ecclesiastical Latin, and believed in the devil whom, she said, she had seen many a time.

Be that as it may, it was during this conventual period that she matured, that she really took possession of traditions, hair-raising stories and ancient legends, which she recounted to me, and recounted to me alone. My brothers and my sister hardly bothered themselves about them.

My father was principal clerk at the Archives Générales. He spent a lifetime there, and after his retirement he carried on his researches and his Benedictine tasks, to which he never put his signature. He worked as a subordinate for historians and genealogists, deciphering and copying for them dusty documents, charters, ancient obituary registers, letters patent, acts of magistrates—work without glory, but of good account.

Such was our everyday background—parchments, yellowed papers, illegible or faded writings that my father succeeded in reading, as though hypnotized, through a huge magnifying glass. As for seals, they were his speciality. All of this in a sepulchral silence, and also there was a smell. . . .

The house was overrun by the souls of these ancient papers.

Was it the odor of History, the odor of the Past?

Once I put the question.

"Rat's piddle," the dear man replied.

But this odor saturated me forever. And I came across it again when in my turn I became an archivist, as I was during twenty or so years. But, more venturesome in spirit than my author, I used these peaceful years to create my theatre, hiding behind files and bundles of papers to preserve appearances.

I fell in love with things of the past as every other child falls in love with his toys. I saw nothing else around me—the great wax or metal seals, and those fine counterseals in their wooden box, these greasy sheets of parchment, these diplomas in weird writing, these letters patent ornamented with coats of arms, at the bottom of which tremendous signatures displayed themselves, the Empress Maria Theresa, Philip II, Charles V, and others—from time to time, a Duke of Burgundy.

My father showed me these astounding relics in all artlessness. With his spectacles on his nose, he would laugh contemptuously, *"Fuerunt."* He also laughed that way because I sat with my behind on a great register in which the sentences of death of the Council of Troubles, or rather the Tribunal of Blood, created by the sinister Duke of Alba, were written. Yes, in this bloody book you could find the minutes of the condemnations to capital punishment of the Counts Egmont and Horn, among hundreds of others. And, in all innocence, I was sitting on it! Again, there were papers that had been pushed away to one corner of the table between the bread and the plates at the evening meal. I remember bundles of letters from Peter Paul Rubens, to some canon, to some Flemish or Italian Maecenas, about the purchase of a canvas, about the disposal of works of art, about grievances, about disputes, with grandiloquent formulas of politeness such as they loved at that time: "Your Lordship's most humble servant . . ."

My father talked to me a little about these things because I was the only one who happened to be close by him and to listen to him. I was something of his reflection during these evening hours, his shadow, like the dog or the cat on the hearth. I loved him for these rare things, just as, at other times, I hated him for having killed a sparrow and a cricket.

Pedagogues fancy, quite wrongly, that a dreaming child dreams exclusively unclean things. What do they know of the world of childhood which they left prematurely and whose paths they would not be able to find again?

I dreamed wildly, but I watched the flight of a bee, a

distant window on fire, or the progress of a white cloud
shaped like a swan. "What are you dreaming about, sir?"
"About Lohengrin, sir"—for I had treated myself to
Wagner's opera at the *Monnaie* one fine Sunday. I read—
something that was little appreciated by my teachers—
but I didn't read forbidden books. I didn't understand
them. They remained foreign to me. I think I have told
you, I didn't awaken to the things of the flesh until late.
I was not born to be of the Don Juan type, not in the
least. Woman has been no more the eternal driving power
in my life than she has been the inevitable subject of my
plays. I have been reproached for this as a defect—yes,
indeed!

I have always loved old churches, in the same way as
theatres. I willfully say the old ones, not the others; in
the same way as old-fashioned theatres, gilded and purple,
with a crystalline prism chandelier. Places of enchantment!

Yes, I have always admired rites, the stage management
of offices, the glamour of processions and funerals. Somewhere in *Fastes d'Enfer* [*Chronicles of Hell*], I think, I
make one of my characters say, "Only the church buries
well," and that is true enough.

I cannot go past one of the churches of the past, one
of our old chapels, without going inside, even at the risk
of being promptly driven out by what I find there in the
way of wretched prayer books and abominable pieces of
art, and because I don't find the lively and radiant solitude without which the presence of the divine does not
operate.

What do I do in these holy places? What would I do
other than tell the golden beads of dreams? And if you
allow that meditation is a form of prayer, you will see
me attentive to the call of the angels, to the secret signal
from a mystic country whither I shall go when the flame
has left the ashes. You should also know that at certain
moments I hear an aerial music which, for me, is another sign, an everlasting language which accompanies the
whole of my life: I hear bells living, breathing, and
rambling on. I am a bell-fancier. A strange passion, isn't
it? Not only religious bells, but civil bells also, those
carillons that Flanders invented, both the tragic bells with
bloody mouths and the triumphant with golden tongues.

Many a time I have traveled to a very ancient and altogether hieratic city of the North, Bruges, where the bells and the carillons are innumerable, and where, more than anywhere else, they speak well, are eloquent. And there, in this medieval city which hasn't changed much, I lived in the sound of these carillon recitals, storms of chimes, funeral forges of All Saints. The bells celebrated by Poe and Verhaeren were not yet electrified.

The Flanders I loved abided in this, nothing but this: bells and their towers. It could not be but so. The Flanders that bowled over Rainer Maria Rilke with its ghostly beauties.

Furthermore, you will frequently come across them in my writings, in my plays. They are like an obbligato accompaniment. They are a musical sign announcing the intrusion, the imminence of the supernatural, the approach of mystery.

My work is no more anticlerical than it is proclerical. If I deal with persons of the cloth in a way that rouses your indignation, I am not aiming at institutions or dogmas—neither those of the Roman religion nor those of any other religion. [. . .]

Why shouldn't people make a Catholic author of me, while they are about it, on the excuse that I have put saints on the stage?

Yes, why shouldn't the fact of having written works with biblical inspiration such as *Barabbas*, or having been the author of plays such as *Saint François d'Assise*, prove me a purveyor of Catholic literature?

No, I don't practice that profession: I don't create that kind of theatre. It is a propagandist theatre, a theatre of patronage.

I no more think of edifying than of corrupting—or of convincing.

My second life began the day I realized that I was destined for one or other of the shabby occupations toward which my brothers were heading—banking, business, commerce, and whatnot. And my worthy father hoped for something similar for his youngest, something safe and respectable. He assumed me to be of mediocre intelligence. In his eyes, a civil servant was the best thing there was in this conformist world.

But, in fact, I was not bothering myself about the future.

More than anything else, I was dreaming.

I had plenty of time, and I believed life was long.

It is.

Moreover, I was already feeling the need for this second life, a secret life that I kept dark, like a hidden treasure. It was the realm of dreams to which, alone, I had found the magic keys. Paternal sermons were obliterated by those of Eulenspiegel, by the preaching of Reynard. And the extravagant discourses of the ingenious Hidalgo completed this topsy-turvy education. Somewhat intoxicated by the discovery of my coming autonomy, I thought about painting, I thought about music, not knowing exactly what, and I was the prey of confused and contradictory aspirations like the young German romantics whose drama was that of not being able to make up their minds between an artistic and an intellectual discipline.

I served the apprenticeship of a painter. Like other youngsters, I daubed about for some years; without result, if not without conviction.

Fervently, I went in for music; but the study of an instrument soon left me disappointed and did not offer an end in itself.

Then I turned toward writing—since that was what I was to do. But I was still unaware of that. One must take it that the time had not yet arrived.

I no longer go to concerts—I, who was so fond of virtuosi! I deny myself this delight. That is because I am very receptive and it has happened that I have been plunged into an inexpressible condition after certain hearings, certain revelations of important works. Prolonged euphoria became a means of atrophying the creative will.

So, I avoid music as one avoids pleasures that are too violent, too powerful. . . .

Still, it continues to help me in the form of phonograph records that I sometimes listen to in my solitude; but I no longer reckon to move out of a particular musical world which is my proper domain and which I do not seek to enlarge, although I am heedful of new forms.

It is the polyphonic world of the Flemings and the Italians, the medieval and pre-Renaissance polyphony of Guillaume de Machaut, of Dufay, Obrecht, Orlandus de Lassus, Palestrina, and others. It leads up to him who dominates all in the past and the future, Bach.

There is my great man of music, Johann Sebastian Bach.

I also retain a very great attachment to sacred music, which is a way of religion to me. Art as religion, and perfectly so.

As for liturgical chant, that is my luxury on selected occasions—like reading Ruysbroeck l'Admirable.

But equally there are kinds of popular music that very often enlighten me—Spanish, for example. And when I am *available*, as M. Gide puts it, I very much enjoy fairground cacophonies, orchestrions, street organs, mechanical pianos, not forgetting nostalgic accordions. I followed a one-man band for days through the alleys of my old city. What a creature!

As for the music of my own time, syncopated music, I acknowledge its existence, but never when I am working. It wearies me very quickly; it distresses me. The silence that follows it is that of the morgue, its odor is that of human carrion. I feel a kind of incurable sadness in it, and I flee this misery of the soul because it is too contagious, too insinuating, and rarely in a pure state as in music taken from its popular sources. They say to me, *Rhythm:* I reply, *Spasm.*

These grindings make me think of outer darkness, of the jerkings of *danses macabres.*

But music, yes! The Mass of Pope Marcellus, The Pastoral Symphony, and the sublime Berlioz, and my friend Moussorgsky. Yes, I would give a half-century of contemporary music for an air by the Chevalier Gluck! But music is constantly present, believe me, it is always there, and it provides, if I may say so, a deep pedal to the whole of my toilsome existence.

A kind of education of the ear leads me to demand a certain music in human speech.

On the stage you can feel very strongly that a musical requirement is prevalent in my prose, in my theatrical language.

Then again, many works have come to me with music in their interstices, an underlying music. This is a fact that has often struck me—while I was writing certain plays, I had old refrains in my head and they followed me and pursued me the whole length of my work.

I can give examples.

The writing of my first theatrical work of any importance, *La Mort du Docteur Faust* [Winter 1924-25], was accompanied in this way by a tune from the fair—a sort of Rhenish dance that a Limonaire organ played doggedly not far from my window.

If such a tune did not really furnish the climate of sound of my play, it helped me to write it all the same. It was sufficient for me, at about three o'clock in the afternoon, to hear this orchestrion which painfully awoke, yawned, then suddenly burst out like a catastrophe, submerging the neighborhood, for me to be hurled roughly, headfirst, into the suspended play. The music literally bore me along, like the torrent from a lock that has been suddenly opened.

I have often introduced refrains and songs into my plays, not as tricks, but from necessity.

That was the case in *La Balade du Grand Macabre* [1934] and in *Mademoiselle Jaire* [1934], where singing actors appeared. I heard them coming. I hummed their verses, their laments, with them. Sometimes the tunes were of my invention, to be sure, and they were probably incoherent; but what mattered to me was that they were in place and held me bound to my writing.

Yet another example: *Escurial* [1927] made me play over in my mind a record I possessed at that time, a harsh and dreary song, somewhat gypsy, somewhat Arab—dreadfully Spanish. I found in it the mephitic, savage, and gloomy atmosphere of a Spain that I wished to raise up, that of a Philip II and contemporary with the building of the Escorial and, indeed, the blazing days of the Holy Inquisition.

But this phenomenon is not very peculiar to me. Many writers as well as the poets have these solicitudes of a harmonic order, admit to similar manias. And if music has helped me a great deal in my work, I will add that it has at the same time remained a kind of recompense and a lasting aspect of my disquiet.

I have already told you, I do not misuse it, and most often I do without it because it torments me. When I am impressed by a work, by a concert that pleases me, I do not sleep. All night I reconstitute the music received as a gift from Heaven, in the same way that I reconstitute poems I have heard and which have ricocheted in my heart as in the depths of a well.

It is, moreover, this same eternal music that we demand from poems that I want to find again in the best theatre, welling up hidden in the dramatic prose, and running beneath it, murmuring and invisible.

There is indeed a certain *Poetic Theatre*—or allegedly so—which is rarely a vehicle for poetry. Let us beware of Poetry announced by placards.

Without the verbal incantation which renders it dependent on magic, the theatre disintegrates of itself, crumbles away in words, renounces its priority over other forms of literature, and disclaims its obsessional or possessional power, its marvels.

A kind of serious accident was necessary in my young life for me to discover my true territory.

This happened toward my sixteenth year, at the beginning of the 1914–1918 war.

I was gravely ill from a contagious malady that almost carried me off, and after having been hanging between life and death during a whole winter, I had to leave my classical studies in the lurch, on the verge of finishing them. It was like a metamorphosis, for, on coming out of convalescence, childhood had gone for me, or, at least, was making off very quickly with long strides; and I awoke a man.

It was then that I took up a pen for the first time, immediately feeling the enchantment and the pathos of this new gesture.

Here, then, was a means of getting to know myself better, of living more generously, of resisting my native sadness better, or of denying the encompassing tragedy, or holding out against meanness and against the ugliness of the so common life—by the somewhat magical use of the "Little Stump of Wood," as Jarry* called the penholder!

Doubtlessly, like all young folk who pledge themselves to the writing desk, I must have begun by writing poems; but I haven't the faintest recollection of them. I can no

* *Alfred Jarry* (1873–1907), French writer who led a strange bohemian life. His most celebrated work is the play *Ubu Roi* which, some claim, had a great influence on French Dadaist writers. The following is a revealing comment of Jarry's, ". . . talking about comprehensible things only serves to weigh the mind down and to warp the memory, whereas the absurd exercises the mind and makes the memory work." [Translator's note.]

longer find any of these attempts—and so much the better.

Similarly, I must have kept a *Journal*. And why not *Memoirs*, after the fashion of all adolescents who haven't yet begun to live?

Meanwhile, I read a great deal, and in a happy enough way. I didn't devour books. I wasn't an avid reader; but I remained under the spell, and I don't know if it was a grace of Destiny's, but I came across decisive works which revealed the existence of myth, of the mythical character, to me. I breathed at a certain altitude to which one doesn't have access until older, and after certain trials.

Thus it was that I discovered *Don Quixote*—and not as an adolescent thirsting after action. I was struck forcibly by the size and the humanity of this intoxicating work which overwhelmed me to the extent of tears. All my life I have reread Cervantes, who never leaves my side, and I always read him in the same way—in the tragic vein. This is one of the works that resolutely pushed me toward pure literature, as the *Colloquies* of dear Erasmus pushed me toward a more theatrical art.

But it wasn't until after the discovery of that other epic tale, Charles de Coster's *Legend of Eulenspiegel*, that I set about writing in a determined way, in 1916–1917— and, to tell the whole truth, the discovery at the same time of the adorable *Gil Blas*.

At the same time I was reading a lot of other things as well, notably the works of Belgians—of Camille Lemonnier, of Georges Eekhoud, who afterward became my master and my friend, of Max Elskamp, of Franz Hellens too, that incomparable taleteller who was going to help me on so importantly. But it was principally *The Legend and the Heroic, Joyful and Glorious Adventures of Eulenspiegel and Lamme Goedzak in the Land of Flanders and Elsewhere* that gave me the desire to practice an autochthonic art, to try to write a work of some resonance —a work which might not be national (a term covering so many mediocrities that it is preferable to ignore it) but a work which might be *patriale*, if I dare use this adjective which is not at all French, but which expresses so well what I want to say: a *patriale* work, in short, a work that might be ancestral and traditionally of my home, while still being accessible to men of my time everywhere.

You can't separate my works whether prose, theatre, or even essay. It all comes from the same mind, from the same sensibility, and I have never attached importance to difference of forms, even though the theatre has taken precedence over the rest.

I went to the theatre from necessity, because this form turned out to suit me—unless the theatre came to me! I didn't take hold of this form: it took hold of me. That is the truth. One doesn't choose. Or so little!

Today it seems that my stories are a preparation for my plays and that in these plays is the substance of stories.

But what is the point of seeking out these cross references?

I sum up for you: I believe my work, looked at from the standpoint that my age permits, is one whole.

[. . .] I hold that to be authentic a play must be able to be recounted, to be communicated as a story—even if it is a cock-and-bull story. Failing this there would only be an incomplete structure, clouds in the flies, smoke on the stage—plays that never begin.

Take note, then, that a being endowed with any poetic sense is sensitive to the supernatural.

It is around us; it is in us.

Have you come across your image already present in an old mirror?

That some people never perceive the encompassing supernatural proves nothing. Let us say that they are impervious to everything, to poetry, to music, to light, to love, to the cries of the world, to the chorus of the dead, to the phosphorescence of the living, to metamorphosis, to anamorphosis.

Only the brute can deny that we are surrounded by the supernatural, that we lose our footing to the extent that reason advances in its sloping territories, its nocturnal borderlands.

You can perceive it, unexpectedly come across its messages in the humblest things, the most everyday things. I have an angel on my shoulder and a devil in my pocket! In order to reassure you, I don't say that everything breathes the supernatural; but could you dissociate it from art without great damage?

I love this solitude in all purity for its own sake. It is necessary to me. It is my security. I can do nothing without it. It is my collaborator, and I believe the artist can do nothing really great outside solitude.

Without solitude I am unable to write—not only at the moment of writing, but well before then, and even afterward, from the time that the dream kindles on my brow until it grows cold again, burnt out.

I have need of these long shores of silence and solitude, otherwise I wander endlessly.

It is a purification, a hygiene of the soul. And even now I still jealously guard this solitude that nothing will make me leave.

I tell you again, my destiny is to be alone, to work in my room.

Montaigne speaks truth. Solitude has its pitfalls. It is a way of life I wouldn't impose upon anyone; but this way of life suits me and confers upon me the state of bilocation indispensable to spiritual adventure and to the writing of art that records it.

[. . .] Death can be put off, one can receive a respite from Destiny, but Death will be back, rest assured of it! Even if you do not love him, he stays with you, and he is the only person of whose constancy you can be sure. Crown him with roses!

From the time I began to think, I have found myself faced with enigmas. To the extent that I have had faith, a reply has been made for me: the Church has replied for me.

But when this faith became diverted, I had to re-think the essential problems of our life, of our human condition —what all things would become, and what would be their end.

And it is with infinite curiosity that I advance slowly toward this last ending—curtain fall or curtain rise! Is that clearly put?

I shall finish by knowing what is behind.

And this fear of the night gives value to our days.

But what name can we rightly give to this fear? Let us say anxiety. This anxiety shows through all my works. Without it, what would be their meaning? They would consist of literary games, little tales more or less neatly parceled up.

And I do not write little tales, for if I take up my pen, committing outrage on my idleness, it is more to fix this fear than to deliver myself from it—this fear so old that I believe it was born with the earth, which is so old.

Fear of that fear which took hold of me at the very beginning and which doesn't leave me, of that fear which each man has on him and which has his odor.

Now you know why I write pages that sometimes appear to be unpleasant and that seem to be cruel; but I cannot do otherwise. This is my art. And not the art of an egoist, for my own private use. I give all to everyone, the sweat of my brow. This art is worth what it is worth; but it helps me to live, in the way I describe—always seeking the puppetmaster and the meaning of the play we are acting.

[. . .] I discovered the world of shapes before discovering the world of ideas.

When I was quite a child, I was sensitive to public demonstrations—processions, parades, fairs, strikes, popular disturbances—to all open-air entertainments, funerals as well, triumphal entries, liturgical pomps, carnivals, masked balls. Equally, I conceded a great deal of importance to furniture, to clothes, to decoration, to the world of things that are believed to be dead. I was struck by everything that ordinarily doesn't surprise other children: dummies in shop windows, electric signs, statues in gardens, the enigmatic Hermes in the old park, the gesticulations of the trees, all that was color or movement— or seemed to contain mystery. And then, I was curious about entertainments that were still forbidden to me because of my age. I might have been twelve years old when I made my way into fascinating halls—where I passed unnoticed. There I gazed on operas which I little understood but which enchanted me. I initiated myself into ballet. I witnessed bloody melodramas like *La Tour de Nesle*. So, little by little, this vocation for the theatre strengthened itself in me. And I must have been well bitten when, at about seventeen or eighteen, I set about reading a great amount of dramatic literature, whose impression I still retain—notably the plays of Schiller and those of Victor Hugo. In spite of his redundancy and all that is laughable today, Victor Hugo greatly impressed me in his time: *Ruy Blas,* fairly enough, and even works which are less defensible but which contained good moments, highly contrived scenes which I accepted without discussion because, at the same time, I was discovering the underground theatre, the world of popular marionettes, where grandiloquence is obligatory, like the plume and the dagger, the poison and the sealed letter!

However, all of this hadn't yet been very decisive, and I insist that it was painting, giving colors to form, that led me toward the art of the theatre.

I had already very quickly made my choice in the galleries.

Naturally, I went to the works of my country, those of the master Hieronymus Bosch, of Pieter Breughel, of Teniers, of Jordaens. And this application accustomed me to the portrayed characters, settings, and lightings that I later found once more when I put my feet on the stage. All was familiar to me, known, on the scale of the vast compositions that I had lately admired.

So, in spite of its small size—but what does that mean?— [Pieter] Breughel's painting entitled "The Parable of the Blind Men" had left me with so intense a recollection that after many years, in 1933, I transposed this touching pictorial anecdote to the theatre, in a few hours and with great ease.

It was the same with *La Pie sur le Gibet* [1935]. A Breughel painting was the origin. Yes, Breughel again. You see that this master has played a very great part in my career. For me he is always present, for his work is not only wonderful painting; equally, it offers a vision of the world, a philosophy.

Yet another of my plays, *Masques Ostendais* [1935], was also inspired in me by a painting; but this time it was a contemporary master, James Ensor, who was born and who died in this very city of Ostend where we are.

The Anglo-Flemish Ensor painted low women, down-and-outs, the fishermen of the port, all the maritime common people who work hard and who allow themselves no less rough compensations.

It is in one of the old interiors of the houses of these fine folk that I set the frenzied carnival of *Masques Ostendais.*

Once again, I had only transposed the vision of a painter.

For me, a theatrical work does not exist without the sensuousness proper to the plastic arts, or, in that case, exists only as a dialogue which can be read and does not call for realization on the stage.

[. . .] Possessing a perfect knowledge of the English language, literature, and, above all, the theatre of the Elizabethan age, [Georges Eekhoud] published several translations and certain scholarly works which, even now, can still be read with profit—notably *Au Siècle de Shakespeare*.

It is thanks to Georges Eekhoud that I was able to recognize the greatness of this age, when passions were extreme, when life was perilous, the Counter Reformation not yet having carried out its ravages.

It was the Renaissance in all its purple glory—but for so little a time.

Also, in spite of the political censorship which must not be forgotten, the authors of the time—these extraordinary contemporaries of Shakespeare—were able to bring onto the stage the picture of the manners of their time, and these manners were juicy in a way different from our own.

This was true for England and equally so for Italy. You only need to read Stendhal's *Chroniques Italiennes* to assure yourself of it. Life had the same savor in Florence and in London. And do you think that it was insipid in Paris under the Valois?

That was what Georges Eekhoud revealed to me, the hugeness of the men of yesterday. It's not so much a matter of the works of an age as the spirit of that age. And that is what made me say that since the Renaissance, man has never stopped on his downward road, losing his autonomy, losing face. . . .

What mattered to me was finding access to an authentic world, to men of great size and powerful voice, with whom nothing was small or mean.

Examine the historical events of that time, reread what the Elizabethan theatre tells us of them, and we are soon forced to admit that in our poor state as modern men we could not any longer bear this way of complete living, in the best and in the worst. And, after all, what are two or three centuries?

Georges Eekhoud, applying himself to *Au Siècle de*

Shakespeare, showed me that these playwrights were not
hindered by rules, by academic instruction. He opened
my eyes not on the theatre, but on the size of the theatre.
He taught me that the theatre was in truth *the mirror of
nature*. An integral nature and in a state of expansion,
rather than a conformist nature read over and corrected
for the use of a society that thinks itself decent because
it has disowned all passions.

A total nature—with all the horror and sublimity that
this entails, for the men of the Renaissance were the an-
nouncers of Romanticism and they swung between two
extremes, the ecstasy of living and the horror of living.
They were perhaps full of sentimentality, especially in
their elegies and their elegant plays; but for the rest they
were prepared for anything, to protect their individuality.
To sum up, this age holds up to us an infinitely complex
and contradictory humanity, florid in colors and strong
in odor. On Fortune's wheel, man is high or low—the
average man is of our time. This is the lesson held out to
me by the Elizabethans, Shakespeare, essentially (or whoever hides under his name—it matters little, and you can't
get away from him) and then Kyd, Marlowe, and Ben
Jonson and Cyril Tourneur, and others as well, Massinger,
John Ford . . .

However, at the same time, I underwent another influence which was as elevating although of a different kind:
that of Spain. The Spain of a Philip II and of a Theresa
of Avila, but also the Spain of Cervantes and of a hundred
other "fools" of the theatre, the dramatists of the Golden
Age, Lope de Vega, Tirso de Molina, Alarcón, Calderón,
and all that illustrious assembly led not only by the
Cervantes of *Don Quixote*, but also by the dramatist
of *La Numancia* and *The Two Chatterboxes*.

I was even more attracted by all of these writers because they freely spoke of Flanders. The theatre of the
Golden Age is hypnotized by Flanders and includes many
military plays in which it is merely a question of honor
and of prodigious exploits, seen from the Spanish point
of view, of course, and always to the glory of the King,
the army, Don John of Austria, Farnese, Álvarez of To-
ledo.

This theatre, notably because of its action, remains
thrilling today. It is little known in French, and the more's
the pity. It contains odd plays that ought to be brought

to light again, considering what some nations have "borrowed" from these lively fellows.

Naturally, I was unable to read all of these English and Spanish writers in their original tongue. I was only able to know them through more or less faithful translations. What did that matter since in these go-betweens there was the essential lesson—set the rules at naught!

Yes, all these dramatists, the Elizabethans in the van, taught the fledgling author to free himself from these rules, which are paralyzing, and it is thanks to them that I have always written plays as it suited me, in accordance with my perspective, and not in accordance with an eventual audience. And since one does not write plays for oneself, I have written for an imaginary public which, perhaps, had existed or could exist one day—not for the immediate public.

No doubt this is why I called this theatre, which was free from the worry of probable performance, *experimental*. It was a poetic form that suited me, a very versatile and a very rich instrument, much more thrilling than the story as I practiced it, or the novel which I didn't "feel."

As a result of the childhood that I have already told you about, that solitary childhood, I loved mystery, I loved drama, I even loved, as I have confessed, my own fear.

That is why, quite young, I came across a whole literature toward which my yearnings were pushing me, and if I haven't the least recollection of the novels of Horace Walpole or Ann Radcliffe, I still feel the dread I experienced during my reading of *The Monk*, by Lewis.

Equally, I remember *Notre Dame de Paris* and *L'Homme qui rit*, which I very much want to read again.

And then, certain of Balzac's stories, his admirable metaphysical stories written under the influence of Jean-Paul. But, more prominently, there were the German romantics. I retain a very vivid recollection of Arnim, and above all of Hoffmann, the master Hoffmann, who was one of my bedside authors, and to whom, furthermore, I remain faithful.

Hoffmann, that staggering man who is so close to us, is badly translated, and it's a great pity. *Le Chat Mürr* and *La Princesse Brambilla* apart, we have only been given abridged versions, adapted to the French taste, as the translators of yesterday put it.

Finally, one must set down among these gloomy writers Barbey d'Aurevilly, Pétrus Borel, Charles Baudelaire, Villiers de l'Isle-Adam, and the master of them all, Edgar Allan Poe.

We are relatives. We make up a huge family. It isn't possible not to be the friend of Edgar Allan Poe. Modern literature is indebted to him for his most acute perceptions.

He was the very first to be able to put down the inexpressible, the unutterable.

His influence has been considerable. Through Baudelaire, for example, Villiers de l'Isle-Adam, and many others, it shines as far as us, it affects our contemporaries. I dare to assert this!

I don't know the theories of Freud. I distrust these specious operations and I protect myself against all the works of science as against the plague.

Likewise, I don't read philosophers. Nor sociologists. In my opinion, the dramatic author has no need to know so much. The theatre is an art of instinct. The intrusion of psychoanalysis, or of any analytical element, into the theatre seems to me harmful. The dramatic author must live by vision and divination only, the part played by the intellect remaining auxiliary. Reason serves to supervise the facts supplied by instinct.

Freud? This must be a fashion, a precarious idea of man defrauded of divine direction. And a fashion is slavery. I saw the birth of this fashion. I have seen the ravages of this fashion. In my opinion, the author who submits his work to a system of this kind is infected, lost. Such a one reverts to political or denominational theatre, always the same mistake: he will create one-way and transitory theatre that may be profitable to the literary man but which objects to Man and denies all liberty of creation.

Directed, premeditated, this theatre feeds on marginal references and hints, on countersigns and annotations. It is a theatre that opens the door to all literatures and to the worst of literatures. No.

My characters are what they are, just as they have come, incorrigible. I don't know if they are psychoanalyzable, as they say, or if they bear with them cholera or poetry. I don't know the current jargon and I don't bother myself about it. To the title of intellectual, which stinks, I prefer that of artisan—which has a good smell. . . .

But beyond this infatuation [with the expressionist novelties of the 1920's] there was the theatre. It was very necessary to return to it, and the principal motive of the theatre was not stage technique, the discovery of unknown accents and strange gestures, the discovery of an unexpected perspective or of lighting of a kind never seen before: the profound motive of the theatre remained man, or humanity. To express the man of one's time, and through him man eternal.

And it was to this unconditional and timeless theatre that I very quickly returned after wandering around for five or six years like all the dramatists of my time for whom the theatre wasn't an industry.

My first work for the Flemish Popular Theatre was a *Saint François d'Assise* [1927]. Johan de Meester, the director and founder of the company, had ordered from me a commemorative play that put the life of the *Poverello* on the stage. I accepted on condition that there was no question whatsoever of an edifying play—the work would be such, naturally, since I was putting the life of a saint on the stage—but I remained free in the face of my inspiration. No style was imposed on me.

Then it became possible to see an astounding thing, a play (which was apparently religious) putting a saint on the stage in the most unexpected ways, the most modern ways, ways borrowed from music hall, pantomime, and ballet. Whence the joy and surprise of the artless country public, because the means set in action were very direct, very simple. Thus one saw at times angels swinging on trapezes, like acrobats. Thus were Francis' miracles expressed through pantomime. And there were clownish irruptions, the alternation of tragic and comic making up a play full of shocks that is still not forgotten to this moment. It was a kind of revolution.

There were incidents. The champions of the old romantic or realist theatre found my ideas of the representation of the life of a saint subversive, or even sacrilegious. The clergy protested, also a section of the press. Henri Ghéon, the well-known author of edifying plays (some of which, moreover, are not without merit), Henri Ghéon, a Protestant converted to Catholicism, was not one of the least scandalized. He had seen Saint Francis dancing! Yes, in a transport of joy, Francis had danced among his brethren. He was happy, and this was his way of praising the Lord and creation: he danced.

That evening, Henri Ghéon asked me, "Would you dare, in the end, to make Christ dance?"

"And why not? I deny myself making Him speak, but not making Him dance. Do you know that He didn't dance, since He had a human nature like ours? He wept indeed; why shouldn't He have known joy? Is dancing immoral in itself? Isn't the mass, in a certain way, a sacred ballet? And is Catholicism a necessarily sanctimonious religion?"

Henri Ghéon made no reply to the infidel he suspected me of being. Since then I have come across many other critics in good faith—and in bad faith too.

To finish with *Saint François d'Assise*, this play was a complete success. From then onward, I was "set up," if I dare say so. I knew the public. Not only the collections of hybrid spectators in the capitals and what is comically called the elite, but also the crowds in the little towns and in the country, in which there moves a collective spirit, or as much of it as remains in our day.

In the end, the essential thing about this experience [of having written plays for the Flemish Popular Theatre] was that on going back into my ivory tower, in 1930, I was going to be able to work comfortably. You must believe that I was not disillusioned. For the future, I was very familiar with the resources of actors, the possibilities of staging, up-to-date equipment, the practical life and the economy of the theatre. It was necessary that I should have gone through all this on the other side of the footlights. But I also aspired to something else. This direct contact, these realizations, left me unsatisfied. In fact, I was nostalgic for the theatrical dream that I had lived in at the time of my studies and that success had been unable to destroy. Now and again I even regretted not having remained the poet, the storyteller, writing plays to be read, plays that were theatrically inept, impractical. And it was toward that, toward the work of art, that I turned back; or at least thought I was turning back. Later, life offered me a rude contradiction in bringing me, in spite of myself, to those crowds from whom I saw myself forever separated. In any case, I preserved the benefit of experience, and in the future my plays were going to be marked by a certain virtue that I shall style workmanlike. They would be organically made for the stage: they would be playable. No doubt my plays would be able to be read, as formerly; but also they would have to be played: they would be above all for playing, even when I gave them an apparently difficult shape. Of course, it has often been maintained that those plays that outrage conventions and demand an effort of adaptation or as-similation do not appear to be playable, even that they are not playable. One has seen, since then: they were made for the stage. But isn't it easier to declare unplayable that which one hasn't the courage to put on because it demands work, because it constitutes a risk of displeasing what is wrongly held to be Public Opinion (never so stupid as directors, actors . . . and authors take it to be)?

Yes, marionettes were the great concern of the whole of my childhood, I'll even say of the whole of my career.

Even today I collect marionettes, dolls, puppets, little rag creatures that the children of today scorn—also dummies with lovely mortal faces of wax, models of hands, adorable heads of young martyrs, severed by what executioner?

I welcome all these human shapes and reminders of hu-man shapes to my home; I collect these image-beings as treasures. They are silent presences—I say they are pres-ences, presumptions.

All these effigies thrill me by the fact of their some-what magical nature, and even though flesh and blood actors can weary me and often disappoint me, marionettes, because of their natural reserve and silence, manage to console me for the cacophony of the play and the crazy glibness of the impudent creatures that theatre people most often are.

Furthermore, I owe them the disclosure of the theatre, the theatre in its pure state, the theatre in its savage state, the original theatre.

Naturally, I wasn't able to understand all this from my first playtime. The marionette was then a toy, my favorite toy, even my passion—other toys gave me no pleasure.

But even then I believed—and this strange belief is not yet dead in me—that objects were sensitive, living.

"Objects," says a poet, "objects are signs." Have you never noticed that there are objects that are hostile to us, and others that are benevolent? And there are some which are still neutral and waiting to reveal themselves.

One has seen objects seeking to do one ill, to hurt one physically, and Hieronymus Bosch has depicted very well for us the inscrutable, redoubtable world of things. He shows you a knife, for example, an innocent and terrible knife, from which legs have suddenly sprung and which comes toward you hypocritically—today it would be called radio-controlled.

Most certainly you yourself have such a knife. Suddenly it wounds you. You don't know why. You will never know why. You will say, "An accident!" but at the same time you can't help noticing how strange all accidents are, and their circumstances.

Aren't there sounds that the human ear cannot hear? Also certain colors remain imperceptible to our eyes. And do you think that we have smelled all the perfumes, all the odors?

You know what I think of the imperfection of our senses. Well, couldn't the most customary objects have a secret life that we haven't the power to make out, a capacity for joy and suffering, a memory, and even nerves?

Listen, I remember having searched in the rain—I was still quite a child—for a wooden horse that I had left outside. I felt how much the horse must be suffering to be thus abandoned, and in the night I went to him and brought him back into the house, to where it was dry. I was at last relieved, and only then was I able to go back to sleep. Forty years later, the horse came back, bright-eyed and laughing heartily! It was he who had grown up—but I too had grown up!

It was the same with the "smaller than I" dolls. Moreover, by their shape and their structure marionettes and dolls cannot be other than the objects that are the closest to us. I regard them as friends, as little familiar spirits. I gave them a name, a part to play in my life, a part that they still play, since I have never been able to dispense with them. Yes, one often has need of something smaller than oneself—the wisdom of the nations affirms as much.

Columbus became a synthesis of all the travelers, all the wanderers, all the "erratics" of his age and of all ages. To my mind, Columbus was the man who escapes. *Escape!* An expression that was fashionable twenty years ago and which has been much abused. However, it's the only one I find suitable at the moment—escape—but isn't this the worry of all men today, isn't it our daily worry? One must believe that the age in which we live, and that the present for the young people of all times, must be hard to spend one's life in and must give few joys in exchange for a great deal of pain, effort, and anxiety, since man has always tried to escape. In my sense, the expulsion—biblical version—of Adam and his mate from the original paradise is in fact an escape—otherwise the Creator's great anger wouldn't have its meaning. Adam escaped. Why? Go and ask his descendants! . . .

There isn't enough love-making in my plays doubtlessly because there was too much love-making and nothing but that—making love and going to bed—in all the French plays that poisoned us and whose fleshly odor still persists. There is a great deal of dying in my plays, but, after all, there is a great deal of dying in real life also. And if we take our age, not to talk of the past to which we so often turn back, don't you see that our age has the color and smell of the corpse, that it accumulates heaps, mountains of corpses? Look, death is everywhere, but they hide it from us, or try to. Happy ending to the innocents marked down for the great slaughter! But it's still the death of the Middle Ages: it's still the same. It's no longer made a carnival character or a character in a popular play. People can give it a scientific appearance, if they like. They can put a white apron and rubber gloves on it, make it a kind of superscientist, Doctor Miracle in reverse. Parsifal has given way to a melodious gangster. In any case, if there is a great deal of dying in my plays, I believe there is a great deal of dying in all plays from the time plays were first made. Moreover, why must everything end happily? I don't write for the box office.

The aim of the theatre—and of mine in particular—is not to comfort, no more is it to grieve. The theatre is a fact. And the definition given to it by Shakespeare remains true across the centuries. I will add that, if it is bad, the theatre gives rise to pleasure, if it is good, to joy.

Low theatre can corrupt, high theatre raises up, gives the spectator the possibility of levitation. Morals have nothing to do with the matter.

Am I lovely? And you? Men are not lovely, not often, and it's very well that they are not even more ugly; but I believe in *Man*, and I think that this can be felt in my work. I don't despair of him, and I find him very interesting, capable of everything—and of its opposite.

THE WOMEN AT THE TOMB

(*Les Femmes au Tombeau*)

A Play in One Act

(1928)

Translated by GEORGE HAUGER

NOTE

The manuscript of this play, written in 1928, bore the reference, "A Play for Marionettes." The author has deleted this indication so that the work is not thought reserved for wooden actors only—although there are certain expressions that belong to them in their own right, such as strange gestures as portrayed by the Flemish Primitives.

CHARACTERS

THE MIDWIFE

THE LAYER-OUT OF THE DEAD

MAGDALENE

MARTHA ⎱
MARY ⎰ *the sisters*

VERONICA

THE WOMAN CURED OF AN ISSUE OF BLOOD

THE WOMAN TAKEN IN ADULTERY

PILATE'S WIFE

YOCHABETH

JOHN

THE OLD WOMAN

SCENE—In a mean house in JERUSALEM on Good Friday evening.

THE WOMEN AT THE TOMB

The house is empty. The door is open onto the street.

THE MIDWIFE. Let's go in here, woman. It's a house that's been abandoned, like so many this fatal day. The angry crowds are trampling women underfoot.

The Layer-Out. This is a Christian's house, I'll bet. The Christians have dug holes in the countryside to hide in. Some are skulking in trees. What madness! The Son of God is dead, but his madness goes on. The ideas have been amputated, but the stumps are still alive. Are you the midwife? Yes, you are. Show your face. Good evening to you, woman, who help children out of the belly and wash them!

The Midwife. There's my face. You help old children to die and wash them. A lot need to die for you to be satisfied.

The Layer-Out. True enough. For you, a lot of women need to swell up under the laughter of the moon.

The Midwife. Yes. Tonight I shall go from door to door. Women who were big will have been afraid. The mountain has cried out and the world has fallen into the depths of a vault. We've seen the moon making strange faces. The bellies of all these women will burst like a bomb, and, tell me, what fruits am I going to bring forth from them?

The Layer-Out. I declare my night'll be as good as yours. The old dead have got up on their rotten legs. They'll have to be put back again—if they're found. In all decency they ought to be laid out afresh. Without counting the living in Jerusalem who will have dropped down dead with fright. Shut the door. To us, who are afraid of nothing, since we know where men come from and where they go to, to us, misfortune will bring forth

31

good fortune, and this black Friday will be a golden Friday. . . . [*Pause.*] Woman, was Christ also born of a woman, in agony?

The Midwife. I don't know. Did he die as others die?

The Layer-Out. I don't know. Who laid him out? The people in his band?

The Midwife. Nobody knows. Did you notice that all the women were out of their wits?

The Layer-Out. It's like that every time there are executions, when they see the wounds. A lot of women'll be making love tonight.

The Midwife. Huh! . . . They were saying that when the graves opened, women threw themselves at the revived corpses and hugged them. You'll see they'll give birth to purple children.

The Layer-Out. We're living in strange times. It's a huge piece of witchcraft.

The Midwife. Quiet! Someone's stopped in front of the house.

The door opens. MAGDALENE *stands on the threshold.*

The Layer-Out. A madwoman, indeed. She's trembling from head to foot, inside and out. Come in, woman.

The Midwife. There'll be plenty of madwomen, and the more the darker it gets. They'll be finding some women strangled and others running around naked in the fields. Why doesn't she come in? [*She makes* MAGDALENE *come in and shuts the door.*] It's nobody's house. D'you want to rest?

Magdalene. Ho, ho, no. . . . Suffer . . .

The Layer-Out. Why d'you laugh when you talk of suffering?

Magdalene. No, nothing but suffering. . . . Ho, ho. . . . I'm at the end of the road. . . . Ho, ho. . . . Gag me! Ram in the sponge soaked in gall. . . .

The Layer-Out. What a disgrace! She's laughing on a night like this! . . . When even the rocks are wailing. . . . Utterly mad! Are you in need of a man?

Magdalene. I'm not laughing. It's in my throat. Ho, ho, ho. . . . [*She slips to the ground.*] Leave me alone. [*She is seized by an attack of mad laughter, spasmodically rolling about and choking.*]

The Layer-Out. Be careful, she might bite. She's beginning to foam at the mouth. Have you been attacked by a mad dog, woman?

The Midwife. She's filthy. She stinks. . . . Who's spit on you? And this mud? Have you been having fun in the cemetery with a passionate skeleton?

Magdalene. Ho! Wicked women . . . He died at the third hour!

The Layer-Out. Who? Your lover? Is he one of the thieves? Get up. The demon's taken possession of you, as he has of the mountain, the city, and the sky. Stop your squirming around or I'll call the police and they'll smother you between two mattresses.

The Midwife. Let her lie on her back. She's holding her belly. She's one of those with a live coal in her backside. What does her carrying on matter to us? Have you a name, woman?

Magdalene. Magdalene. [*She raises herself a little.*] I'm ill, ho . . . [*She falls back.*] O Thou, bleed again, ho! bleed on me! [*A moan followed by a laugh.*]

The Layer-Out. D'you hear? She's reached her climax.

Magdalene. When he was alive he froze you; now he's dead he sets you aflame. . . . [*She lies motionless.*]

The Midwife. She's lost consciousness. What if she were dead?

The Layer-Out. I'd lay her out. She's not dead; she's asleep. It's an illness. Touch her. Like wood.

The Midwife. When she comes to, we'll ask her what it is that puts her in trances. [*Pause.*] She looks lovely now.

A knock at the door. Two women in deep mourning hesitate, then enter.

Martha. Whose house are we in?

The Layer-Out. Nobody's. Come in; it's a shelter.

Mary. What darkness! We only have this little lamp. Can we stay here and keep quiet?

The Midwife. Stay. As for keeping quiet for long . . .

Martha. We have nothing to tell.

Mary. Who is this dead woman? [*She leans down.*] Oh! Magdalene! . . . We must be on our guard, Martha.

Martha. Pretend not to know her. Public attention mustn't direct itself toward us. [*Pause.*] What are you waiting for in this room, women?

The Layer-Out. For the crowd to calm down. There are drunks and fanatics in the streets. We're afraid of a serious hurt, that's all.

The Midwife. And the victims are always women, you know. You two are undisturbed, quite indifferent, eh?

Mary. We're merely women in mourning.

The Layer-Out. Brand new crepe? A recent bereavement? Did you know the dead've been raised up by the score? Just think of it! If your deceased were among them and came back in the hope of a bite to eat or even . . . a kiss! Go and see quickly!

Martha. Is it money you want? I'll stuff some in your hideous mouth. . . .

The Layer-Out. Hey! My mouth isn't a money box. . . . [*To* THE MIDWIFE.] These are respectable women. Whores have already been seen in mourning, and it was standing them in good stead. . . .

Mary. Let's go, Martha.

Martha. No, outside it's worse. . . . And Magdalene might wake up. She's capable of wild talk, of mentioning names that should be kept quiet at present. . . . Is it late?

Mary. It's completely dark. People can only get around with lanterns. No one'll sleep tonight.

Martha. Let's stay here. Peace between us, women?

The Layer-Out. If you want. . . .

Mary. There's a certain odor in this house. . . .

Martha. Yes, an odor we've already noticed on someone. . . . An evil odor . . .

A knock at the door.

The Midwife. Another woman more or less doesn't matter, it's a big room. Come in!

A woman comes in.

The Layer-Out. She has a way with her, this one! Shut the door again!

Veronica. I beg your pardon? . . . I am the one they call Veronica.

Martha. Veronica? Mary, it's her! Show us quickly, Veronica, show us the imprint you've stolen!

Veronica. Impudence! I've never stolen anything!

Mary. Where's the cloth? There's a hundred witnesses to what you did.

Veronica. Is doing an act of charity doing wrong? . . . Anyway, what have I stolen?

Martha. His holy Face.

The Midwife. It's clear enough she's a thief! Isn't she pregnant?

The Layer-Out. Yes, indeed, my girl! One's got to steal, pregnant or not. Why've some got all and others nothing? I want justice and equal shares. No one's going to blame you, my girl, but you must share it out. . . .

Veronica. You can't divide a face. How? The nose for you, an eye for you, the beard for her. . . .

The Layer-Out. How stupid to steal a face, instead of lifting a flatiron or some forks!

Veronica. Besides, I haven't stolen. The cloth belongs to me.

Martha. It used to belong to you before it received the imprint. After that, it became a sacred cloth which reverts to the Christian community. Give it to me. I undertake to deliver it to the Christians when they gather together.

Veronica. The cloth and his imprint remain my property, and the imprint is my reward, for among so many lamenting women—you know, these women you find at all the calvaries for the pleasure of whining—I was the only one who went up to Christ to rub off the sweat of his death agony. . . .

Mary. We were among those women. . . .

Veronica. You were there, and for you with your exaggerated lamentations, Christ spoke these words, "Weep not for me, but weep for yourselves and for your children. . . ." He knew that women never weep except for themselves and what immediately concerns them, that they shed tears as they make water!

The Layer-Out. Well said, Veronica.

The Midwife. That's for you, women in mourning! Keep your image, Veronica, you've well earned it. Suppose you were to show us this cloth?

Veronica. I haven't got it here. It's better not to see it. The face of a person in agony isn't lovely. . . . I won't dare to look at it often. What a terrible gift!

Martha. Mary, I tremble to think that such a relic abides in this woman's hands. . . .

Mary. What can we do about it? She too is a Christian.

Martha. There are too many women about our Master's person, about His life and His death. We two were enough. . . .

Mary. Who's going to drive them away? Let's hold our peace. We're not in our own surroundings. But rather this house than the street. . . .

The Midwife. Suppose we consult the cards to see whether your master will rise again?

Martha. Let's go, Mary. Better the street and its dangers. . . .

The Layer-Out. You've had enough? Go on then. We're staying, we are. [*A knock at the door.*] Another one?

A fat woman comes in.

The Woman Cured of an Issue of Blood. May I, my dears? I'm dead beat. Are you holding a meeting? A meeting of holy women? [*Deep sigh.*] I've come from Calvary. . . .

Martha. We too. . . .

The Cured Woman. Well, I never! But I saw everything! I was in the front row. More than that, I helped in the taking down from the cross. My hands here have touched the body of the Crucified, love. . . .

Mary. In the front row, as always, outdoing the Son of God in his painful Passion with your grimaces and your sighing. Didn't he die for you alone? And tomorrow you'll be relating that he came to your bedroom, that you taught him his doctrine. . . .

The Layer-Out. What've you got to say to that, tubby?

The Cured Woman. I don't know this black creature. I despise her. More than that, I forgive her. We know how to forgive, we Christians! All this snarling because I had the honor of being a witness of the Passion? . . . It was public, wasn't it? I've had other honors! If I wanted to talk . . .

Mary. We know. Who doesn't know? . . . You were the sick woman, the authentic one, the only one who had the right to be so.

Martha. But she didn't mean to die. She was in the best of health, furious that people saw her looking so well!

The Cured Woman. Are you talking about me? Go on. Afterward, I'll tell the story of the sisters, Martha and Mary. . . .

The Midwife. We're going to hear some good yarns about them!

Mary. This woman of the Pharisees saw Christ going by surrounded by a great crowd. Since there was a crowd, she touched Christ's robe and found herself miraculously cured—sorry at the cure, but happy at the great crowd crying, "A miracle!" and looking at her with admiration. Since then, she's no longer the sick woman: she's the woman who was sick but who has been cured and who wants to cure the whole world. She caught the madness of charity. And the poor roared with laughter at the spectacle of her haughty charity. When she came along, the poor gathered up their crutches and made off somewhere else. Don't be charitable in front of her; she can't abide the competition. Soon she in her turn will be working miracles. She's plump, quite ruddy. Charity fattens one. . . .

The Layer-Out. Congratulations! Are you going to answer back, cured woman? Don't you hear yourself being insulted? I'd answer back, I would, and with a sharp tongue. . . .

The Cured Woman. I do not deign to. I said that we Christians know how to forgive injuries. . . .

Martha. And what was she doing on Calvary? Did she collect souvenirs? The thorns, the nails?

The Cured Woman. If I had all that! The whole of the cross, and the spear, and the cloth that a woman called Veronica . . .

Veronica. I'm Veronica. You shall not have that cloth.

The Cured Woman. You? Congratulations. If I had the veil of the Temple as well, the reed they mocked Him with, the pieces of the seamless garment. . . .

Martha. You'd organize a lottery for the furthering of your works, wouldn't you?

The Cured Woman. Poor Martha! To say such things this night! . . . I shall pray for you.

Martha. No thank you! Just tell us why you're running about the streets tonight instead of sleeping at your husband's side?

The Cured Woman. I have my reasons. And all of you? You're not in bed either! [*On the floor,* MAGDALENE *moves and groans. Attention is directed to her.*] A sick woman?

The Midwife. Will you see to her, charitable woman?

The Cured Woman. Bah! No! Not to that one! . . . My hands, which have touched Christ, must not touch a prostitute. . . .

The Layer-Out. Cut your hands off and put them under a globe, on account of the flies. . . .

A knock at the door.

The Midwife. Come in! It's a free house! No charge!

A woman comes in carrying a little pearl funerary crown.

The Woman Taken in Adultery. May I? They told me that women were gathering in this house.

The Cured Woman. Who is this crown for?

The Adulterous Woman. For God who is dead. Are they going to bury him? Or has it been done already?

Martha. You must wait. We're going to his tomb, to-night or perhaps at dawn.

The Adulterous Woman. If you don't want me to come with you, accept the crown. I loved Christ very much.

The Cured Woman. We all loved him. And I was loved by him.

The Adulterous Woman. So much the better for you. I won't dare say as much, although he showed goodness toward me.

Mary. Who are you?

Veronica. The woman taken in adultery, I think?

The Adulterous Woman. The very same. That's who I was; that's who I remain henceforth.

Martha. Sing hosanna! For Christ saved you from the justice of the priests.

The Adulterous Woman. I won't sing hosanna! Why did they take me to Christ? They could have stoned me and have had done with it! Now I'm an object of public scorn, and the men make obscene gestures when I go past.

The Midwife. Committing adultery's nothing; the crime's letting oneself get caught.

The Adulterous Woman. In the heat of love-making I lose all discretion.

Veronica. To each her sins. We're all impure. Some draw the curtains and others forget to do it. You've been forgiven, haven't you? This crown shows the kindness of your heart. I have nothing, not even a candle.

The Cured Woman. I'll buy whatever's necessary.

Martha. What is necessary is to be able to get near to the tomb in the potter's field. There are sentries. . . .

The Cured Woman. The soldiers? With money . . .

Mary. Romans? I doubt it. . . .

Martha. We've got to get to the tomb in spite of the guards. The corpse isn't washed. I've got perfumes and paint.

The Layer-Out. I'll help. It's my calling.

The Midwife. D'you want to know how to fix the soldiers? Take them some drink.

Magdalene *has gotten up during these last exchanges.*

Magdalene. What are you talking about?

The Cured Woman. Not ill any longer? All the same, I don't think you'll be coming with us to Christ's tomb.

Magdalene. I'll go all alone.

Martha. No, let her come with us. The soldiers know her. You understand me, Magdalene?

Magdalene. Yes, Martha. They'll let me past and you'll all follow. [*She laughs.*] I'll do what certainly none of you would do. I'll go up to their lantern and fasten my stockings up. . . . When the soldiers have seen my legs, they'll go wherever I lead them, with their tongues hanging out.

The Cured Woman. Horrible!

The Midwife. Magdalene knows what life is.

Magdalene. And doesn't the end justify the means, as the priests say?

A knock at the door. A woman comes in.

The Layer-Out. Come in! There's still room on the mantelpiece!

The Midwife. Just look! This one has a hat and gloves!

Pilate's Wife. I was wandering around, ladies. . . . My insomnia is persistent. What a dreadful day! They wouldn't believe me. Nevertheless, the dream book explains a lot of occurrences. What does one do to get to the tomb?

Mary. You shall come with us. I promise nothing, because of the sentries. . . .

Pilate's Wife. I shall order the soldiers not to see us.

Martha. Without being tactless, who are you?

Pilate's Wife. A stranger. [*Pause.*] If you wish, I shall go.

Veronica. Stay. Every woman is sick at heart tonight.

Pilate's Wife. Yes. [*Pause.*] Tell me, what are the people saying about Pilate?

Martha. They say he showed himself a very shrewd politician in the case, but they take him to task for having washed his hands ostentatiously with the air of an actor.

Pilate's Wife. Is that all? Listen: I am his wife. [*Pause.*] Normally a wife admits her husband to be right. I do not. I don't care much for him. He is a neurasthenic. [*Pause.*] You were Christ's friends?

The Cured Woman. Some of us were. This meeting was not planned, you realize? Come with us. You can be of great assistance to us, Madame Pilate. . . .

Pilate's Wife. Don't talk to me like that.

The Layer-Out. When will the procession be?

Veronica. After midnight, no doubt?

The Midwife. I can see now that by then we'll all have fallen asleep! [*She yawns.*] I'm drowsy. . . .

Martha. Put your hand in front of your mouth. No one is sleepy tonight. No one has any right to be. He is in his tomb, he is watching . . . He is waiting. . . . [*She yawns.*]

Magdalene. What's he waiting for? . . . [*She yawns.*] It's catching. . . .

Mary. The resur- [*she yawns*] -rection. Pardon.

Pilate's Wife. In spite of myself . . . [*She yawns.*]

The Midwife. Don't worry. [*She yawns.*]

All the women yawn. Silence falls. The door opens. A young man appears.

The Layer-Out. People knock before coming in! No, lad! Nothing but women here. The pub for the men!

The young man is followed by an OLD WOMAN *whose features are hidden by a dark shawl.*

John. Hush! No arguing or complaining. [*He leads* THE OLD WOMAN *to the back of the room.*]

The Cured Woman [*pointing to* THE OLD WOMAN].
Who is she?

John. Ask the angels.

Veronica. Give her this chair.

John. Don't talk any more, and have no misgivings. I'll
take care of this woman, who has been entrusted to me.
If you have anything to do for better or worse on this
incredible night, do it without delay. . . .

Mary. Yes, let us move. To the tomb, women! And
let the maddest go in front.

The Cured Woman. Follow me.

The Midwife [*to John*]. Isn't your old woman going
there?

John. She's come from there.

*The women gather together and prepare to go out. A row.
The door is flung wide open.* YOCHABETH *enters, full of
fury.*

The Layer-Out. I know her! She has cattle. . . .

The Midwife. It's Yochabeth. Now there's going to be
fun. . . .

Yochabeth. All these women in my house, my house!
. . . All these trollops! . . . Outside, or I'll smoke you
out! . . . Whores, I say, whores, female pigs! . . . Get
out!

The Midwife. Why did you leave the door open?

Martha. Mary, the odor?

Yochabeth. Never mind that. Which one's stolen my
husband? He's hiding under the skirts of one of you. . . .

John. Search no further, woman.

Yochabeth. You, apostle, will you tell me where he
is, whole or in pieces? If not I'll denounce you. . . .

John. Get yourself to the morgue straight away. Your
husband's lying there in ice and formalin.

Yochabeth. He's been killed! What happened?

John. The devil knows what happened. Your Judas went
to a swampy field, a field where mushrooms grow and
toads weep. . . . And there he hanged himself wretchedly
from a rotten tree, and all the time he was filthying his
breeches!

Yochabeth. Ah! The skunk! I'm a widow. . . . Help!
[*Jostling the women, she goes out yelling.*]

The Cured Woman [*guffawing*]. Ho, ho! . . . Filthied
his breeches!

John [*stamping his foot*]. So the drama goes on, poign-
ant and occasionally ludicrous. Go along in your procession, women—that's your part. . . . Hurry if you still
want to find a corpse to bathe in your tears. . . .

Martha. We're going. Come along, worthy and unworthy; all is logical. . . . Let us go with all our feelings.
. . . Let John take care of the old woman who has no
name.

*Slowly they go out, and the last closes the door. John
watches* THE OLD WOMAN, *Mary, for a long time, then
makes one or two unfinished gestures, not knowing how
to begin. Finally:*

John. It doesn't matter whether their grief is rose-
colored or white, of the pearls of love or of gilded paper.
[*Pause.*] Mary, are you going to come out of your daze?
I am your son now, and I am asking you. . . . [*Pause.*]
All is accomplished. We've got to make the best of it.
We are alone, and even if he rises again, he won't be your
son any longer, nor my friend, but our God. . . . [*Pause.*]
Mary, you old mother, are you going to stay like that
with your eyes shut, between life and death and without memory? Do move! . . . [*Pause.*] And your face
shut up like a tomb? [*Pause.*] Mary, mother, they arrested,
jeered at, tortured, then killed your son Jesus. You saw it
all without flinching. And not a tear fell on your cheek!
. . . Will those who set down the story of these dreadful unparalleled days have to write that the mother of
the living God never shed a tear? . . . [*Pause.*] Mary,
you frighten me. . . .

The Old Woman. What time is it?

John. What a question! There's no longer any time.
We're just sailing on in the dead of night. . . . [*He
yawns.*] I've been wanting to go to sleep so much . . .
for days. . . .

The Old Woman. Sleep, John. I shall stay awake. . . .

John. Thank you. What are you going to do?

The Old Woman. Sweep out this room. [*She gets up,
takes the broom from a corner, and, as though she were
sleepwalking, begins her task.*]

John. The traitor's room? As you wish. . . . [*He sits
at the table and immediately falls asleep, his head on his
arms. He can be heard murmuring.*] We shall awaken, it
is written. . . . We shall indeed awaken once more. . . .

A long silence. A cock crows nearby. Dawn filters in and there is a pale light in the room.

The Old Woman [*who has caught sight of the Apostle puts down the broom.*] It is morning! John is asleep. He can no longer watch over me. . . . [*She kneels.*] Jesus, my child, I have forced back my sorrow as much as was needful. Now, away from the sight of all, I weep over you. . . . I am no longer the mother of God whom they crucified, I am the mother of the condemned man. . . .

BARABBAS

A Play in Three Acts
(1928)

Translated by GEORGE HAUGER

INTRODUCTORY NOTE

. . . . It was in 1928. [The Flemish Popular Theatre] had asked me to provide a work that could be played during Holy Week, a Passion, or something similar. Once again, I had complete freedom of choice and inspiration. Not wanting to write a classical Passion, and above all not wanting to steep my pen in holy water and make a pastiche of the old mystery plays, I thought of writing something provoking, unexpected, and yet popular. I saw the other side of the Passion, the Passion seen through the eyes of the people, seen from below. Instead of being on Calvary with the Honorable Witnesses, I went to the foot of Calvary with the rabble. I wondered how the crowd, the lower orders of Jerusalem, had stood that dreadful and sublime day, in its consequences the most tragic in human history. And naturally I found Christ and all the actors of the Passion on my way. I did not make a speaking character of Christ—something I would refuse to do—but Christ appears in my play like a ghost, a presence: he is a light and, at the same time, a nightmare. He is not the Christ we know from the plaster figures of Saint Sulpice, from the religious pictures of the Munich school, but a Gothic Christ, the Christ of the Grünewald of the Isenheim altarpiece, bloody, befouled, covered in spit, crowned with thorns, actually murdered, but still living because he has not suffered enough. To embody the people, the mob, that violent emotive crowd in its state of trance, I chose the character no one ever speaks of, and whom the Scriptures no more than name, Barabbas, he who was preferred to Jesus, he who was released instead of Jesus. For some years now a literary fate has been created for this obscure Barabbas, as one has been created for Judas. But in my time nothing like it existed. What do we know about Barabbas? Little. That there was a brigand of this name, and that the crowd, urged on by the priests, set him free by virtue of an old tradition, in place of Jesus.

It was the history of this bandit that I wanted to exhibit on the boards.

In so far as I was a poet, I was able to imagine what became of him after his liberation. He couldn't have gotten far, for society doesn't easily let go of a gentleman of this kind, suddenly enriched by a new popularity in addition to his old criminal glory.

Moreover, what did Barabbas think on learning that he had been set free in place of one called Jesus, an ideologist? That was the starting point of the play.

When this theme was proposed, the Flemish Popular Theatre accepted it right away. I brought a new, unusual vision of the Passion, while respecting the data familiar to the masses through religious teaching. And I fell in with the masses. They accepted this vision. It was a very great success. It was moreover admirably played, forcefully, without flourishes, by very primitive actors, a little barnstorming, perhaps, but that was suitable; it had great attraction in an unerringly beautiful décor and with supers fond of making a great noise. *Barabbas* has left such an impression in Flanders that this play is still performed there nowadays. It has become one of the customs. The character Barabbas has raised himself to the level of popular types, like certain criminals or heroes who have become famous through plaints and Épinal figures.* It is known that a popular play *Barabbas* exists, a play that tells the story of the brigand; but it has been forgotten that it is the work of a contemporary author, and it is played somewhere in Flanders each year on the occasion of the Easter festivals. Nothing can make me more proud. For it is played here, there, and everywhere in the world, in all tongues. The bandit has made headway!

. . . . This play *Barabbas* is moreover made of cries, and is no more than the embodiment in a play of a yearning for purity. I do not claim to be incarnated at any moment in this work; but all the same I wrote it under the influence of a certain accepted hallucination.

I carried it within me for a long time, and I sought the pretext for putting this superhuman tragedy on the

---

* Épinal (N.E.France). "An industry peculiar to Épinal is the production of cheap images, lithographs and engravings." —*Encyclopaedia Britannica*. [Translator's note.]

stage. And the motive, the deep-seated driving force of this work, could well have been this terrible obsession with the death of Christ—of which I don't possess sole rights, do I?

From *The Ostend Interviews*

CHARACTERS

BARABBAS, *who talks a great deal*

CAIAPHAS

PILATE

HEROD

JUDAS, *an apostle*

PETER, *an apostle*

JOHN, *an apostle*

MAGDALENE

YOCHABETH

PILATE'S WIFE (*Procula or Procla?*)

THE GOVERNOR OF THE PRISON

THE WATCHER

THE GOOD THIEF ⎫
THE BAD THIEF ⎬ *Iothas and Maggabias*
⎭

THE PRIEST

THE CLOWN

THE SHOWMAN

THE OTHER APOSTLES

THE BEGGARS

THE SOLDIERS

THE CROWD

and

JESUS, *who says nothing*

The supposed names of Pilate's wife and of the thieves
are without historical value and do not come from the
Scriptures. They are only indicated above as a matter
of documentation, and in accordance with Apocryphal and
legendary sources.

BARABBAS

ACT ONE

SCENE—*A jail with huge bars, surrounded by a raised inspection walk. Granite steps in the center of the cage. Gloom. Deep silence. Then, in the distance, prolonged whistles, as though signals, followed by calls like hoots.*

VOICES. Barabbas! Barabbas! Barabbas!

A shadow stirs in the cage. A roar. A man has stood up and stretches himself.

Barabbas. Barabbas! [*He yawns.*] They are calling Barabbas? I hear you. It's me, Barabbas, in my cage, in my chains! Shout my name in all directions! [*He walks around heavily.*]

A Voice [*dying away*]. Barabbas!

Barabbas. Yes, be quiet! Leave me to sleep in my endless night. Like the beasts, I can only sleep or gnaw my chains. Are you coming to set me free, you morning hooters? Do you want to give me a warning? Of what? Why can't you tear down this prison, rescue me from torment?

A Voice. Barabbas!

Barabbas. And this name of mine that you call out endlessly, are you claiming to teach it to me? It's me, Barabbas, under sentence of death, disgraced, bound hand and foot, but still terrible. And I shall go on being terrible, right up to my shameful death, before these priests and these judges and these crowds I have made tremble and who still tremble—this death which will be great and moving like a stage play, this purple and riotous death which will be my triumph. For I shall die without yielding, in the full force of my hatred, blaspheming, and, just as I lived, above the law.

51

A Voice. Barabbas!

Barabbas. Meanwhile, Barabbas greets you, my brother malefactors, my dear rabble! Greetings from the depths of my pestilential darkness! I can no longer see you, but I can sniff your musky smell and I know that you are multiplying abundantly, that your kind will never allow itself to pass away. Make crime live forever, for as long as man himself! And let me serve as example! Have my shamelessness and my cool head; have my contempt for all justice. I am pleased with you, who are mounting a guard of honor around my prison. Spread my glory in your hovels and your dens. Steal and kill pronouncing my name, the name that brings good luck. Be at my torment, happy and threatening, insulting the lovers of Justice and praising their victim. In return, you shall see me spit out my soul; you shall see the most astounding grin that ever appeared on a human face. And on that day you shall hold a gallows feast, as though in honor of a bloodthirsty god. I do not ask too much: strangle some priests and doctors of the Law, desecrate the Temple, set fire to the city that will have seen my end. Do these things so that your good deeds may accompany me in eternity.

A Voice. Barabbas!

A trumpet sounds. A long silence, made deeper by the sound of dragging chains. BARABBAS *stops walking around.*

Barabbas. Dawn. . . . Are they going to come? Perhaps it's to be this morning. Thieves, you must make the best of it. They will come armed, in grand array, with bonds and gags, knowing that Barabbas will not die like a bleating lamb. You shall see the scuffle. I am fit enough, myself. And you, thieves, what will you do? Do you remember our trial? A royal escort, an unparalleled day for Justice. What a fine gallows bird! Will they ever find another of this cut? Are you asleep, thieves? No doubt you are dreaming that they will open your cage and say to you, "Come, gentle prisoners, go and be free. . . ." It's better not to wake you.

One of the Thieves [*whimpering*]. Barabbas!

Barabbas [*laughing*]. What? Are you expecting me to comfort you? Think of the torment; think of that, and be comforted! It is written that we shall not rot much longer in this hole.

The Thief. Barabbas!

Barabbas. Are you going to go on moaning? Are you bandits—yes or no? If you are, follow your destiny right to the end steadfastly, with dignity, and tell yourselves that the torment is, logically enough, part of your calling. And if you are not bandits, what are you doing meddling in the business of murdering your fellow men? Dying a hard and bitter death is nothing to one who is prodigal with death. [*Furious.*] Or—but it's beyond belief—are you feeling remorse?

The Thief. Light, Barabbas. . . .

Barabbas. Thieves, you make me feel sorry for you. If you go on whining, I will make a complaint about you and get the judges to grant me the favor of dying alone, without the absurd hangers-on that you are. Doesn't my presence fortify you? Aren't you proud to be executed with me?—when the most you deserved was a hurried execution on some accursed waste plot, before the gaze of mangy dogs. After all, how do you justify your title of condemned men, what's the inventory of your exploits? Can you honestly call yourselves murderers? I doubt it. Me, I *am* a murderer. My exploits? Seek them in epics and endless rhapsodic songs. I am covered by as many wounds as there are nights in the year. And when I was taken, I struggled alone against an army whose soldiers fled crying that I was aided by demons. [*Violently.*] Me, I *am* a bandit. [*Shaking the thieves.*] Why don't you applaud? [*The thieves feebly clap their hands.*] Thank you! Still, they'd have done better to make jailers of you. [*One of the thieves bursts into tears.*] Come on, we're friends? I didn't mean to humiliate you. Tell me, why did you kill?

The Bad Thief [*getting up*]. He doesn't know. But I know why I killed. Because I wanted to!

Barabbas. Like that, eh? Is killing child's play, then? One kills by fate! One kills in accordance with an ideal! One kills by vocation! One kills in order to play one's role in society! One kills because one has genius! Miserable creature! [*He spits on the thief.*] I can see your loathsome action from here. And whom did you kill? An old man? A drunk? A client in a brothel who couldn't defend himself? Get out of my sight, you object of disgust! [*He lays hold of the other thief and forcibly stands him up.*] And you, sniveler, are you worth any more than your mate? Have you killed as well?

The Good Thief. I killed, and I didn't know that I

was killing. At that time there was limitless despair in
my heart. I was weary of existence, and I was in truth
a poor wretch. Why did someone I didn't know make
game of my distress?

Barabbas. And you killed?

The Good Thief. I killed because it is infuriating for a
man to insult another man's distress. Yet, Barabbas, I
never even harmed a beast.

Barabbas. Sleep in peace! By killing you meted out
justice. So why these regrets, why this dejection? You
are puffed out with tears, and you weep over your victim
even though you acknowledge he was detestable. Miserable
stupidity! I pardon you; but I can't stop myself from
belching you up. [*He spits on the thief. Pause.*] If I was
one of those who let themselves be affected, my last days
would be pretty miserable and your presence would have
taken the heart out of me. I don't want to know anything about misery. I am happy. I am healthy. You two
are morbid. And how sinister you are! It's you who have
tarnished the radiance of crime. It's your fault if crime
is a rejected doctrine. You are strayed sheep and not
the bandits you are made out to be. Have you for a
moment thought of escape, of wrenching the bars of this
cage, as I try to do, hour by hour? The idea never even
comes to you. You are resigned. You are dead already.
Let them finish you off. On the other hand, see how I
go on, and tell me if I'm not in good heart.

The Bad Thief. What good does that do you?

Barabbas. It torments the owls who watch over me. And
then, if a bar were to give way . . . [*He rushes at the
bars and shakes them violently, grunting as he does so.
Suddenly a dark lantern lights up, and its beam strikes
Barabbas' face, blinding him. The bandit is still.*] The
owls are lighting up? [*He tries to escape from the circle
of light which follows him and reveals his movements.*]
Who has got that lamp? Who is it who feels bold outside
my cage?

A Soldier. What were you up to?

Barabbas. I was testing the strength of these bars. Is it
true that this cage was forged in my honor? They
couldn't make the bars strong enough, for if they should
happen to break, you would see the jailers swallowing
their tormenting lantern.

The Soldier. What pride! May you keep it up!

Barabbas. I invite you to my funeral, cave-dweller. Are you willing to come closer, so that I can study your features before I go to the brigands' paradise? I feel some tenderness, some gratitude toward you who have watched over me with so much concern. Haven't we become brothers by virtue of living in this cess pit, this stinking darkness? I love you as I love everything that creeps about in this jail, the rats, the lice, the spiders. . . .

The Soldier [*who has come closer to the cage*]. Sneer . . .

A cry. The light goes out. BARABBAS *has managed to lay hold of* THE SOLDIER, *who can be heard struggling for breath.* BARABBAS *laughs, the thieves become agitated, but immediately three lamps from above join their beams together and concentrate their brightness on* BARABBAS, *who releases* THE SOLDIER *and draws back, fleeing the light. He wanders around, followed by the lamps. Shadows come down the inspection walk.*

Barabbas. Galley slaves! Come on then, with your pitchforks and torches! The wild beast is ready for you!

But the lamps go out and the light of an ash-gray dawn falls from above. THE SOLDIERS *stand fast, holding their spears toward the cage.* THE GOVERNOR OF THE PRISON *comes forward.*

Barabbas. Who's that? The executioner?

The Governor. He will come, don't fear. But when he will come, that I couldn't tell you. Now, why this uproar? Are you trying to escape your destiny? Take hold of yourself, Barabbas!

Barabbas. I am in control of myself, even in my colossal bursts of anger. You ought to know that, governor—you who pretend not to know me, you, my old comrade, a thief washed as good as new! You have made good! Here you are a servant of the State! What progress! The trouble with living here is that your complexion grows pale and you finish up looking like the criminals you are guarding. Keep calm? I am enormously calm. I would break your back calmly and gently. I would suck your brain through your nose, if the happy chance came to me.

The Governor. Be quiet!

Barabbas. I am condemned to die, not to keep quiet.

The Governor. True enough. Listen, Barabbas. You are condemned to death . . .

Barabbas. Then let them kill me and not go on talking about it.

The Governor. I want to talk to you about it and you shall listen to me. Believe me, it would be better for you to adopt an attitude of resignation and to display the outward signs of repentance.

Barabbas. To pretend?

The Governor. If you did that, perhaps you would move the judges to mercy.

Barabbas. Then let me die straight away!

The Governor. Still, it wouldn't be a matter of indifference to you to see the sun again, the roads, the countryside, to find once more all that makes up life?

Barabbas. Tell these things to miserable wretches, but not to Barabbas who had a price on his head and who was condemned by your judges seventy-seven times! Would Justice deprive itself of such a fine and moral example? Does a man of my stamp die in his bed? No, no! . . . The governor is having his joke. Good night.

The Governor. Be reasonable. It is not the governor of the prison who is speaking to you, but your old comrade in arms.

Barabbas. Well, what do you mean?

The Governor. I am not a prophet, but I say again, "Have hope!" [*He moves away.*]

Barabbas. Governor!

The Governor [*coming back*]. What?

Barabbas [*falling to his knees*]. I am uneasy. I am suddenly bathed in hope. See if I have understood you! I am shattered. Terrible images walk through my sleep. In shame I confess to you that remorse is gnawing at me. I am not worthy of the good judges' clemency. I am aware that I shall not escape the bitter death that is going to be; but I am strengthened by the generosity shown me. Governor?

The Governor. What now?

Barabbas. You know that custom demands that those who are going to die should be heartened—as you have just been doing. I have courage. On my gallows I shall sing the praise of Justice and its upright judges. I shall tell the crowd to hate evil. But let me address a plea to

you, Governor. Would you refuse the plea of him who
is going to die?

The Governor. No. What can give you pleasure now?

Barabbas. That which gives you pleasure. Come here.
Blow in my face. [THE GOVERNOR *draws near and blows.*]
Oh, delight! Give me, oh, I implore you, give me what
you love!

The Governor [*laughing*]. You are thirsty?

Barabbas. Thirst! Thirst! Remorse has taken this tormenting shape. Thirst is my punishment. Am I thirsty?
I accept being condemned to death; but to be allowed
to die of thirst, I rebel against that. My worst crimes have
been paid for long ago. No, I don't want pardon, nor
sunlight, nor liberty, nor life. I want to drink, drink,
drink!

The Two Thieves [*who have come forward*]. Drink!
. . . Drink! . . . Drink!

The Governor. You shall drink, Barabbas. I shall give
you some of the wine they give the soldiers before battle,
a heavy wine, a cloudy wine, that tastes of sulphur, a
wine that nails drunks to the floor.

Barabbas. Give it here! Through you, through the
power of this wine, my agony will be splendid. I shall sob
and weep. I shall beseech the Lord. Give it here, and give
me a lot of it. My throat is like a chasm. My brain is
like a rock, and it needs the tides of your wine to sub-
merge this rock. Give it here! Let it not be a robber that
is crucified, but a drunk! Let it not be blood but wine that
spurts from my five wounds!

The Two Thieves. Give it here! Give it here!

Barabbas. Governor, I want to kiss your feet. You are
magnanimous! I shall proclaim your generosity, the
nobility of your spirit, the greatness of your character,
from the depths of the outer darkness where I shall be
flung. Quick! My mouth is like a blazing furnace. I am as
thirsty as a whole caravan!

THE GOVERNOR *gives a signal to* THE SOLDIERS. *One brings
a tall jar; another opens a grille at the bottom of the
cage, through which the jar is passed.*

The Governor. Here is your wine. Drink! And with
drunkenness may good resolutions come to you. It is
time for them. Soon, one of the doctors of the Law who
condemned you will be coming. Those people like defer-

ence. Drink and hope! [*He goes along the inspection walk and, followed by* The Soldiers, *disappears.*]

Barabbas [*pressing the jar to his bosom*]. I shall drink and hope will be born. [*To the thieves who are creeping around him.*] Why are you acting like serpents? What's wrong with you?

The Two Thieves. Thirst! Thirst!

Barabbas. You are lying! I alone am thirsty. This wine belongs only to me. Drink your stagnant water.

The Two Thieves. Thirst! Thirst!

Barabbas. Ah, so your eyeballs are aflame? What evil designs are you harboring? Your madmen's goings-on don't impress me a bit.

The Two Thieves. Thirst! Thirst!

Barabbas. Get back! Let go of my legs! Anyway, who was this wine given to? To Barabbas, who deserves it! Have you a reputation? Not at all! You are just underhanded pickpockets.

The Two Thieves [*threatening*]. Thirst! Thirst!

Barabbas. Look here! [*He puts down the jar. Short scuffle.* The Two Thieves *roll on the ground and moan.* Barabbas *picks up the jar again.*] And now, swallow your saliva. Watch me drink and your thirst will be quenched. [*He drinks.*] Oh, good! . . . How good it is!

The Good Thief. Have pity, Barabbas. You are superior to us and you deserve the wine; but are we not all equal before death?

Barabbas. Fine talk! [*He drinks.*] Ah, it flows gentle and harsh; it is icy and it is boiling.

The Bad Thief. Barabbas, you are handsome, you are big.

The Good Thief. Barabbas, you are strong, you are a lion.

Barabbas. Let the lion drink! [*He drinks.*]

The Bad Thief. Barabbas, I'll let you into a secret. Give me some?

Barabbas. I'll drink as I listen to you. [*He drinks.*]

The Bad Thief. A secret! The soldiers said that at the feast of the Passover, Justice would release a criminal. A drink?

Barabbas. What's that to me? It won't be me.

The Good Thief. It's the truth, Barabbas. If you let me have a drink, and if I'm the one set free, I'll get them to pardon you in my place. A drink?

Barabbas. What self-sacrifice! [*He spits out a jet of wine.*] Pah! This wine is a thick poison. You must taste it.

The Two Thieves [*leaping with delight*]. Thank you, Barabbas!

Barabbas. But you won't stand up to it. This black liquid, this puddle of bitterness will break your arm and leg, better than an executioner. They will have to drag you drunk to the place of execution, and what a revolting sight for the crowd! [*The thieves try to lay hold of the jar.*] Hey! For this wine? Would you be parricides, fratricides, regicides?

The Two Thieves. Yes! And worse still!

Barabbas. A proud cry from the heart! Drink, then. . . . [BARABBAS *raises the jar and pours wine into the gaping mouths of the kneeling thieves.*]

The Good Thief. Better than the spring leaping forth in the burning desert.

The Bad Thief. Better than the morning dew.

The Good Thief. Better than the rain on the dry earth.

The Bad Thief. Better than the music of cymbals and sistrums.

The Good Thief. Better than springtime stitched with bees, and than the dance of the stars.

Barabbas. Enough! You are talking like the prophets in the holy books! Are you raving already? Drink, but in silence! [*He pours some more.*] Simpletons! It's the height of their aspiration! Let the poverty-stricken gleam of conscience that wavers in their dark heads, like lanterns in the night wind, go out as quickly as possible. Reel and jerk like scarecrows in the fields! And if blasphemies leap from your ugly mouths, nothing will be more pleasing to me, dear thieves. Draw nearer to the animals, brothers, to the beasts with their absolute instincts! You've drunk enough! Leave some! [*He drinks greedily.*]

The Two Thieves. More! More!

Barabbas [*giving them the jar*]. Pah! This wine tastes of prison, of sweat. It's certainly the wine of the condemned, believe me. No doubt they pressed the accursed grapes for us, the ones the lightning had burnt. What does it matter? This wine makes you drunk. Don't you feel your thoughts becoming sticky and red? Me, I have a taste of blood in my mouth, a scent of blood in my nose. Is there anything better? I feel brisk and lithe like

the wild beast whose cunning and cruelty I possess. What
do you say?

The Bad Thief [*passing the jar to* THE GOOD THIEF].
Good heavy wine! My head has caught fire. I am stone. I
was like this on the night of my crime.

The Good Thief. My heart is huge. It is ringing like a
shield. I would like to sing as I used to sing not long ago,
before my crime.

Barabbas. Sing? You don't know how to sing. I do! My
voice is like the forest winds or the march of a barbarian
horde. It is melodious and violent. But the most beautiful songs are the hymns they sing at carnage. I am going
to sing, thieves. Do you like the laments of pariahs? Unless I make up a solemn and imprecatory funeral song
that I shall bawl as I go to my execution, a song . . .
[*Tears come to his eyes.*] Am I absurd?

The Good Thief. Barabbas! What's the matter with
you? If you weep, what must we do?

Barabbas [*clasping them*]. Comrades . . . my poor comrades . . . Don't think I'm weakening. It's the wine. It's
also an indescribable uneasiness that has taken hold of my
senses, for I'm thinking that we are three criminals and
we don't know why we are criminals. Not long ago we
were children and no one knew we were going to become criminals. No one told us what to do not to become
these. Then one day the judges accused us. And now they
are going to kill us, who are harmful, in the name of
laws we are ignorant of. And yet we know that crime
reigns over the whole length and breadth of the earth,
and that no one hinders crime from reigning. We have
always been hungry, ignorant, dupes, slaves. And we are
criminals because there are those with full bellies, smart
alecks and bosses who proclaim so. And no one has
wanted to change it at all. The priests and the judges
have always respected the Tables of the Law, but no one
has taken thought about our crimes and inquired into our
misery. And when the Lord appears to us, it is to announce His vengeance, it is to let loose His scourges on
our frightened crowds, it is to set alight the faggots of
hatred.

But I tell you, we are criminals because injustice gov-
erns the great throng of mankind. And, in truth, I don't
know that the most shocking crimes are really ours. What
I do know is that we are strays, fools, imbeciles, who are

lied to, led on. In short, what I know is that men won't stay what they are. [*Raucously.*] Is there still any wine? Sometimes it's good to talk nonsense. [*He thrusts the thieves from him.*] Enough tragedy! Which of you will sing? We've got to laugh! Are we going to pass our last hours arousing our indignation, dwelling on our ancestral wrath? Let us sing! And let our voices even shock the soldiery. Let them ring out above the walls and go and wake up our masters in their palaces. Do you know the songs of the executioners? I'll sing you those of the murderers. Human songs, songs from life. They are songs that are magic to the extent that everything described in them comes true. The song of crime, listen! You begin by singing and you finish by killing. Listen. . . . [*Silence. Tragic dumb show by Barabbas; then he sings.*]

> When Barabbas ran the roads,
> Jostling the darkness,
> The earth cried out harshly
> And it breathed in agony—
> The earth that laps up blood!

The Two Thieves. Go on singing, Barabbas; your voice thrills our bowels!

Barabbas. Ah! Ah! . . . It's the song of crime. . . . Don't be surprised at anything. At the last verse I kill someone. Listen, but watch as well. Now I'm going along the road. Follow me closely. [*He imitates a clumsy, dubious walk; then he sings again.*]

> Now my fist is a club
> And my breast is a snuffer
> And my ten fingers are a garrote.
> I have more weapons than the devil.
> Now the earth is madly athirst for blood!

The Good Thief. Barabbas, where are you heading for?

Barabbas. Wait. Don't you see anything? I've already seen the victim. Or would it be the drunkenness from the wine mixed with the spell of the song that makes me see him? Listen and watch. . . . [*He advances, singing.*]

> A man lies in the road,
> A traveler at the end of his tether.
> A man lies there! He is the prey
> That will quiver in my hands.
> The thirsty earth will drink his blood!

The Bad Thief. It's true! Go on, Barabbas! There really is a victim! Are we so drunk?

BARABBAS *goes on, but hesitates. Not certain of himself, he looks attentively at a mass that lies motionless at the end of the jail and that none of them has so far noticed.*

Barabbas. Someone there? Then the crime is about to take place. Listen to the last verse. . . . [*He sings in a choking voice.*]

> Sudden crime bursts out of me
> Like the sea—like a rose.
> My nerves hurl me like a catapult.
> I have the prey. Crrk! . . . He's dead. . . .
> The earth drinks, is drunk with blood!

The Two Thieves. Kill him! The prey! Come on!

There is a heart-rendering cry. BARABBAS *draws back and stammers.*

Barabbas. Who cried out? The prey? Thieves, did you cry out? I was singing. . . . The darkness cried out. . . . Did I commit a murder?

The Good Thief [*indicating the mass*]. The prey, Barabbas! Witchcraft!

The Bad Thief. I'm still frozen from it. Men don't cry out like that. Oh, what a moan! You have killed, Barabbas! You weren't singing, you were killing!

Barabbas [*frightened*]. I don't know. It is horrible. I touched flesh, bones. I'm frightened. Hide me! Perhaps I have killed. Is it a man that I have killed? I don't know. I have killed and I didn't mean to kill this time. No one ever cries out like this one who cried out. My hands are burning. Go and see. I daren't. Something incomprehensible is going on in this prison.

The Good Thief. It's the wine. And it's the song. . . . You were crying out, "A man lies there!" A ghost, more like!

Barabbas. A ghost that cried out, whose carcass I felt?

The Bad Thief. Be quiet! There's a man there. He's moving. It would be better to kill him.

Barabbas. You don't kill ghosts. He's moving. . . . Yes. . . . [*Howling.*] It's one of my victims come back from the dead! I only want to fight with men, not with ghosts.

*All three go and flatten themselves against the bars. The
mass has moved. It is a man. He gets to his feet, slowly,
mysteriously.*

The Good Thief [*dully*]. Get out of this cage. . . . Yes,
it's a victim! Mine!

The Bad Thief. Mine! The man I murdered . . .

Barabbas. Remorse has taken on flesh in order to show
itself to us. Does remorse exist? Either it's a ghost or
else . . . it's an accomplice the judges have put in the
jail . . . to hoax us! [*Furious.*] I am Barabbas! I'll go for
this ghost. I'm not afraid! [*He slowly goes toward the
man, who is on his feet.*] Who are you? Are you in this
world or in another? Answer! [*He stops, fist raised. The
man staggers and little by little sinks to the ground.
BARABBAS rubs his eyes. He goes back toward the thieves.*]
Let's be quiet! I understand. He's one of ours. Look! He's
not moving any more. This man, I declare, this dying
man, is the same as we are, a wrongdoer, or a murderer.
Yes, a man condemned to death. They put him in our
cage while we were asleep. What has he done? What is
his name? Do you know him? There's no doubt he's
dying. Let's be quiet. It's a man. . . .

*They stay still and attentive. The man is now lit by a light
that comes from below. It is JESUS. Long silence. Then:
trumpets outside. The sound of arms. The three do not
budge during the happenings that are going to take place.
Two people, JUDAS and THE PRIEST, come along the cage.*

Judas. Where are you taking me, priest? This is a
tomb.

The Priest. It is the gateway to a tomb. From here, one
goes to death. Where am I taking you? Where you
wanted me to take you. Are you afraid you will be shut
up in your turn?

Judas. Do not mock, priest. I am not easy.

The Priest. What have you got on your conscience
that is troubling you, Judas? Gaze at your ease on these
prisoners, and among them him you are so interested in.

Judas. You have put him among these tramps, in this
cage? Him?

The Priest. Yes, indeed, it is a mistake to put a poor
thirty-penny wrongdoer among these wicked fellows. But,
you see, it had to be a secure cage, since he excels in

working wonders. The cage has held out. And the wonder-worker doesn't look in sparkling condition. What a woeful posture for the founder of a kingdom. Do you see him?

Judas. Where is he?

The Priest. There! That humiliated creature.

Judas [*hiding his face*]. I dare not look. He is unrecognizable. Rend yourself, my soul!

The Priest. Your soul? It is well known to us, Judas. Your soul isn't the sort that rends itself. It sleeps in your purse. Gaze at your ease, at your complete ease, on him you sold us. What morbid sentiment makes you want to see him again? Do you want to give him another kiss? Do you want to spit in his face? Or count your thirty pence under his nose? Do you want to feast on his downfall? It would be in your line, all that. But I do not want to deprive you of these delights, you who served our plans so well. I leave you to your contemplation, Judas. Make yourself at home here. [*He withdraws a few paces.*]

Judas [*after hesitations and gestures through the bars, speaking in a toneless voice*]. Master! [JESUS *moves imperceptibly.*] Master! [JESUS *tries to rise to his feet, but falls down again.*] Master, do you still please to know me? I am Judas, Master. Judas, your apostle. In short, Judas! I wanted to see you again to explain to you. . . . The kiss I gave you . . . I didn't know what I was doing, but an unknown force made me give you that kiss. Did I betray you? Yet you knew in advance that one of us would betray you. At that time you had an ineluctable expression that seemed to order me to betray you. Why did I do these things? What fate did I have to submit to? [*Pause.*] Why won't you listen to me? Master? All the apostles have betrayed you. They have all taken to flight. You no longer have any apostles. I am the only one to dare to rejoin you. Why do you not upbraid me? Why do you not show your anger or your contempt? [*Pause.* JUDAS *flies into a passion and raises his voice.*] I am Judas! Get up and curse me! Ah, if you cursed me, I would ask your forgiveness; but you say nothing. That is because there is no pardon for such a betrayal. That is what you allow me to understand. There is no more hope for me? And I am unable to weep. Weep? I have an overwhelming desire to do that. Perhaps you would listen to me if

I could weep. But I remain frozen, insensible, and I revolt myself. Master! You must explain to me the meaning of my actions, for I can understand nothing of what I have done. By what secret will, stronger than my own, did I act? And who would have betrayed you if I had not done it? Judas alone was able to betray you. And no doubt I have played the role to which I was predestined? I have performed my frightful duty. And now? What am I to do? Betray you again? Master? Or abandon myself to my despair?—for I am in despair, although frozen and insensible. Master, I shall have strength. I shall go to the bottom of Hell if you wish it. [*He moans like a child.*]

The Priest. Judas, you are wasting your time. Haven't you had your pay? Then leave your old Master to his fate.

Judas [*startled*]. What fate will you prepare for him, priest?

The Priest. The one that political sagacity dictates.

Judas. But he isn't guilty!

The Priest. Are you trying to save him? Why did you deliver him up?

Barabbas [*who has imperceptibly drawn near, seizing* JUDAS *by the arm*]. Judas! If the man who lies near us doesn't recognize you, I recognize you well.

Judas. Get back! I'm not of your kind.

The Priest [*laughing*]. Barabbas, have pity on this wretch overwhelmed by despair.

Barabbas. What a pleasure to see you again, Judas. Do you remember? You weren't an honorable brigand or a cunning pickpocket—only a pale and obscure fence; but you were always quaking and you were satisfied with an indifferent profit. Old Judas! What shady motive brings you to this prison? And what have you done to the dying man you are pleading with?

The Priest. Not much. He delivered the fellow up to us, and for a reasonable sum.

Barabbas [*thrusting* JUDAS *away*]. Scorpion! You sold him? Get out of this prison! There are murderers in here, not traitors! We kill our neighbor, we don't sell him.

Judas [*fleeing beneath* THE PRIEST'S *ironical gaze*]. There has been a mistake, I assure you. I am not the one who . . . [*He disappears.*]

The Priest. Yes. . . . In all peoples and in all ages there

will always be those who will deliver up the weak. I
congratulate you on your loyal disposition, Barabbas.
What a pity you have to be executed! For it seems likely
that you will be executed, even though . . . it's not
absolutely certain. . . .

Barabbas. That's all right. When?

The Priest. Today, perhaps. It is the Passover. There
will be a great crowd. Could we have chosen better? We
shall order the ceremony in such a way as to satisfy your
pride. All the magistracy in the front row. Me too, your
admirer. For I do admire you. I admire your powerful
faculties, your radiant state of mind. Ah! if it only de-
pended on me! I wouldn't leave you in this cage. One
can do something with men of your stamp.

Barabbas. I'm deeply moved. Yes, I could have been
someone. Now if you were to give me clothes like yours,
I would be the ornament of your caste. Eh? You agree?

The Priest. You are on one side of the cage, I am on the
other. For the moment it is better that each of us stays
where he is. Still, one never knows what may happen.

Barabbas. Stop your hinting. You came to give me
notice of the execution. I know what it's necessary to
know.

The Priest. You don't know everything.

Barabbas. Get on with you! This jesting passes the time.

The Priest. What you don't know is that they will
execute, at the same time as you, one of the most extraordinary of characters, whose popularity exceeds
yours.

Barabbas [*annoyed*]. You're lying. There's only one
Barabbas. Find me a killer, priest, whose exploits are as
grand and as many as mine. Are you trying to get at me
through my self-respect? A crude trick! Or, if this condemned man does exist, what crime named in your laws
has he been able to commit? Where is this criminal, this
rare bird? Show me this superman!

The Priest [*indicating* JESUS]. There he is.

Barabbas [*with a ringing laugh*]. Him? He shouldn't be
flung into a prison, but a lazaretto. Him? A criminal?
Him, Barabbas' competitor? Him, my equal, my rival?
And he has done more than me, better than me? Do you
hear, comrades? Shame is burning my brow. Priest, if it is
as you say with such seriousness, let me out of this prison
for a few hours, time to commit a new heinous crime

that will surpass all the others in horror, an indescribable crime that will give me back the rank I have a right to, the prestige I have been robbed of. After that, I'll come back quietly to my cage.

The Priest. You couldn't do anything that would make you as guilty as this man.

Barabbas [*distraught*]. But if he is stronger than me, if he is more glorious than Barabbas, what is he?

The Priest. The enemy of the Nation!

Silence. THE PRIEST *goes out slowly. Trumpets outside.* BARABBAS *is all at sea. He goes around* JESUS, *trying to make him out.*

Barabbas [*stifling his anger*]. Comrade! It's not certain that you will have the honor of sharing my punishment. Get up, enemy of the Nation! I'm the enemy of Society. Let us measure our strength. But I shall only fight if you undertake to defend yourself. We must fight. On your feet! [*He is going to lay hold of* JESUS.]

The Good Thief. Stop, Barabbas! The man isn't able to fight.

The Bad Thief. Understand! He's not a tough. Nor one of the boys. The priest came to incite you against this pale brother so that you would do him harm. I am going to reveal the truth to you. This man isn't like us.

Barabbas. You are right, thieves. He's a brother in misfortune. You can see that well enough. And then, he's an enemy of the Nation. From the moment he's the enemy of something . . .

The Good Thief. What I know is that he's going to die, like us. And if the four of us are together going to die the same death, I see a good reason for fraternizing, for all that.

Barabbas. Yes! Have we still any wine? [*He takes the jar and holds it out to* JESUS.] Drink, man. It's your share. You will forget your troubles, and in drunkenness you will find courage. Don't stay crumpled on the ground like this. Is your suffering different from ours? Has life less value for you than it has for us? Or has death already broken you? Cheer up, friend. I'm going to help you, to teach you how to go on.

He raises JESUS *with difficulty, and sets him on his feet; then he draws back. An unreal light shines around* JESUS,

*who seems blind and moves staggering toward the stone
steps. When he reaches the steps, he falls to his knees;
then he becomes still in a praying position from which he
does not henceforth move—the statue of Grief.*

The Good Thief. Take care, Barabbas.

The Bad Thief. He's not a murderer, that one; he's one
of the murdered!

Barabbas. He has the shape of a man, the death agony of
a man; but what is this light that surrounds him, what is
this dawn in our mortal darkness?

The Good Thief. And why are you trembling, Barabbas? What are you afraid of?

The Bad Thief. I have seen this man; but where and
when?

Barabbas. I know this man and his legend. We have all
seen him. I recognize this man.

The Good Thief. Barabbas, this prison is no longer ours.
And our infamy is no longer the same.

The Bad Thief. Yes, they said this man was insane. I
remember. He talked about redemption, and the people
asked him for bread.

Barabbas. Wasn't he an ambitious fellow who wanted
to set up the crowd against authority? But he talked too
much to the crowd instead of commanding it to act. This
man is the victim of dreams; leave him to his dreams.
[*Pause.*] Listen to me, comrades! I'm going to tell you the
whole truth. This Jesus was the leader of a band, like
me, a rebel. . . . His only mistake was to want to manage
things with gentleness when violence was what was
needed. If he had come to see me, and if he had said,
"Barabbas, let us join together," we wouldn't have been
long in reigning over the kingdom he talked about so
eloquently. But here we are. . . .

And whom did he pick out to help him? Men who were
humble, timid, hotheaded, incapable of action. Think
whether the judges and the priests didn't have an easy
time of it. He only cost them thirty pence. That's the
story of this man. . . . [*Pause.*] It grieves me to see him
in this state. Did he at least defend himself? He seems
indifferent to what happens to him. After all, even in this
prison, couldn't he melt the bars and throw down the
walls by means of his magician's skill if he wanted to?
We could save both his kingdom and our skin. But I
don't dare suggest it to him. [*Pause.*] And then, who says

that his wish is not to die? [*Pause.*] Not so us, comrades! Whatever we may say about it. We die because there's no means of doing anything else. [*He seizes his chains and stares at them stubbornly.*]

The Good Thief. Death is haunting you, Barabbas. Is it the presence of the other?

Barabbas. I don't know. I've got a feeling I've never had before.

The Bad Thief. We were counting on your example, Barabbas, on your moral strength, in order to remain brave in our last moments.

Barabbas. A harrowing feeling. It's because of the wine, because of this man. . . .

Trumpets outside. Music strikes up, bagpipes and kettle-drums. There is a distant hum like the noise of a town waking on a holiday morning. BARABBAS *moves to the steps where* JESUS *lies.*

Barabbas. I ought to explain to him. . . . But will he, can he still, hear? I would like to explain what is wretched, insane, delusive, about our death, our annihilation. We have been unavailing, like tracts of land that contain nothing but stones and dead remains. We haven't been able to alter anything of all that we found baneful, sickening, and hateful. And after our useless death, Justice will still not be done, and untruth will reign no less supremely than it has reigned since human beings have existed. That is what drives this man to despair, and that is what drives me to despair also. [*He drinks of the wine and throws away the jar, which breaks.*] The festivities are beginning. Listen to the bands. The crowd is merry. And have they really a reason for making merry? The time is about to come. Soon nothing will remain of what we are. There is nothing more to do than to wait and to offer no resistance, just as he is offering no resistance.

THE TWO THIEVES *draw close to* BARABBAS.

The Good Thief. Barabbas, death is dreadful! We don't want to disappear, not this way. . . .

The Bad Thief. Tell us, Barabbas, how will you die?

Barabbas [*bawling*]. Like a pig under the knife! [*Coming to himself again.*] That doesn't matter any more, my friends. . . .

Trumpets. The sound of arms. The two thieves lie at
BARABBAS' *feet as though to protect themselves.* BARABBAS
gazes at JESUS.

Voices Outside. Barabbas! Barabbas! [*Prolonged whistling.*]

Barabbas [*not hearing*]. But you, Jesus? . . . [*Pause.*]
We must see if the crowd is pleased with me, if I hold
out. . . . [*He goes and sits on the steps near* JESUS.] And
what do you want me to say when you keep silence, you,
Jesus of Nazareth, the man with the golden mouth? . . .
You who certainly know more than ordinary people.
. . . [*He hides his face in his hands and remains motionless.*]

Desperate Voices Outside. Barabbas! Barabbas! Barabbas!

The Two Thieves [*moaning dully*]. Barabbas! Barabbas! Barabbas!

Great and sudden light. SOLDIERS *come along the cage.
Heavy rhythmical march. Drums beat funereally.*

ACT TWO

The street and, set back a little, the entrance to PILATE'S
*palace, the edge of whose pedimented porch can be seen
to the left. In front of the entrance and extending into the
main area of the stage, a terrace, which one can reach by
steps. A fire is burning on this promontory, making* THE
CROWD, *massed on the other side, invisible.*

*A woman stands motionless in the light from the fire. A
confused noise can be heard in the distance. A shadow
passes swiftly below the terrace—*YOCHABETH, *the sordid
and hideous wife of* JUDAS. *The woman watching by the
fire is* PILATE'S WIFE.

YOCHABETH [*like a dog on the scent*]. Where is the
money? Judas! Where is the money? Where are you,
Judas? You have deserted me. You love money. You don't
love me any more, Judas. The first day, and the only day,
that you have money honestly come by, you desert me,
me your wife. Do you reckon on being rich without me,

Judas? Judas! Judas! [*She goes up the steps leading to the terrace.*] But I shall find you. I shall go after you, even into the depths of the slums, even into the Temple, for you haunt both of them, you man without a conscience! [*She sets foot on the terrace.*]

Pilate's Wife. Guards!

Sound of arms. A SOLDIER *appears and bars the way to* YOCHABETH.

Soldier. What do you want?

Yochabeth. The money! And my husband, Judas, as he's called! He is rich by thirty pence. He possesses money, and money possesses him. I need both of them. [*She slumps to the steps and weeps openly.*]

Pilate's Wife. Go, soldier! [THE SOLDIER *goes, and* PILATE'S WIFE, *her ears pricked up, comes to the flight of steps.*] Thirty pence, woman? Was it a wage?

Yochabeth. The one wage, the only wage, he ever earned. [*She gets up.*]

Pilate's Wife. The wage for what task?

Yochabeth. For a good deed, a good piece of work. Listen, you who seem to be interested in my fate. Judas—he's my husband—no longer has a trade. He has wasted his time, made a mess of his life. He followed an adventurer along God knows what roads. He abandoned me in want. But this time, I vouch for it, he has done a good deed. He has done a great service for the priests and the senators. He has redeemed himself, re-established himself. He sold . . .

Pilate's Wife. Do not mention that name tonight!

Yochabeth. He sold the adventurer. The priests rewarded him. Hmph! Is thirty pence a reward? Judas has saved the Nation! For, you know well enough, the adventurer wanted to do away with the established order and found a kingdom after his own heart.

Pilate's Wife. What do we know about it? This is what you say, and the Jewish rabble along with you. This is what the Jewish priests say.

Yochabeth. Listen! This fellow whose chimeras Judas shared wanted to try a stroke of violence. That has been well understood since the triumphal entry into the city of a cohort of his apostles. But Judas' conscience came back to him. He had a presentiment that opinion disapproved of the adventurer's plans. I am truly proud of him. For once he acted according to his conscience. And I would be

happy if he hadn't fled with the money. If he goes off
again, that's his business—but not with the money! Help
me, woman, help me! Haven't you come across anyone?
[*She takes* PILATE'S WIFE'S *hand.*]

Pilate's Wife [*drawing back*]. Do not touch me. I am
not of your kind.

Yochabeth. Then who are you?

Pilate's Wife. The governor's wife.

Nonplused, YOCHABETH *quickly goes down the steps and,
without a word, goes and sinks against the terrace wall.
Pause. Another shadow slips furtively below the promenade. It is* JUDAS. *He does not see his wife and kneels near
the wall a few paces from her; then he sets about counting
his money with exaggerated motions.* YOCHABETH *has
flattened herself against the ground.*

PILATE *appears on the terrace. He is lean and smooth. He
walks toward the fire and stops in front of the flames. His
wife joins him. Their faces are lit up. They look at each
other coldly.*

Pilate. What are you doing in front of this fire?

Pilate's Wife. I am waiting for the dawn.

Pilate. Why not sleep?

Pilate's Wife. For fear of the nightmares that assail me.
[*Pause.*] And why are you not sleeping tonight, Pilate?

PILATE *does not reply and goes back, close-mouthed, into
his palace. His wife follows him. Below the terrace,* JUDAS
has begun to speak.

Judas. Money . . . money . . . money . . . five . . .
six . . . seven . . . money . . . twelve . . . thirteen . . .
fourteen . . . fifteen . . . money . . . twenty-eight . . .
twenty-nine . . . thirty . . . money! Thirty pieces of
happiness . . . Thirty pieces of bitterness . . . [*He laughs
painfully.*] Ah, who says money has no color? It glitters
with red sparkles! And who says it has no smell? It smells
of carrion! It is fiendish money, bewitched metal. And
these thirty pence weigh heavier than thirty millstones.
I dare not read the inscription cut in this gold. I dare not
look at the image shining on this gold, Caesar's head,
death's head or Judas' head. This gold is baleful. This gold
is accursed!

I wanted to give alms, and the cripples and the blind men pushed my hand away, as though I had offered them a burning poker. I wanted to drink, and the innkeeper shouted at me that an unnamable liquid was flowing from his casks, a stream of sweat mixed with spit. I was hungry, and the baker yelled in my face that his bread had just changed into blocks of granite. [*Harrowingly.*] I have been cheated! I have been cheated! I sold my Master, and the money they gave me for this piece of work is no use for anything, neither for good . . . nor for ill. . . . I have been cheated! [*He weeps and throws the purse in front of him;* YOCHABETH *leaps on the purse.*]

Yochabeth. The money!

Judas [*erect*]. Stop, thief! it's mine! The money belongs to me!

Yochabeth [*defending herself*]. To the two of us, Judas, to us two.

Judas [*striking her*]. To me alone. My money is mine, like my crime.

Yochabeth. Give me the money; keep your crime.

Judas. It's not money. It's no longer money. It is filthy stuff that I am going to fling into the sea.

Yochabeth. You are a liar, Judas. It's good money; my nose tells me so. Count the pieces. Or have you already spent some without me?

Judas. Take it! Take it! And be a thing possessed like this that you covet! But leave me a few farthings, enough to buy a rope.

Yochabeth. Why buy a rope, unless it's to strangle yourself with? Believe me, Judas, you are not worth the rope at whose end you'd swing. Have yourself strangled by the devil; it would be a saving. Come on now, give!

Judas. No, indeed! I won't give it to you! This money is going back to the priests. I am going to give it back to them, or I shall fling it into the Temple. But can't you see that I am suffering?

Yochabeth. Suffering? You? If you were capable of the least feeling, would you have deserted your wife?

Judas. I acted according to my heart.

Yochabeth. Your heart? Did you become a lousy wretch, a tramp, a thief, according to your heart? No fear, Judas, by a feeling for money, yes, by mean interest. By hatred of work. By delusions of grandeur. For all these reasons, you shabby little Jew. Dung! Son of a pig! Did you even for a single instant believe in him you called Master and who thought to become king?

Judas. Yes. He was light. He was warmth. He was Justice.

Yochabeth. Did you act according to your heart when you delivered him to his enemies?

Judas. Hold your tongue! Women are too stupid to understand a thing about this tragedy. The Son of Man had to be delivered up. It was written. And I knew that this wicked yet supernatural mission had devolved on me, down all eternity. And even if I had fled to the bowels of the earth, my treachery would still have been accomplished.

Yochabeth. A fine explanation! And how well you talk! But why did you discuss the price of the betrayal so keenly? Was that written?

Judas. Do not plague me, Yochabeth! Or if you find me loathsome, why do you want to have the money from my crime? Yochabeth, you are despicable. Go . . . go . . . go!

Yochabeth [*grinding her teeth*]. I shall follow you, you and your gold, as far as the darkness where you are going to strangle yourself. And you will indeed be forced to let go of your treasure when you choke.

Judas. Slut!

Yochabeth. Judas! What is this horrible mask stuck on your face?

Judas. It is the true face, the imperishable face of Judas. Be proud of your husband! Be proud of him who sold the Son of the living God!

Yochabeth. Your God is a seducer, a madman.

Judas. Take the gold, but hold your tongue; do not blaspheme!

Yochabeth [*seizing the purse and letting it fall*]. Ah! It's burning!

Judas. Yes, it's burning. Indeed, it is Hell already declaring itself in that purse. Take it, do take it, my beloved wife.

Yochabeth. No, no. You take it! We must go. Take it!

Judas [*picking up the purse*]. We are rich! Well, well! Rich in infamy! I love you, wife, I love you. . . . [*Full of hatred.*] You are not worthy of a rope either. You are not worth the claws of the devil. I am going to prove my love to you. [*He tries to strangle her.*]

Yochabeth. Murder! [*She gives vent to hideous cries.*] *Sound of arms.* JUDAS *lets go of* YOCHABETH's *neck. Pause. The noise dies away.*

Judas. Pity! [*Uneasy.*] Shadows are gliding toward us. [*Lights brush the terrace wall.*] These folk know I have gold. Come, Yochabeth!

Yochabeth. I am afraid of the gold—of your hands! You are a murderer!

Judas [*dragging her along*]. More than a murderer, Yochabeth, much more. I have the death of a God on me! [*They go out.*]

Silence. The shining circles from dark lanterns, like stars, come and sweep the stage sinisterly; then shadowy forms come in. They are indefinable. Their faces are hidden by
    black dominoes, and they are covered by cloaks.

A Voice. Brethren!

Another Voice. Brethren!

An Apostle. Put out the lights! [*The lamps go out.*]

Another Apostle. Darkness is within us, thicker than over the world.

Another Apostle. The dawn will not break again.

An Apostle. Where is the prison? We shall wail before its walls and the walls will moan with us.

The Apostle John. Moaning will not do any good. Did our Master utter a single moan?

An Apostle. We shall never understand the reasons for his suffering. And if he dies, his death will remain inexplicable.

An Apostle. Why did he speak so mysteriously to us about all things? Here we are forsaken! And if the shepherd is stricken, what will become of the flock?

Another Apostle. We are in the pit of the night, and no one knows what ought to be done.

John. Listen! We are crying like children. We are crying because his voice is still. Here we are incoherent. Did his word never enter into us, then?

An Apostle. Who will lead us to the Promised Land?

An Apostle. We shall never reach that kingdom. We shall be wiped out, one after the other.

An Apostle. All is finished, brethren. We shall become poor men again, workmen, fishermen. One of us was a traitor. Another pretended not to know the Master. There were those who slept while the Master was at the point of death. Where are the others? Where are the crowds that followed Jesus in the countryside, more numerous than the stars in the sky?

Another Apostle. Oh, Master, joy is dead, and hope. What have we done to you?

John. Enough! Did he not foretell that he would rise from the dead? Then what will he say if he finds you quaking and shivering in your shoes? And if he does not rise again, has he not left us his flesh and his blood in memory of him? Haven't we the promise of eternal life?

An Apostle. Brother, do you say this in truth, or do you say it in order to raise our courage again?

A lamp lights up the apostle JOHN.

John. I say this because I believe it, for Christ affirmed it. Nothing will prevent the fulfillment of our Master's Passion. It was enough that the drama began for your faith to find itself shaken. Well, you who are in tears, you who have doubts, tell me: was Christ the Son of the living God? He confounded the learned men and the doctors of the Law.

An Apostle. He gave back life to Lazarus.

An Apostle. Sight to the blind.

An Apostle. Limbs to the paralyzed.

An Apostle. He calmed the tempest.

An Apostle. He walked on the waters.

An Apostle. He multiplied the loaves and satisfied a whole multitude.

An Apostle. He unmasked the hypocrites.

An Apostle. He spared the adulterous woman.

An Apostle. He changed the water into wine.

An Apostle. He drove the merchants from the Temple.

John. You were witnesses of his miracles and you remember them with wonder; but which of you could repeat to me the profound words he spoke on the mountain? He knew, brethren, he well knew that we were weak. He well knew that our fear and our dispersal were close. But did he not prophesy that we should depart to the four corners of the earth to bear witness to his glory?

An Apostle. Perhaps we shall set out tomorrow for this world of his dreams, but where are we to run this constricting night?

Another Apostle. Has anyone considered or even thought of rescuing our Master?

An Apostle. Who would dare?

Another Apostle. We would dare, if we knew that was what he wanted.

John. Wretched men! Did he not go out to meet his enemies? Oh, do not act unless a divine command orders you to. It is written, I swear it, it is written that the Son of Man shall be sacrificed. It is dreadful and it is right. And the stars would go out in the sky, and the earth would break up, if this sacrifice were not accomplished.

An Apostle. There's the fanatical disciple for you. Words! Who is going to act, then? Christ furthermore prophesied that the city would be destroyed, that his kingdom was at hand. Who knows that it isn't we who shall destroy the city and found the kingdom? Who knows that our Master's voice is not going to ring out imperiously from the depths of the prison, that we are not going to collect the crowd, rouse it, and hurl it against the prison to deliver him who will be king! [*He lights his lamp.*] Let us answer violence by violence! Light your lamps! [*All the lamps light, except one.*]

John. Fear to perish by the sword! Recall the example of our Master, I beseech you.

An Apostle. No, no! It's we who are disregarding our human duty. It is better to perish, better that our blood flow in purity. Or must we go back to the common herd as shamefaced men, after all the mirages we have glimpsed?

John. Hold your peace, brethren; put out these lamps!

The Apostles. No! Swords! Torches!

Uproar. PILATE *appears on the terrace. Sound of arms. Military commands. All the lamps go out.*

The Apostle. Quiet! [THE APOSTLES *are still.*]

Pilate [*haggard, gazing on the scene*]. Shadows? More shadows? My palace is haunted.

An Apostle [*in a low voice*]. Perhaps this foreigner who rules us will decide life or death. Who will speak to him? [*Shouting.*] There are judges at Rome!

Pilate [*making movements like one asleep*]. What do these shadows want of me? This is persecution. Soldiers! Drive these phantoms away!

A Soldier *looms up.*

The Apostle [*rapidly mounting the steps to the terrace*]. Pilate, there are judges at Rome!
The Soldier. Halt!
Pilate. Drive them away! I don't want to hear anything. . . .

The Apostles *scatter and go.* The Apostle *who called on* Pilate *is thrown to the foot of the steps and makes off, running. Pause.*

Pilate. Dawn. . . . Ah! Let dawn come! What a night! What an age! Soldier! Is dawn showing itself?
The Soldier. Not yet.
Pilate. I want it to appear. I order the sun to rise. Soldier, have reveille sounded!

The Soldier *withdraws. Orders are shouted in the distance. A trumpet sounds. Other trumpets reply and sound reveille.* Pilate's Wife *enters silently.*

Pilate's Wife [*to* Pilate, *who is standing in the glow of the fire*]. Pilate!
Pilate [*starts and turns around*]. You! Will you finally go to sleep?
Pilate's Wife. I shall not sleep. Didn't I hear reveille sounding—even though the night isn't over? . . . Or did I hear these trumpets sounding on the borders of my dreams?
Pilate. Your dreams?
Pilate's Wife. Yes, my dreams. You must know about them.
Pilate. I don't want to know about a woman's dreams. My own cares are sufficient for me.
Pilate's Wife. Your cares and my dreams have the same cause. You know well enough what I am going to tell you. What torments me is tormenting you as well. The man I have dreamed about to the point of obsession has entered into your memory.
Pilate. The Galilean?
Pilate's Wife. Take care, Pilate! I dreamed that you were condemning an innocent man.
Pilate. I shall only condemn him who is worthy of condemnation by virtue of the laws which I administer and which I safeguard. Just now a voice cried to me from the

depths of the night that there were judges at Rome. That is all that matters to me. . . . [*Pause.*] As if there weren't enough gods without this Galilean!

Pilate's Wife. Cruel gods. . . . But, Pilate, we still look for a God who is better than us, more just; we await him eagerly, in spite of the fact that there are so many idols among so many peoples, so many virtues in Rome.

Pilate. Be quiet! Dreams are your business. Reason is my domain.

They gaze at each other for a long time. Finally, PILATE *closes his eyes.* HEROD *enters below the steps. Day breaks at last. The ringing of bells greets the dawn.* PILATE'S WIFE *withdraws into the palace, while* HEROD, *the short-winded tetrarch, climbs the steps.*

Herod. Greetings, Pontius Pilate! Up already, dear Governor? Or haven't you been to sleep yet?

Pilate. Greetings, Herod! I have not slept. All the coldness of the night is flowing through my flesh.

Herod. I have not slept either. Sleep is too much like death, and life is too short. Life is made for pleasure. Do you know that, severe Roman? The city by night had a most extraordinary appearance on this festival eve. I mingled with the riffraff. Very laughable! But what a crew these Jews are!

Pilate. You are one of them, Herod, and you even govern them.

Herod [*in an artificial manner*]. Oh, I share their origin, so noble, so distant; but not their smell, not their manners.

Pilate. As for manners, to tell the truth, you are worthy of the Roman aristocracy. As for smell, Herod, you have scented yourself with musk like a third-rate courtesan.

Herod [*laughing heartily*]. Oh! . . . Pilate! . . . You will never like the Orientals. I pity you for having to live in this land.

Pilate. Indeed I am to be pitied when Herod makes me gifts like the one he offered me tonight.

Herod [*falsely ingenuous*]. What? What Herod sent to Pilate? The Galilean? [*He laughs.*] But . . . I thought this fantastic character was going to amuse you. Only you should see him at liberty. I have not been able to get anything out of him. He was tired and close-mouthed. What could I do with him? And what fate could I set

aside for him—unless to clothe him in the fool's robe? It
was in that costume that I sent him to you. Come, Pilate,
you certainly must have seen other madmen in Rome, at
theatres, at baths, at feasts, at circuses?

Pilate. Everything is merely a joke to you. You would
see your people slaughtered without your pointless smile
leaving your painted lips.

Herod. Is that a reproach? Am I not, as you describe me,
a true friend of Rome? Pilate, you gloomy man, you are
the victim of too frigid an education. You are from the
Occident. [*He taps him on the stomach.*] Well then, have
you expelled your Galilean from this city? Or shut him
up in some padded cell?

Pilate. No. I can't. The priests demand that he be tried.

Herod. The priests have nothing to demand. The quar-
relsome rascals! And if they are demanding that their prisoner be tried, why did they send him to me?

Pilate. And why do you send him to me? No one seems
to know by whom or on what grounds this man ought to
be tried. What is his fault?

Herod. His fault is not being like the rest. Between ourselves, he is a careerist. What a clumsy one! Well, try him.
But go about it carefully; the Galilean is very popular.
And on the other hand, the priests don't wish him particularly well. So find an elegant formula. Good night. I
am going to bed. [*He is about to go.*]

Pilate [*holding him back*]. An elegant formula . . .
compatible with the laws. Which laws? The ancestral laws
of the priests, or the laws of the Roman senators?

Herod. Ahem! Take what can be of use to you from all
the laws, and interpret it according to the circumstances.
Don't try to have the wisdom of old King Solomon. Ah!
Our times are no longer times of wisdom. [*In* PILATE's
ear.] And think of your position.

Pilate. What are you trying to insinuate?

Herod. I mean that the priests will leave nothing undone
to influence you. Would you like a piece of advice, a
piece of Oriental advice? Set the public going. Make use
of the nerve-racking atmosphere of this feast of the Passover, of the state of feeling of the crowd. Remember the
customs.

Pilate [*interested*]. Ah, yes. Let the crowd ask for the
liberation of the Galilean?

Herod. In this way you will be covered and you will have the inward satisfaction of having thwarted the plans of the priests. As for the poor Galilean, he will betake himself to other territories.

CAIAPHAS *appears below the terrace.*

Herod. Didn't I tell you they were on the lookout? This one who is coming is their great chief. He doesn't come without a reason. [*Ostentatiously.*] Pilate, look at the sky. What fine festivities we are going to have! [*He yawns fit to dislocate his jaws.*]

Day has broken. The hum of THE CROWD *can be heard.* CAIAPHAS *climbs swiftly to the terrace.*

Caiaphas. Greetings! Yes, fine festivities. Herod, what have you done with the man who was brought to you?

Herod. I ridiculed him. That is all that one could do. Then I sent him to Pilate.

Caiaphas. From Herod to Pilate, as always. And what are you going to do with this man, Pilate?

Pilate. I don't know. What is there to do, Caiaphas? What do the priests think about it?

Caiaphas. The priests think he must be tried.

Pilate. Is that indeed your will?

Caiaphas. Our will? Oh, no! It is the will of Israel, of the people.

Herod. Of the people? What are the people going to do about it? Where are your people?

Caiaphas [*indicating the back of the stage*]. There they are!

HEROD *and* PILATE *turn around. Suddenly, as though on a signal from* CAIAPHAS, *the noise of a great* CROWD, *which was already loud, is heard.*

Pilate. Is it you who have called this servile rabble together, priest? Why this pressure?

Caiaphas [*humbly*]. There is no pressure, Governor. There is only a crowd alarmed by happenings whose gravity will not escape you. It is in the name of the people that I question you.

Pilate. Drop these orator's manners. What does this crowd want?

Herod [*feigning indignation*]. Why, that you try the

Galilean! That's clear enough. . . . As for Caiaphas, he's not only waiting for you to try him, but for you to condemn him as well.

Pilate. So be it! I shall try him. Condemn him? I seek in vain for this man's faults. On the contrary, I can clearly make out the motions of your hatred, Caiaphas.

Caiaphas. What you call my hatred is my desire for order and Justice, the love that I bear to my Nation.

Pilate. Very well; but the faults, the faults of this madman?

Caiaphas. He is not mad, but seditious. This man has blasphemed against God, against the divine laws, against the principles of our religion and our secular authority. This man is the enemy of the Nation and therefore the enemy of Rome. Has he not raised his voice against Caesar? Consequently, Pilate, it behooves you to try him.

Pilate. He has spoken against Caesar? That is what I shall try to find out. Your charge seems well thought out, and nothing in this case, whose importance I do not wish to exaggerate, seems to have been formulated in a hurry.

Herod. Not even the arrest of the offender, sold by one of his fellows at the suggestion of the priests. For how much, Caiaphas?

Caiaphas. I know nothing about these things.

Herod [*sarcastically*]. Not even the gathering of this early morning crowd, drunk with . . . Justice. This crowd that is here, good for paying tribute and bringing offerings in ordinary times, good for being insulted and ill-treated. Today, quite suddenly illuminated, it is good for unerringly calling out for Justice. Ah! Ah! But this crowd is intoxicated with wine! Who gave it drink? Who brought the crowd before this palace?

Caiaphas. I know nothing about these things. Nothing will divert me from my duty. May you accomplish yours, Pilate. It is useless to talk to you of your duties, Herod. You are a peacock, a gourmet, a fat invalid. All the same, a first-rate friend, aren't you?

Herod [*softened*]. Ah, Caiaphas! . . . We have indeed learned to appraise each other.

Pilate. Stop it!

Caiaphas. It is I who ask you to stop it, to re-establish peace and security in the land. It is the moment for it. And if you falter, or if you seek to escape your responsibilities, we priests will claim Justice elsewhere.

Pilate. What do you mean?

Caiaphas. Governors are made and broken according to Caesar's whim, according to whether Caesar has a good or a bad digestion. Take care that Caesar doesn't digest badly!

Pilate. Quite so, Caiaphas.

Caiaphas [*bowing*]. Your very humble servant, Pontius Pilate. [*Naïvely.*] What must I accordingly announce to the people?

Pilate [*nervously*]. To the people? To your people?

Caiaphas. To the people of Israel.

Herod. We could begin by making a speech to them.

PILATE *goes toward the back of the stage, appraises* THE CROWD *at a glance, and comes back quickly.*

The Crowd [*exploding, invisible*]. Pi-late, Pi-late, Pi-late!

Pilate [*to* CAIAPHAS]. Announce that, faithful to the traditions of the Passover, we shall deliver to them a prisoner of their choosing.

Caiaphas. And is Jesus among those you select?

Pilate. Yes.

Caiaphas. Then that is an admission that Jesus is condemned?

Pilate. So he was, by you.

Herod. This will be very merry. But you must leave the initiative to the crowd and offer them various victims, otherwise where is the free choice, the gamble?

Pilate. That is provided for. There is another. A criminal.

Caiaphas. This criminal is Barabbas, of course?

Pilate. It is Barabbas.

Herod. He's a champion, is that one. [*He pretends to disembowel* CAIAPHAS.]

Caiaphas [*smiling*]. I thought you were better informed, Pilate. Do you at least know the feeling of the crowd with respect to Barabbas?

Pilate. I know your feeling with respect to the Galilean.

Caiaphas. The crowd will choose. The crowd also knows how to judge, and its judgments are without appeal.

Herod. You might as well hold a meeting of tigers, jackals, and vultures.

Pilate [*out of patience, to* CAIAPHAS]. Announce, then . . . announce . .

Caiaphas. Don't be harassed, Pilate. Speak with confidence!

Pilate. Announce that, following tradition, the governor will have two prisoners exposed to the generosity of the people. That the people may release one. That is all I can do.

Caiaphas. It is more convenient than judging.

Pilate. Less dishonest. Even though I might have washed my hands of it.

Herod. Ah! Fine festivities! Fine festivities!

PILATE *withdraws toward the porch.* CAIAPHAS *goes toward the back of the stage.* THE PRIEST *who was seen in the jail, in the first act, enters and comes up on the terrace.* HEROD *seems delighted.*

The Crowd [in chorus]. Cai-a-phas! Cai-a-phas! Cai-a-phas!

CAIAPHAS *holds out his arms toward* THE CROWD. *Silence falls immediately.*

Caiaphas. People. . . . Holy people. . . . Chosen people. . . . Persecuted people. . . . People of suffering. . . . People of kings and prophets. . . . [*He meditates, his face in his hands.*]

Pilate [to a SOLDIER]. Go to the jail. Bring the one who is going to die today: Barabbas. And bring as well the one that the priests want to put to death: Jesus of Nazareth.

THE SOLDIER *goes. From now on,* PILATE *remains apart.* THE PRIEST *who has just come greets* PILATE. *The latter does not reply.*

Caiaphas. People! Listen, Israel, to the voice of your priests . . .

The Priest. Of your priests . . . The voice of God who speaks through the mouth of your priests . . .

The pair of them look at each other with satisfaction, then suddenly begin to emit doleful cries.

Caiaphas. Aya . . . aya . . . ayaya . . . poor people! Poor priests! Let us fear the wrath of God! Let us fear calamity! . . . Aya . . . ayaya!

The Priest Ayaya! Let us fear the vengeance of God.

Huge is our fear! Stand by your priests and render yourselves pleasing to God! Ayayaya . . . ayaya . . . aya!

Caiaphas. Aya . . . calamity . . . aya . . . God . . .
ayaya. . . .

Herod [to PILATE]. Do you hear this menagerie?

PILATE *shrugs his shoulders. The two priests beat their
heads and their breasts with their fists, in simulation of
vehement sadness. They speak amid excessive gesticulations.*

Caiaphas. For now, people, for now . . . we must
crush the snake beneath the stone that hides it. We must
sacrifice the black sheep that taints the flock. We must
strike down the renegade from his ancestors, from his
Nation, from his God. Him whose ridiculous name sullies
your mouths.

The Priest. Him whom you unanimously denounce to
the justice of the governor, and who is called . . . [*He
puts his right hand to his ear.*]

The Crowd [howling]. Je-sus-of-Na-za-reth!

Caiaphas [violently]. Yes. . . . Jesus of Nazareth . . .
the king of the Jews! Do you hear, people? The king of
the Jews . . . the Son of the living God. . . . Your king,
O people!

The Priest. And we are threatened by the scourges of
Heaven, thunderbolt, famine, plague. We are threatened
by Caesar's repressive armies, because the arrogant fellow
for whose death you ask does not only raise himself
against God, but also against the highly enlightened power
that protects our destiny. Woe upon us!

The Crowd [in chorus]. Woe . . . woe!

Herod. I feel myself overcome by emotion.

Caiaphas. God has ordered us to warn you, O people.
And I appeal to all your faith, to all your patriotism, to
set apart for this crime of treason against the Divine the
consequence for which it calls. Alleluia!

The two priests withdraw to one side.

The Crowd [swelling up]. Alleluia! Alleluia! Alleluia!

Herod [to CAIAPHAS]. My congratulations on this fine
piece of eloquence.

Caiaphas [haughtily]. Do you not see that I am suffering?

Herod. Me too. In my stomach.

Pilate [*to* CAIAPHAS]. Here are the prisoners. Begin your show, so that my palace may be cleared without delay!

The Priest. We shall finish it on Golgotha.

JUDAS *enters and runs and hides himself against the terrace wall.* BARABBAS, *in chains and escorted by a* SOLDIER, *comes up the staircase. He masks his eyes, which are hurt by the light, with his elbow.* CAIAPHAS *and* THE PRIEST *go to meet him.* PILATE *wears an expression of disgust.*

Barabbas [*groaning*]. Aye . . . aye . . . it hurts, the light. Is this another court? What more am I going to be condemned to? My eyes . . . Why didn't you leave me in the darkness? Why didn't you execute me in the darkness? [*To* THE SOLDIER.] Hold me less tightly, my friend. . . . You can see that you aren't used to it.

The Priest. Bear up, Barabbas.

Barabbas. I would like to see you in my place, pighead!

The Priest. Don't brag. I wish you courage because you seem depressed.

Barabbas. Me?

The Priest. Yes, you have lost your pride. And that at the moment of being shown to the crowd.

Barabbas. The crowd? Well, here goes! [*He swaggers.*] Still Barabbas!

The Priest. No, don't act that part. Be natural. Are you sad and dejected? Stay like that. It is for your good. In a few moments you will learn things. . . .

Barabbas. The time of the execution, the place, the kind of torture, and the order of the procession?

The Priest [*dictatorially*]. Don't jeopardize your cause. Be woeful, dismal, exhausted.

Barabbas [*with simplicity*]. I am as you say, and with no effort at all. [*He has come before the crowd. Tremendous clamor.*]

The Crowd. Ba-ra-bbas, Ba-ra-bbas, Ba-ra-bbas! [*Applause. The outcry continues.*]

Barabbas [*disconcerted, trying to assume a pleasant expression*]. In person! Very nice of you to have come to see me die. Gaze on me completely at your ease. I'm not very merry. But next time I certainly shall be. [*To* CAIAPHAS.] Will you tell me, you venerable skunk, why I am

exposed to the gazes of this crowd? If I had known, I
would have cleaned myself up a bit.

Caiaphas. Don't worry, Barabbas. Wait, bow your head
and, if you can find it in you, weep . . . weep . . .

BARABBAS *bows his head and sniffs powerfully. Appearance
of the second prisoner:* JESUS, *escorted by a* SOLDIER.

Pilate [*to* THE SOLDIER *escorting* JESUS]. Quicker. . . .

THE SOLDIER *hustles* JESUS, *who is led before the people.
The two priests move aside from him with scorn.*

Barabbas. Him as well? I no longer understand. [*To*
JESUS.] Comrade?

The Crowd [*in frenzied chorus*]. Boo! . . . Down with
him! . . . Down with him! . . . Boo! . . . Jesus! . . .
Boo! . . . Down with him! . . . Down with him!

Herod [*to* PILATE]. The choice is already made.

PILATE *advances toward* THE CROWD, *thrusts aside* CAIA-
PHAS, *and stations himself between* BARABBAS *and* JESUS.
*The sun lights up the group strongly. The silence is com-
plete.*

Pilate. Jews! On the occasion of the feast of the Passover, I have condescended to grant you the release of a
prisoner, and I have had the two most notorious of the
condemned brought to you. Choose, then! Whom do you
want? Jesus or Barabbas?

The Crowd [*exploding*]. Ba-ra-bbas! Ba-ra-bbas! Ba-ra-
bbas! Ba-ra-bbas! Ba-ra-bbas!

Judas [*in a tiny high-pitched voice*]. Jesus! . . . Jesus!

JUDAS *shrinks, fearing he has been seen. Astonishment of*
BARABBAS. PILATE *makes a motion of resentment. Satisfaction of the priests. Sneering of* HEROD.

Pilate [*to* CAIAPHAS]. Yes, I hear. I am not deaf. This
odious crowd could do no better. But it must confirm its
choice. This crowd has been drinking. This crowd is
drunk.

The Priest. Be calm, Pilate.

Herod. He has had a bad night.

Pilate [*who does not hear them*]. It's not finished at
that. . . . [*To* THE SOLDIER.] Take this prisoner back
below, to the soldiers. Let him be scourged. Let him be

covered in blood. Let him be treated with the utmost brutality. And when he is disfigured, let him be brought back here!

THE SOLDIER *drags away* CHRIST, *who has not ceased to remain withdrawn, as though he were outside the drama.* THE CROWD *snarls dully.*

Herod [*to* PILATE]. Are you going to vent your spleen on the Galilean?

Caiaphas [*to* PILATE]. This is unnecessary suffering that you are inflicting on the condemned man.

Pilate. Is it you, Caiaphas, or I, the governor, who is presiding at this tribunal, if I dare call it such?

Caiaphas. It is you, indeed.

The Crowd [*in unappeased chorus*]. Ba-ra-bbas!

Pilate [*furious*]. It is a conspiracy, a parody! [*To* CAIAPHAS.] What were the names this Christ called you, and with reason?

The Priest [*simpering*]. Oh! He wasn't affectionate toward us. He called us a race of vipers, whited sepulchers. . . .

Pilate. That's it! Vipers, sepulchers, and even worse. [*He rushes back into his palace.*]

The Crowd. Bar-ra-bbas! Ba-ra-bbas! Ba-ra-bbas!

Herod. This Barabbas has a popularity that I envy. . . .

The Priest [*to* CAIAPHAS]. Let us make haste! Soon they will bring back Christ to us. The people are warmed up.

Caiaphas [*going very quickly toward the crowd*]. Do you understand what is going on, Barabbas?

Barabbas. Less and less.

Caiaphas. Try to. The crowd is greeting you. The crowd loves you. The crowd is protesting against your condemnation. The crowd wishes you well.

Barabbas. If by any chance it was my judges who wished me well!

Caiaphas. We do wish it, fool! Keep your confidence: leave things to me. But I beseech you, groan, whine, complain!

The Crowd. Ba-ra-bbas!

Barabbas [*after a hopeless piece of dumb show, holding up his chains to* THE CROWD, *and wailing*]. Aye . . . aye . . . I am a villain. . . .

Caiaphas [*clasping* BARABBAS]. What? . . . You a villain? On the contrary. We pity you when we see you

in company with this Galilean whose crimes are
without equal. There is only one villain here, and the
crowd has pointed him out. [*To the people.*] People . . .
people . . . they are going to bring Jesus back to you.
. . . You will not allow yourselves to be duped. People!
If there is a man who has fallen, who is dejected, hopeless,
devastated, tormented by the approach of death, it is
Barabbas, Barabbas whom you wanted to set free—what
am I saying?—whom you have set free!

Barabbas. Set free?

Caiaphas. Yes, set free. Barabbas, the famous bandit,
paid for his reputation. Yes, Barabbas was the victim of
his legend. He was the expiatory goat. False witnesses were
not lacking at his hasty trial, and public opinion was so
incensed at that time that we condemned him in order to
set the population at rest. Oh, how happy I am to be able
to disclose this judicial error, this denial of Justice! I
declare to you, Barabbas deserved neither death nor even
prison. Barabbas' only error was to allow himself to be
caught. To be sure, he has done some pillaging, he has
done some fighting and used violence, he has led a band
of bad boys—but it wasn't to do evil. Barabbas is a man
who loves adventure. His greatest fault is to love living
dangerously; and in living that way one always finishes
by running into the police. Barabbas, O people, has come
from your ranks. He is a man of the people. He has your
instinct, your good nature, your courage. People, he is
true to his country, like you. He is a good patriot. He
never revolted against the priests or the senators and
those who lead you with the help of God. He never spoke
against Caesar. He never insulted holy things. He never
attacked God. He is savage in his strength; he is good in
his heart. And if I said to him, "Barabbas, your unwhole-
some life is over, you are washed clean. . . . Barabbas
you are free, work. . . . Barabbas, you are worthy of
living among us as a good father, a good citizen." . . . I
truly declare that that would be the case. [*To* BARABBAS.]
Is that not so, Barabbas?

Barabbas [*weeping bitterly*]. Yes . . . yes . . . yes . . .
that . . . would . . . be . . . the . . . case. . . .

HEROD *weeps also.*

The Priest. Do you see these tears of repentance, O
people? Does a bandit weep? And is it this so sensitive man

that they wanted to execute? Ah, how blind, how harsh we have been. Barabbas, your judges ask your pardon for their doings, for their zeal.

Barabbas [*not ceasing to weep*]. I forgive you.

The Crowd [*in joyful chorus*]. Ba-ra-bbas! Ba-ra-bbas! Long live Ba-ra-bbas! Long live Ba-ra-bbas!

The Priest [*quickly, to* BARABBAS]. Fall to your knees. Speak. Say something—it doesn't matter what. . . .

Barabbas [*falling to his knees and yelling hoarsely*]. Pardon, pardon! I am guilty! Mercy, people! Pardon, people! May God judge me! God bless you people, and bless your priests. Mercy, good people!

The Crowd. Ba-ra-bbas!

Caiaphas [*helping* BARABBAS *to get up*]. Weep no more, my son. You touch us. Forget your despondency. Is it joy that's choking your voice?

Barabbas. Thirst!

PILATE *reappears. Trumpets. Silence falls.*

Pilate. Where is the king of the Jews?

At this moment CHRIST *is brought back, covered in blood, hideously crowned with thorns, the reed between his bound hands, a pitiful and inhuman nightmare figure, as if ready to slump down.*

Herod. They have carried out your orders well, Pilate. He is truly royal, and he has received in outrage what real kings receive in flattery.

All step aside from CHRIST'S *path.*

Pilate [*to Caiaphas*]. Hasn't he been punished enough?

Caiaphas. The people will decide.

Barabbas [*nonplused on seeing* JESUS]. What have they done to him?

The Priest. They have proceeded to his coronation.

JESUS *has arrived before* THE CROWD.

The Crowd [*whistling and jeering*]. Boo! Down with him! Boo! Down with him! Down with him! Boo! Boo!

PILATE *goes toward* THE CROWD. *He raises his arms. Silence falls.*

Pilate [*indicating* JESUS]. Here is the man! [*Long silence.* THE CROWD *snarls dully and threateningly.*] And now

tell me, tell me whom you want me to release to you?
Jesus or Barabbas?

The Crowd [*in triumphant chorus*]. Ba-ra-bbas! Ba-ra-bbas! Ba-ra-bbas! Ba-ra-bbas! [*The chorus is prolonged.*]

Judas [*in a tiny voice*]. Jesus!

Pilate [*shouting above the uproar*]. Then . . . then . . . what must I do with the other?

The Crowd [*thundering*]. Cru-ci-fy him! Cru-ci-fy him! Cru-ci-fy him!

PILATE *draws back in distress, and goes toward* CAIAPHAS.

Pilate [*to* CAIAPHAS]. It is useless to go on defending him. You have what you wanted. I deliver him to you. Go on. Crucify. Kill. There is your prey. But go, go quickly! Take this wreck from my sight! Go! [*Muttering incoherent words, he goes abruptly into the palace.*]

The Crowd. Long live Barabbas! Long live the priests! Alleluia!

Caiaphas. God has spoken; God has judged! To the executioner with the impostor! To liberty the prisoner whom your generosity has released!

The Crowd. Ba-ra-bbas!

JESUS *is slowly led away.*

Caiaphas. Barabbas, you are free.

Barabbas. Free? Just like that?

The Priest. Free as a bird in the air. Let the soldier tear away his chains.

Barabbas. My chains? I earned them well. . . . Free? Then you're not going to execute me?

Caiaphas. Not only do we grant you your life, but also your freedom, as the people wished.

Barabbas. Freedom? No, no. Don't make game of me. Take me back to my prison quickly. [THE SOLDIER *has taken off his chains.*] Hey, soldier, they are mine! [*He takes the chains back from* THE SOLDIER *and presses them to him.*]

Herod. I congratulate you, Barabbas. May our race produce some more fellows of your stature. I have always preferred a downright bandit to a hundred scurvy judges.

Barabbas. Thank you. I am that bandit—and such I remain—in spite of what has happened to me. But the other, the one they took back, is he free too?

Caiaphas. Jesus? Condemned to death.

Barabbas. Him? To death? You are joking!

The Priest. He dies on the gallows that was set aside for you.

Barabbas [*dumbfounded*]. That's not funny. [*Trying to make things out.*] All this wasn't a show, then? In that case who is being deceived? [*He runs toward* JESUS *who is going down the steps.*] Hey, comrade! It's not my fault. . . . [*He holds out his hand.*] No ill feeling?

JESUS, *insensible, disappears along the foot of the esplanade.* BARABBAS *seems dismayed.*

The Crowd [*rhythmically*]. Ba-*ra*-bbas! Ba-*ra*-bbas! Ba-*ra*-bbas!

The Priest. The crowd is calling out for you, Barabbas. They want to admire you. Look what a long face you are pulling. Laugh! And be quick about it!

BARABBAS *is pushed toward* THE CROWD, *who burst forth in acclamation.*

The Crowd. Long live Barabbas!

Barabbas [*raises his arms; silence falls*]. Friends! I express my complete gratitude to you! I am moved by your enthusiasm and I discover with satisfaction that my popularity is more lively than ever. In future, I shall strive to maintain it, and even to increase it . . . by my deeds— I mean by my deeds in the path of virtue! I shall do my utmost to be, as in the past, a good citizen, a good patriot, worthy of the glorious name of Barabbas. And these chains, my friends, I shall keep as a souvenir of my captivity. I shall gaze on them each day, and they will have over me the mysterious power of preserving me from the spirit of evil, if it tried to lay hold of my cleansed heart again. And finally, I give thanks to God, who made the world, the sky, the stars, the sun, the people of Israel, and its upright judges. [*To* CAIAPHAS.] Is that enough?

Caiaphas. Long live Barabbas!

The Crowd. Barabbas! Long live Barabbas! Long live Barabbas!

Barabbas [*coming back downstage and laughing hugely*]. Ha! . . . Ha! . . . Long live Barabbas! I am free! I run off. I leap. I race. What a lovely morning! [*He waves his arms.*] I am regaining my strength. The air is sweet. I move. I stir. I breathe. . . . [*Lyrical.*] Ah, inasmuch as you have never been condemned to death, you don't know how excellent it is to feel yourself alive! [*He throws himself at* CAIAPHAS' *feet.*] Thank you, good priest. I have learned the lesson well. I shall never again let myself be caught. [*He gets up.* HEROD *and the two priests can hardly hold back their laughter.*]

Caiaphas. Go, Barabbas! Be happy! And if you have any vexations, come and seek us out.

Roughly, CAIAPHAS *pushes* BARABBAS *to the terrace steps.* BARABBAS *tumbles down nimbly; then, bewildered, he staggers a little on the stage.* HEROD *and the two priests come down the steps.* HEROD *throws a purse to the exbandit.*

Herod. Here, have a drink! And drink to Justice, my friend!

Barabbas [*picks up the purse and stands stammering*]. Thank you! This is too much kindness. My friend! May you be blessed seventy-seven times seven. [*He kneels and assumes an appearance of inspiration.*] God, your servant humbles himself. The culprit has received his pardon. God, be blessed in your priests!

HEROD *and the two priests go out, laughing at this comedy.* BARABBAS *breaks off and watches them go. At once, his expression changes.*

Barabbas [*alone.*] God . . . God . . . give me a glimmer of intelligence to understand what the priests have done. God, give me the gift of hating more still and of cursing better still. They have set me free and I can't understand why. They appeared to be rendering good; but in rendering good they were rendering evil at the same time. They rendered good when they ought not to have rendered it. They condemned a man without sin to acquit another who was covered with sins as a crocodile is covered with scales. And I was the plaything of these men, and perhaps their accomplice! No doubt they think I am their dupe. Not a man like Barabbas! They have removed my chains, but not my fangs and my fury. Not my gnarled arms, not my bandit's heart, not my violent blood. And they know it. God, You whom I shall insult every day, give me strength, courage, wickedness. O Thou of whom we only know the crushing anger and the unquenchable thirst for vengeance! [*He gets up.*] I am free. Crime has been set free. Yes, there is a justice. The one the criminals will mete out. Justice! Barabbas will dispense it! Long live murder!

BEGGARS *rush on the stage and surround* BARABBAS.

The Beggars. Barabbas! Free! Come on!

Barabbas. Comrades! My old comrades! Fine beggars! Haughty scoundrels! Dear rogues! What bliss! I meet with you again. I recognize you. I feel you. I sniff your scent. I see your vermin crawling. How sweet it is! Ah! . . . Ah! . . . I am your leader. Worship me, acclaim me! Give me something to drink!

A Beggar. Here is some wine, the wine of your liberation! [*He gives* BARABBAS *a jar.*]

The Beggars. Barabbas is drinking! Long live Barabbas!

Barabbas [*throwing the jar away*]. And give me a dagger! [*He is given a dagger, which he kisses.*] Comrades, I am an honest man, a good citizen. The priests said so, and you know that they never lie. I am white, I am like a lamb, like a dove. I am going to be a judge or a senator. With my renown, that will be easy. What a future, what luck! I shall be mixed up with politics, morals, reforms, laws.

A Beggar [*offering him flowers*]. Celebrate! The underworld is lit up in your honor. There is going to be drinking. You will be gloriously drunk!

The Beggars. Come on! The crowd wants to see you. We'll take you through the city, and the city will be yours!

Barabbas. Comrades, a new age is beginning. It is the advent of the beggars. Everything has been overthrown. I am your king . . . not like the other that they are going to crucify . . . but a redoubtable king, with troops, weapons, a friend of the great, protected by the judges. It is paradise regained. We shall burn the Books of the Law. We shall break up the Ark of the Covenant. We shall sack the Temple. Everything is going to change. Crime will be legal. The wrongdoers will be the just. And I, Barabbas, am the one who will smash up the universe!

The Beggars. Long live Barabbas!

Barabbas. Let us open the prisons! Let us smash the chains! The rich and the powerful are not in the prisons. In the prisons there are only people like us, beggars, unfortunates. Make way for the beggars! Make way for the unfortunates! Let us give back to the people those who are the people. I want to dance. I am huge, invincible. I have a dagger. I am Barabbas. The free man rehabilitated! So much the worse for those who wanted it so!

A Beggar [playing the accordion]. Dance, Barabbas! Dance your freedom!

Amid the savage yelling, BARABBAS *begins to leap like a wild beast.* THE BEGGARS *shout with him and clap their hands. In the distance,* THE CROWD *makes answer. And the excitement reaches its climax.*

The Beggars. Barabbas is dancing! Long live Barabbas! The free man is dancing!

ACT THREE

There is a fairground atmosphere; but the shadow of Calvary will hover over the stage. We are in a hollow in Jerusalem. In this place the actors will be as though in a cistern, and since everything is strange and panic-stricken during this act, they will have the manners of madmen or sleepwalkers. People will go by almost continually in the gloomy rear part of the stage. The murmur of a CROWD *will be heard, like a deep organ pedal, almost ceaselessly and with silences that heighten it. Now and then, shouts, jeers, trumpets, and percussion instruments that emphasize the dramatic action.*

On the left of the stage, the little entrance to a portable booth with a platform, colored panels, red lantern, and cracked bell. THE WATCHER *will remain permanently on a ruined wall, right. He is the commentator on the divine drama that is being performed on Calvary.*

At first, the street is empty. THE SHOWMAN *beats the big drum on the platform in front of his booth. He yells through a megaphone.*

THE SHOWMAN. Walk up! Walk up! Come and see the men of the moment portrayed by an incomparable illusionist! Come and see the celebrities, murderers, and politicians! The true likeness of Barabbas! Walk up, you pay as you leave! The parade is about to begin, and after what

we are going to show you, you will judge what you can
see inside! Walk up!

The Clown [*coming into view from the booth, bursting
with laughter*]. Ha, ha, ha, ha! . . . What did he say?

The Showman. Shut up, Coco. Not worth beginning.
[*Indicating the stage.*] Nothing. This means bankruptcy.
The public is on the mountain. The show has gone to
the winds. Why would anyone come to my booth when
death sentences are being carried out? That's what's
needed, strong sensations and the feeling of impunity. For
our next turn we must prepare something with the characters of this butchery. Understand? Go and lie down,
Coco!

THE CLOWN *disappears.* THE WATCHER *enters. When he
sees him,* THE SHOWMAN *bangs his big drum.*

The Showman. Walk up. . . . Come and see. . . . Hey,
passer-by! Dear passer-by, come and see, I beg you. . . .

The Watcher. See? See what? If today you can't show
very Heaven or Hell, give up hope and shut your booth!
[THE WATCHER *goes and stations himself on the right, on
some ruined steps, and becomes motionless.*]

The Showman. Things are bad. Things are done for.
[*He sits on the platform, his head in his hands.*]

THE CLOWN *reappears. Bugles sounding the salute are
heard in the distance.*

The Showman. The fair is a failure. Cursed Calvary!

The Watcher. The sky is opaque. What trains of darkness are rushing from the horizons? Is a drama unfolding
in the clouds just as one is unfolding on the earth? It is
no longer day; it is not night. The city lies prostrate at
the bottom of a pit. [*Distant outcry.*] The crowd is
swarming like vermin on the wounded mountain. And its
outcry seems to rise up from the depths of time, for
never before has a crowd rattled in its throat in such a
way. Would you not think it was humanity itself that was
being executed and that gave the death rattle?

The clamor mounts like an acclamation. MAGDALENE *enters.
She is disheveled and haggard. She points to the skyline.*

Magdalene. The crosses! The crosses are rising up! The
crosses! [*She runs to the steps on the right.*]

The Watcher. The crosses! There are three of them,

and one is bigger than the others. It is still going up. It is huge.

Madgalene [*quietly collapsing, exhausted*]. Jesus!

The Watcher. A body is nailed to it. This body is dazzling. You would think it was nailed to the foot of the sky. Is it a man? This body hovers and shines far above the world. This cross opens its arms to all the peoples of the world. O woman in tears, look at this cross that is set up! And this mountain that is turning crimson. And this crowd attacking its flanks, like a stormy sea. It is the mountain that is yelling. With fear, with joy.

Magdalene. I want to see nothing more. It is my God they are murdering. [*With her hands on her eyes, she gets to her feet again and is going off, staggering; but when she reaches the front of the booth,* THE CLOWN *begins to dance.*]

The Clown. Ah . . . ah! What did she say?

MAGDALENE *takes fright and flees.* THE SHOWMAN *punches* THE CLOWN, *who blows kisses.* THE CLOWN *drops back into the booth.*

The Watcher. The sky is growing darker. The sun is losing strength. It is a light in its death agony. It is a sepulcher lamp. And all these lanterns, incoherent semaphores . . . Whom are they crucifying for the elements to assemble into a mob, then to break up like this? What is everything waiting for? What are Heaven and earth waiting for? What deliverance is awaited? It is impossible to breathe and the angels are flying very low.

The darkness becomes thick. The showman lights a lock-keeper's lamp. An APOSTLE, *masked, glides onto the stage.*

The Apostle. Magdalene? [*To the others.*] Come, brothers. It is better that we hide ourselves in the very bosom of the people.

Two more masked APOSTLES *enter.*

The Second Apostle. There are soldiers at each of the city's gates. Where are our brethren? How can we recognize them?

The Third Apostle. We shall recognize them by their masks. Treat every man who is trembling as an apostle. Brethren, what have you learned?

The First Apostle. What do we know, unless it is that our Master is on the cross? That our common fate reaches its end this evening at the foot of Calvary?

The Watcher. The earth is rumbling. The moon is rising, pale. Crows are flying around the crosses.

MAGDALENE *returns.*

Magdalene. Brothers, brothers, where are your pure apostles' faces? I no longer know you. You are strangers.

The Second Apostle. Magdalene? We are lost children. Do not call us by our name any more. We must find a house to hide ourselves.

Magdalene. Hide yourselves in the tombs that the dead are forsaking.

The Watcher. For how many hours, how many centuries, how many thousands of years have these crosses been set up?

The Third Apostle. Magdalene, our sister, do not blame us. Where is Peter? Where is John? Where is Mary?

The First Apostle. Speak, Magdalene! What do you know? What have you seen?

Magdalene [*with a savage laugh*]. He was going along under the crushing weight of the cross, heavier than the sins of the world—and he fell.

The Second Apostle. And then? How did he climb the slope of Calvary?

Magdalene. The soldiers flogged him. And the crowd laughed. And he began to walk again because he had to go on to the end. But the cross, heavier than the sins of the world, crushed him again, and he fell for the second time.

The Third Apostle. Be quiet, Magdalene! Don't tell us any more of what you saw then.

Magdalene. You have got to know. The cross crushed him. And he fell for the third time. Ah! He was no longer a man, no longer a God . . . but a walking corpse.

The First Apostle. Be quiet, Magdalene!

Magdalene. Veronica wiped his face and his face burned the cloth. The head of a dead man in a smoking cloth. Then, on Calvary, they tore his robe from him. And all his wounds reopened.

The Apostles. Be quiet, Magdalene!

Magdalene. And then they sacrificed him. . . . [THE APOSTLES *hide their faces and turn away.*] They laid him

on the cross. I no longer remember. The hammers echoed
like thunder. I only remember the first spurts of blood.
The nails entered his wrists, his feet. His body trembled
for a long time. And the cross was set up—with what an
effort! There was talk of fetching horses. [*She opens her
arms like a cross.*] And I am crucified like him. My flesh
is pierced. For such is my love that his torture is mine,
that his woe is joy. For such is my love that I have not
ceased to love him, and it is in his suffering that my love
rejoices. And I await his death. . . . [*Exhausted.*] Apostles, I am a woman, a sinner. My heart is crushed. But I
cannot despair. [*She points to Calvary.*] And if you look
on Calvary, you will be without fear. Jesus is seeking your
gaze. Apostles, dare you not look on Calvary?

The Apostles. Why talk to us like this? Madwoman!
We haven't done any harm. We too love our Master. But
we no longer know who we are nor what we ought to
do. Should we tear him from the cross? Our reason is
tottering, Magdalene. We are delivered up to our enemies.
We are run to earth.

The Watcher. Darkness, darkness, darkness! The mountain is bleeding. The sky is bleeding. Is it the blood of
the Crucified that is spattering the universe?

Ominous trumpet calls.

Magdalene [*who has returned to reality*]. Apostles, are
you bewailing yourselves? Why are you not praying?

The First Apostle. Praying? How? Saying what? Wasn't
Jesus himself like us, in the Garden of Olives—seized with
terror? Didn't he implore the help of the angels?

Magdalene. Speak forth his name. He will hear it. Perhaps he thinks he has been forsaken by everyone. By
everyone! [*Calling toward Calvary.*] Jesus, do you hear
me?

The Apostles. Jesus! Jesus! Jesus! Do you hear us?
Jesus! [*Their voices grow louder.*] Jesus! Jesus!

The Clown [*coming into view from the booth*]. Jesus?
Ah . . . ah . . . ah . . . ah! What are they saying?

THE SHOWMAN *pushes* THE CLOWN *back into the booth.*
THE APOSTLES *take fright.*

The Showman. Don't bawl so loud. Are you followers?
Come into my booth, Christians. I'm showing a picture of
the false miracles of your sage, in there. And for a penny

I'll do subtle tricks as well as him. It would be better to come into my booth while the patrols are surrounding the fairground. Take care! You are suspects.

The Apostles [*rushing toward* The Showman]. Silence! Mocker! Lie merchant!

The Showman [*answering back*]. Go and set your king free! Show the faces you are hiding under your masks!

Magdalene [*restraining them*]. Apostles, what are you doing?

THE APOSTLES *come back*.

The Watcher. The shadows of the cross lie on the countryside, on the seas, on the vastitude. The cross is making signals of distress. And the world is choking. And the darkness creaks. And the mountain grows livid. And the vaults of Hell are in ferment. . . .

Drum rolls from a passing patrol.

The Apostles. Soldiers! Our enemies are seeking us! We must leave the city!

Magdalene. Flee! But if you went to the borders of the universe, you would still see Calvary. Men of fear! You are afraid to see your Master die. But you were close by him, joyful, when he entered the city, among the palms and the hymns. Like a king. And yet, here is his advent. Flee! Hide yourselves! What shameful caverns will you be buried in when he rises from the dead and calls you?

Without paying attention to her, The Apostles *disperse.*

The Apostles [*going*]. We are ignorant, Magdalene, wretched.

Magdalene [*going up the steps*]. Watcher, you who strangely keep your eyes open, will you tell me if my God is dying?

The Watcher. I see . . . I see that they are offering him a sponge on the end of a lance. Why are you waiting for him to die, woman?

Magdalene. Because then I shall awaken. I shall be able to love him as it is fitting that I should love him, unconditionally. Oh, let him die. . . . [*With a painful laugh, she comes down the steps and goes, as though she were drunk.*]

The Watcher. Let him die! What is there still to hope

for in such moments? O spasmodic city! Leaden mountain! Volcanic earth! What is there to hope for in the depths of this nightmare where the world's reason is foundering, if not your death, O Crucified One!

The Showman [who has unhooked his lantern and has come down on the stage]. Misery! I'm ruined! Shall I ever again find a suggestive enough attraction? My clown is doleful and stupid. The only thing left for me is to make a false god, since humanity seeks other claptrap, shows like these they are playing on the mountain. What is going on? *[He bursts into tears.]* Wah . . . wah . . . wah!

PETER *has come.*

Peter [sobbing like the other's echo]. Oh . . . oh . . . oh!

The Showman [annoyed, going toward PETER*].* Are you burlesquing my grief?

Peter. I am weeping. It is my right. It is all I am able to do now.

The Showman [lighting him up]. A mask?

Peter [tearing off his mask]. No, I am no longer a follower, for I denied Jesus before the servants and the soldiery. Because of the cock . . . Before it crew . . .

The Showman [laughing coarsely]. Ho, ho! All the city is infected with this madness. This Messiah has turned all heads. The followers come out of the paving stones. And they have all betrayed him, they have all denied him! Ha, ha, ha! Is it worth the trouble of weeping for such a second-rate adventure?

Peter [seized with fear, trying to master himself]. But I am not weeping.

The Showman. You are not weeping? Then are you shamming? Don't I see tears flowing down your cheeks? It's true that my clown does that like you.

Peter. I . . . am . . . not . . . weeping! *[He falls to his knees and his tears are redoubled.]*

The Watcher. Fires are lighting up on all the towers.

The Showman. I see. In denying Jesus you have saved your skin. Rejoice! Or are you lamenting the lost kingdom?

Peter. My Master, my poor Master! *[Savagely, he gets to his feet and takes a strangled cock from his cloak. Angrily.]* But he has paid the penalty of his baleful song.

I have wrung his neck. Maleficent beast! Fowl of the devil!

The Showman [*roaring with laughter*]. What did this tiny beast do, except greet the dawn?

Peter. It fulfilled a fatal prediction. Alas! . . . [*He screws the cock's neck.*] Cock, you will not sing the time of denial any more! [*He holds out the cock toward Calvary.*] But you, Master. . . . Are not you, whom I denied, denying me from the height of your cross? [*He bursts into tears again.*]

The Showman. I've never seen weeping with such vehemence. You with the cock . . . Stop it! You're affecting me. [*He too bursts into tears.*]

The Watcher. The storm is blowing up. The stars have spent their lives.

The wind is heard mingling with the clamor of THE CROWD. JUDAS *appears: he is livid. He holds a rope. He weeps bitterly, and his cries join with the lamentations of the other two.*

Judas [*jerkily*]. Yochabeth is pursuing me. She beat me, the hideous creature. I am like a leper, like a mangy dog that people chase off. [*He groans.*] And my flanks, my loins! [*Pitiably.*] And my damned soul! I publicly proclaimed my offense. I boasted of it, and everyone turned away from me. And wherever I go, I catch sight of Calvary. I see the instruments of torture. And these three. And him whom I delivered up.

Peter. Judas!

Judas [*frightened*]. I am not Judas. Judas is a dirty Jew. He is someone else who looks like me. Why, he is an apostle! [*After a struggle with himself.*] It is me, Judas. And you, you are Peter.

Peter [*frightened in his turn*]. No, I am not Peter. He is someone else, an apostle. . . .

Judas. Brother, I betrayed him! The Master had foretold that one of us would betray him. It was on me that this task devolved. Spit upon me, Peter!

Peter. And I—I denied him. The Master had foretold that one of us would deny him. I am as despicable as you. The cock . . . Look!

Judas. And this rope . . . My last possession!

The Showman [*withdrawing to the booth*]. They are madmen or drunks.

Judas. Wretched, yes, wretched the man for whom God no longer has mercy!

Peter. Oh, Judas, there is no sinner nor crime for which God is without forgiveness. I have the fervent hope that my Master will forgive me. I shall weep. I shall pay my penalty until death—even beyond. But I know there is forgiveness for my misdeed.

Judas. There is forgiveness for you, for all men, except me. I am damned. I make my way amid unfathomable depths. From one moment to the next the earth might open under my feet and swallow me up. Then what can I do in this abominable existence? Terrify people? What can I still do in this humanity from which, although still living, I have banished myself? I have not even the sweetness of remorse and tears, your tears that I envy.

Peter. You do not feel remorse?

Judas. My heart is a stone, a cracked vase. Remorse—can I call an immeasurable disgust of myself by this name? And I even vomited the silver from my crime in the Temple. Inconceivable sacrifice! [*Rebelliously.*] But did not God will that I should be what I am? [*He stretches out his hand toward Calvary.*] He compelled me to sell him. Was not this thing written before my birth, that I should betray the Son of Man? I am marked out by fate as excluded from redemption. I have no doubt accomplished a horrible and necessary task. My mission is completed. I am obliterated, abject to the very limit, since there is no God left for me to betray. [*Overcome.*] And yet I followed him, I believed him, I loved him. While betraying him, I loved him still more than ever. While giving him that kiss, I loved him perhaps better and more than any of his apostles!

Peter. Oh, Judas, I pity you!

Judas. Now I no longer love him. I was by his cross. I saw his limbs twisted with suffering, his bloodless flesh, and I remained unmoved. I no longer love him, and I do not hate him either. He is a stranger to me, just as all the men of creation have become strangers. Perhaps I am no longer of their kind, or have I already the nature of the devil? I don't know at all. I know nothing more than my name. I am Judas. Everlastingly!

Peter. Shut your mouth, Judas! Don't utter these sacrilegious words! Whatever you have done, you are still my brother, the most wretched of my brothers.

Judas. No, I am no longer your brother. Even if you prayed for me, even if the Son of God himself interceded for me, nothing would wash my infamy from me. Besides, is it the right time to talk of prayer and forgiveness when this cross casts its shadow on our brows? I am only waiting for one thing, that is for Jesus to die. Then all will be indeed finished. I shall feel more at ease. And I shall be able to plunge calmly towards Hell, Hell in which I firmly believe—for if it did not exist, God would create it for me. [*He laughs bitterly.*]

The Watcher. Oh how slow, eternal, this death agony is! Will you die? When will you die, O Crucified?

Judas [*making a slipknot*]. Yes, let him make haste! Or let them finish him off! The quietus!

Peter [*terrified*]. Judas!

Judas [*sneering*]. Pardon, Peter. It is the demon talking already. Peter, if you are my brother, if you love me, spit on me! I beg you! [*He kneels before Peter.*] It would do me good to feel your contempt—for your friendship is unbearable to me. It is my last wish, Peter. Don't be like Jesus, indifferent, without anger, without reproaches. That is what has hurled me into despair. Spit!

Peter [*drawing back*]. No!

Judas [*getting up*]. Ah! I am not worth the spittle? I understand. The spittle was for Jesus. [*He wanders about.*] But the first passer-by who comes will give me this spittle. This one who is coming, there, will spit in my face.

BARABBAS *enters. He is a little drunk, has flowers in his hair, and carries his chains around his neck like the collar of an honorific order.*

Judas. Yes. This one! This one, above all! Barabbas, I am Judas. Spit on me. And I shall bless you!

Barabbas. Get out, dung fly! [*With a thump he knocks* JUDAS *into the road.*]

The Clown [*appearing on the booth*]. Eh! What did he say? [*He leaps very swiftly to the stage.*] Spit?

Judas [*lying on the ground*]. I am Judas, the ordure!

The Clown. Here we are! [*He spits in* JUDAS' *face and, laughing until he cries, runs to the booth. He disappears.*]

Judas [*getting up and making ready to go*]. Good-by, Peter. Mysterious forces are drawing me to the trees. I am going to hang myself.

Barabbas. Hang yourself, you? You are too cowardly.

Judas. With this rope.

Barabbas. Good riddance! Look sharp! And if you are not hanged by tonight, I shall break your neck. [*He seizes* JUDAS *by the nape of the neck.*] Like this!

Judas. Mercy!

Peter. Let him go, man! If Justice is to be done, it will be done. It does not rest with us to dispense it.

JUDAS *flees.*

Barabbas [*mocking*]. Whose business is it to dispense it? The judges'?

Peter. God's.

Barabbas. Who are you to speak with this assurance?

Peter. The apostle Peter, who denied Jesus.

Barabbas. Well! I am the one they excused so as to be able to put your Jesus to death. You can imagine whether I can speak of Justice.

Peter. Barabbas!

Barabbas. Exactly. You must excuse Barabbas. He's not very bright. He's a bit depressed. But he knows what he's up to. You too seem to have been drinking, apostle Peter.

Peter. I have wept. Drunk with grief . . .

At the name of BARABBAS, THE SHOWMAN *has become attentive, and* THE CLOWN'S *head appears.*

Barabbas. You have wept? There's something to weep about, comrade. There is indeed something to weep about. [*Furtively he rubs his eyes.*]

Peter. You too?

Barabbas [*making a face*]. They are drunkard's tears, old man. And then, I have regrets.

Peter. For your crimes?

Barabbas. What a thought! I have regrets.

The Watcher. The crowd is swirling. Filthy dust. The crowd is choking.

Barabbas. Do you understand? I am Barabbas, the supreme brute; but I am not an idiot. I express myself badly, but isn't that because I confusedly feel too many things?

Peter. The way you speak astounds me. Are you really the criminal they set free?

Barabbas. I have that honor, that sad honor. These are my chains. I was happier when I had them riveted to my

body. Now I am free, purified. And things are no longer
all right. I don't recognize myself. I don't know what to
do with this liberty. No, I am not happy [*ambiguously*]
. . . because events are happening that are bringing me
into subjection, because I am mixed up in a terrifying
drama whose meaning I can't discover and in which I
play an unpleasant part, contrary to my taste. [*He shakes
PETER's arm.*] Isn't he your pal, the one who's dying on
the cross up there?

Peter. It is my Master. The gentlest. The best.

Barabbas. I believe it. Look, I should be able to be glad
to see another put to death on the gallows that was in-
tended for me. I am not glad. It makes me spew, bandit's
honor! I have different principles. And I promise you on
my chains that this dirty bargain will be paid for with
judges' flesh and blood. Or I am no longer Barabbas!

Peter. The judges will be judged. God weighs our
deeds.

Barabbas. Leave God in the clouds. Try to understand
me right to the end. My liberty is all humbug, comrade.
I am not free. They pretended to set me free. But before
I submit to the lot they are reserving for me, I will have
meted out Justice to the extent that I understand it by instinct. . . . My liberty? [*He indicates a person clad in a
black cloak, who slips to the back of the stage.*] I am
followed step by step. I am overheard. You can imagine
whether my liberators feel at their ease. It's not with impunity that you loose an artist of my status in the crowd.
Ha! They think I'm drunk, mad with joy. They fancy
that I have grasped nothing of the farce in which I have
had the walk-on part. Go, comrade, it's not good for you
to be found in my company. You are no more pure than
the next man, you, the friend of Christ. Go!

Peter. I shall flee, Barabbas. But do no evil. I ask it of
you in the name of my friend, Christ, who is also yours
since, like him, you suffer injustice.

Barabbas. That is beyond our control, old chap.

PETER *goes off quickly.* BARABBAS *remains, musing.*

The Watcher. Total night! Horror! Everything is con-
vulsed. He is not dying. He will never die. The Crucified!

The Showman [*coming down from the booth and approaching* BARABBAS]. It's really you, Barabbas? The

famous Barabbas? What a happy surprise! Do you know that you are the most popular man of the age? Your name is on everyone's lips.

Barabbas. I'm not stuck up about it. What do you want with me?

The Showman. Only good. Don't trouble yourself any more about what is going on on the mountain. You must be practical. Think of your life in the future. Are you hungry?

Barabbas. No.

The Showman. Thirsty?

Barabbas. Yes. But it's useless for me to drink any more. I can't manage to get drunk today; my heart isn't in it. [*Suspicious.*] Anyway, who are you? Another cop?

The Showman. I am an exhibitor of monsters and phenomenons. [*Admiringly.*] You are a phenomenon.

Barabbas. Of my kind, yes.

The Showman. The man who has been condemned to death! Extraordinary! The murderer at liberty! Brr! The discharged convict!

Barabbas. These titles are as good as any others. I am the king of the murderers and they reinstate me. The other is the king of the Jews and they execute him. It's comical, isn't it?

The Showman. Unbelievably comical, ho, ho, ho! But what are you going to do, Barabbas, now that you are free?

Barabbas. To make myself worthy of my judges' generosity. Become honorable, respectable, estimable. And, between times, to amuse myself, I shall do a little bit of murder.

The Showman. You are joking?

Barabbas. I have no other vocation.

The Showman. Do you want me to make your fortune?

Barabbas. The Pharisees are granting me subsidies.

The Showman. Then would you like to know success, great success? Whiffs of incense? The public worships you. The women are mad about you. You are handsome, you are muscular, you are eloquent. Furthermore, what a reputation, what an indisputable reputation! You are a man of gold. To prove to you how popular you are, you can see a wax bust in your likeness in my booth.

Barabbas. I don't give a damn. I would rather my name were forgotten. I would like to become a nobody. Or to rebound. Barabbas stronger than Barabbas. To perform unheard-of feats. That is what I choose. You will hear about me soon.

The Showman. You can perform these feats here, on the platform. You can wrestle with a bear or lift weights.

The Clown [*from the booth, cutting in*]. Yes, a champion!

The Showman. I shall advertise, banners, a roll of honor of your most outstanding crimes. And a great fresco depicting your release.

Barabbas. My release? [*He bursts out laughing.*]

The Clown [*leaping from the booth*]. Yes, it will be splendid. And in my clown's brain I have thought of an astonishing scene that will make the crowds flock here.

Barabbas. Having been the victim of the judges, I shall be that of the mountebanks.

The Clown. For you can guess, the trial of Christ and your release are events you won't see again in a hurry.

The Showman. Exactly! You are historic! Come on! It will be fun!

Barabbas. All right. It's a good thing for me to laugh, or for me to cease grinding my teeth. It will be fun? All right. But if you don't make me laugh, I'll pull your booth down. [*He allows himself to be dragged to the platform where* THE CLOWN *is lighting lanterns.*]

The Watcher. And if you die, O Crucified, will Heaven and earth destroy themselves along with you?

THE SHOWMAN *rings the bell.*

The Showman. Let's go through it. The ceremony on Calvary will soon be over. The crowd will flock to the squares. And they will need a joyful contrast to the bloody spectacle. The crowd will want to amuse itself. [*He struts around.*] First of all I'll lecture them. I'll sing your praises. I'll proclaim your virtues.

Barabbas. My long martyrdom, my sensitivity, my good citizenship . . .

The Showman. Not forgetting your patriotism! What high-sounding words!

THE CLOWN *appears. He is dressed in a red robe and is crowned, in parody, with dead branches.*

The Clown. And here is the king of the Jews. Do I look all right?

A masked APOSTLE *goes by furtively.*

The Showman. Screaming with truth! What a hit! And what a pity I haven't been able to engage the real king of the Jews. Well, my clown is quite as ornamental. And since the one who's dying on the cross foretold that he would rise again, in a few days I shall be able to maintain that my clown is the genuine king of the Jews come from his tomb. You can see we know how to manage things, Barabbas! [*He seizes the big drumstick and strikes hurried blows.*]

Barabbas. So far it's neither cunning nor funny.

The Showman. Wait. Next I'll do the trial of the king of the Jews. And I'll ask the public, after enumerating the charges pressing on the false Messiah . . .

Barabbas. You mustn't forget that.

The Showman. After proving that this fellow is dangerous, I'll announce to the public . . .

Barabbas. That it can choose Jesus or Barabbas.

The Showman. No! That there will be a collection.

The Clown. Hey! Doesn't the tribunal have to have its wages?

The Showman. After that, the public will be authorized to choose. But since I am full of compassion and want to save the Nazarene, notwithstanding the charges that weigh him down, I'm going to try to move the crowd to pity. [*He turns to* THE CLOWN.] Eh? Eh? You dare to maintain that you are the king of the Jews? Take that, lunatic! [*He boxes* THE CLOWN'S *ears.*]

An APOSTLE *goes by.*

The Clown [*howling*]. Mercy! Don't kill me!

Barabbas [*laughing*]. Badly played! Christ was silent under their blows. I'll show you how. . . . [*He seizes* THE CLOWN *by the throat and hammers his face with his fist.*] Be quiet! Take it! Like the real one. If you squeal, I'll tear your guts out and make you gobble them up!

The Clown [*freeing himself, horrified*]. Help! Murder! That's not just a performance, that isn't!

The Showman [*frightened*]. Don't injure my clown, Barabbas! Listen . . . To finish with, the public will again choose. And it will be you that they choose. There will be another collection in your honor, and to thank the public for having set you free . . .

Barabbas. Good . . . I am free? Then I'll pocket the collection and make off.

The Showman. Humph! . . . You'll go back into the booth, and then you'll begin your number with the weights and dumbbells.

The Clown. No, this will hurt too much. The real one only suffered once. Do I have to be ill-treated every night?

Barabbas. Your part's not interesting, man. The moment I am free, I shall make use of my liberty as seems good to me. I'm going on with the game for what I get out of it, and that's all. The public will be satisfied. As for the clown, we say no more about him. He is condemned to death. [*He seizes* THE CLOWN *by the seat of the trousers and flings him into the booth.*]

The Showman. Calm down! Explain yourself, Barabbas. . . .

A man dressed in a black cloak and with his face covered hides himself against the booth.

Barabbas [*who has noticed the man*]. Didn't I tell you success was guaranteed to us? Here's someone listening to us already. I'll explain myself. You will declare that I am without stain, perfect, absolved, the best chap in the world.

The Showman. Bravo, bravo!

Barabbas. To which I shall reply that that is the truth, but that I haven't been able to cure my passion, that the taste for crime has remained with me, and that I am going at once and with all legality . . . [*He takes out a dagger.*]

The Showman [*terrified*]. Stop! You're going to jeopardize yourself.

Barabbas. The public will thrill with pleasure. It will adore that. It will encourage me, stir me up. The crowd loves a crime. I'll pretend to commit a murder, to please it. For instance, I'll give proof of my gratitude to my judge, to you indeed, and I'll neatly cut your throat. [*Brutally, he throws* THE SHOWMAN *down.*]

The Showman [*trying to flee*]. Help!

Barabbas [*holding him*]. And I'll ask the public if I should finish you off. It's likely that the people will enjoy seeing your comatose gestures. I'll bleed you like a pig. And then I'll make a collection [*He lifts him up again.*] You understand?

The Showman [*choking*]. I want to get out of here.

Barabbas [*holding him back*]. No! Soon Christ will be dead and the show can begin. But I think there's something even better. We must crucify the clown. [*He stretches his arm into the booth and drags out* THE CLOWN.] Why not, since the crowd has decided it? [*He makes* THE CLOWN *open his arms.*] I'll need nails and a hammer. I'll nail him to the wall, like a bat.

The Clown. Help! A madman!

Barabbas. To teach this wretch to want to mock Jesus! [*He flings him to the ground; then, in a thundering voice.*] And since the darkest of portents weigh on us, since the light of the heavens is going out, since it is foretold that the last scourges will come sweeping down on the city, since the world is at bay, as though it were going to come to an end, since the time has come when the Just dies on the cross and the murderer goes free—for all these reasons, I shall grandly play the most baleful of farces, the most philosophical of entertainments.

The Showman [*bleating with fear*]. Very good, Barabbas! Long live Barabbas!

Barabbas. Without you. Without your clown. Without anyone. I begin! . . . [*Like a bull, he smashes in the sides of the booth with one thrust of his shoulders. He fells* THE SHOWMAN *and tears the robe and the crown from* THE CLOWN. *These two characters disappear among the sudden collapse of the booth's canvas and planks.* BARABBAS *laughs vehemently. He has leaped to the platform.*] And now I'll light up. I like fire. I like destruction. Let the fire consume the booth and spread to the city and to Calvary. Let nothing but ruins be left. Let calcined bones be the only things still in existence from this tainted society!

Laughing heartily all the time, BARABBAS *takes a lamp from the debris. Another laugh answers him.* BARABBAS *stops, nonplused. The man in black has run off.* HEROD, *made up and covered in jewels, has just arrived. He laughs tremendously.*

The Watcher. Truly, he will not die until the end of the ages. The crowds will disappear. Other crowds will arise. But after the empires and the ages, the cross will remain erect, and the earth will sail madly in the infinite, with this cross catching the stars.

Herod. Fancy meeting you, my friend! What were you doing on this platform?

Barabbas. You've arrived too late, my lord. It's a pity. But you haven't missed anything. You'll still see fine things. [*He gazes at* HEROD.] I am touched to see you again, you who took such an interest in me. Am I not the dear child of the Nation? Do the priests and the judges trouble themselves about my future, as you do? Tell them I am in the best of health—unless they have sent you to me to give an account of my movements. [*He strokes his dagger.*]

Herod. No, Barabbas, I'm not of their kind. If you see me prowling around this hollow, that's because I like to frequent places where the stinking rabble swarm. I like fairs and clowns, robbers, scoundrels, prostitutes, crazy folk. They are the only tolerable humanity. And I like you, Barabbas, the habitual criminal, the old lag. Your eccentricities are proof of your original character. They have removed your chains, but not your savage power, your tenacity of purpose. Also, I reckon that you will bring yourself to the attention of your liberators without delay.

Barabbas. You're joking!

Herod. I'm not joking. You could murder the whole Jewish people tonight, and I would suavely laugh at it. As far as I, Herod, am concerned, the fire of Heaven can destroy us. I would laugh as I died. I am too civilized, Barabbas, and that is why your barbarous anarchy is so attractive to me. Do you believe me? It wasn't to be that you should be crucified—even though the picture would have been a very beautiful one. But here you are flung into the crowd. Your glorious name must not fall into oblivion. [*He rubs his hands.*] What a significant meeting! Barabbas, formerly condemned to death . . .

Barabbas. I am still condemned to death, whatever you think.

Herod. Ho! You seem to me very clear-minded for a man whose breath smells of wine. How is it that you're not drunk?

Barabbas. I tried to be. I danced, I sang, I drank. No! I regret my prison for reasons that I am the only one to understand. Reasons . . .

Herod. Sentimental? You? A killer? The terror of Israel? Is it really Barabbas who is talking?

Barabbas. Yes, it's Barabbas. The murderer. Here is my dagger. But I'm not the same murderer as before. [*Darkly.*] There are other murderers in this kingdom.

Herod [*delighted*]. You speak a truth, Barabbas, a holy, relentless truth.

BARABBAS [*dragging* HEROD *toward the steps*]. Look, my lord, up there. That's where they are committing murder. [*Dejected, he wanders about.* HEROD *follows him step by step.*] This Christ was duped. I was duped. The crowd is duped. It's a dirty trick. A sad business. A loathsome deal. It's me that says so. . . . [*He indicates Calvary.*] That poor wretch there, they've got him. They'll have me at some street corner. But it won't be so easy. There'll be some unpleasantness. And I'll avenge this crucified comrade, him who was left in the lurch by his friends, sold, jeered at, insulted, beaten when he wasn't able to defend himself. We're like that among our sort, my lord.

Herod. What! You are becoming a lover of Justice?

Barabbas. I am reinstating myself.

Herod. You are hotheaded.

Barabbas. No, I'm fevered, weary, worn out. I'm heart-broken. The beggars that I have met again are wary of me. They think I am a creature of the Pharisees, a protégé of the priests. The contemptibility of my judges reflects on me. I am the accomplice, and that wounds me, that makes me suffer. They eye me distrustfully. They all seem to say to me, "What are you doing in the city? Your place is on the cross." And it's true. And furthermore what disheartens me is that the other, Jesus, didn't see the hand I held out to him. He didn't see it. And I wouldn't want him to hate me. Him!

Herod. Are you troubled about that?

Barabbas. Yes. To the point that I almost climbed Calvary and faced the people and shouted all that is hatching out in my heart. I made up my mind to pull up the cross. But I was struck with fear. I was paralyzed when I saw his mother. The fellow's mother. I was afraid of him. Afraid that he would accuse me from the height of his cross.

Herod. Barabbas, you are unrecognizable. You, afraid? You are afraid of Jesus?

Barabbas. It's mad. Yes, I'm afraid. Of him. Of everything. Of nothing. For the first time in my life. I am

afraid of the darkness, of the living and of the dead. I
am afraid of myself.

Herod. You, the stouthearted? What a revelation!
You are suffering from the contagion, Barabbas. And
your nerves are out of order from the long time you have
spent in jails. Tell me what you have done since this
morning.

Barabbas. Nothing. I drank to drown my anxiety. I
wandered around. I wanted to leave the city, and I don't
know what it was that held me back. Perhaps Calvary.

Herod [*intimately*]. Come along! You seem really
thrown off balance. That distresses me. Such a fine, such
a proud bandit. I am sincerely interested in you, Barabbas;
not like the priests, who will have their claws in you at
the first deviation, but as a friend, as an authority on the
human animal. Will you come with me? You know that
I am rich and influential. Become my servant. From time
to time I need a handyman for certain jobs. Afterward
I'll send you to Rome, where you can fight in the circuses, where you will make free of the stews and the
taverns. Agreed?

Barabbas. I won't take anything of what you are offering
me.

Herod [*nervous*]. Then what do you want?

Barabbas. To be enlightened.

Herod [*bursting forth*]. Oh, no! You are absurd! To
be enlightened—about what?

Barabbas [*bewildered*]. To be enlightened about what is
happening at this moment in this city, about what has
been happening in the people's consciousness for three
years, about what is happening in the world. For a happening as mysterious and majestic as the evolution of the
stars is taking place, as secret and as sovereign as the
juggling of the stars in the universal night.

Herod [*unsettled*]. Yes, something is happening. . . .
But I don't give a damn about it. I don't want to know
anything about it.

The Watcher. The storm clouds are clawed by lightning. Chew ashes; sweat salt! The empty tombs are singing in chorus!

Barabbas. You are troubled just as I am, Herod. Will
you answer me? Do you know him they are putting to
death on Calvary?

Herod. I know him. He claims to be the Son of God,

the king of the Jews, the brother of all men. Perhaps it's true. But I tell you again, I don't give a damn about it.

Barabbas. Is it also true what the people say about him? Did he raise the dead and cure the sick? Is it true that he is dying for the redemption of souls? Did he say, "Blessed are the poor"? Did he say, "Blessed are they that hunger and thirst after Justice"? Is it true that he foretold the rewarding of the just and the punishment of the wicked? That he would probe our hearts and our loins?

Herod. Yes, he made all those remarks. And it is for those remarks that he is nailed to the cross.

Barabbas. And if he spoke the truth?

Herod. Perhaps he did speak it. Are you trembling, Barabbas? What's the matter with you?

Barabbas. The matter with me? Hunger and thirst after Justice. And why didn't you, Herod, who knew this man was speaking the truth, although it displeases you to acknowledge it, why didn't you rescue him from the hands of his executioners? You had the power to do it.

Herod. Doubtless. . . . I wanted to see how far the priests' roguery went. It is too late. Besides, would I have been able to prevent this immolation that Christ himself had foretold and invoked? There is none of us who is not splashed by the blood of this just man. But nothing more can affect me. Look, you who hunger and thirst after Justice, you can cut my throat in this very place. [*On edge.*] I am no more merry than you are, Barabbas, and I search in vain to dispel this horror of living. I am sick. The world runs fatefully to its end. Nothing good can come to pass any more. The light will never come back again. Then let this God of the last days, who will judge the terrified nations, appear amid the falling of the skies. And let it finish! [*He laughs bitterly.*] And I who had come to watch your antics! Ha . . . ha! Here you are talking to me . . . talking to me like one of these visionaries, like one of the disciples of this incomparable madman. . . . [*Furious.*] What is wrong with him that he troubles people's brains? [*He calms down.*] Good-by, Barabbas! Pursue your fate. Seek and find your happiness, in crime or elsewhere, it's of no importance!

Barabbas. My fate? And who is the master of it?

Herod [*going without turning back*]. May you end up brilliantly, carrying out a master stroke!

HEROD *has scarcely gone when men in black cloaks maneu-ver and creep about.* BARABBAS *sees them.*

Barabbas. A master stroke? That's what I'm thinking of. You'll see the gesture, Herod, but you won't understand a thing about it. [*He becomes motionless.*] Come here, shadows, I am not afraid of you. [*He lays hold of a board from the demolished booth.*] Who are you? Who ordered you to follow me? What are you hiding under your cloaks? [*Suddenly he relaxes and leaps toward the shadows.*] Come and fight! Me alone against the lot of you! Aren't you hiding priests' robes under your cloaks?

The shadows scatter in panic.

The Watcher. Die, man or God! God made man or man become God. No royal accession was so grand. O Cruci-fied, panting in time, with your torrential wounds!

Barabbas [*climbing the steps*]. Let him die so that I may be freed from this obsession!

The Watcher. Die! For they who gaze on you suffer your agony and are tortured unspeakably.

Barabbas. Let him die! Let this dreadful and false night clear away! It was proclaimed that Christ would be killed, but not the sun, the moon, and the stars.

THE APOSTLES *return with their dark lanterns and their masks. They conceal themselves as they go along.*

An Apostle. This way, brethren. It is even darker in this hollow. What did he cry from up on the cross?

The Second Apostle. Where do you expect people like us to hide?

The Third Apostle. He cried to his Father. I know nothing more. His language was no longer of this world.

Flashes of lightning begin to light up the scene faintly.

The Second Apostle. And later? But later? What will happen to his body?

The Third Apostle. Later? What will become of us?

Barabbas [*on the steps*]. There's a sort of lump in my throat. Watcher, my eyes can't make out anything other than phosphorescent crosses, crosses, multitudes of crosses, a forest of lurching crosses.

The Second Apostle. Brethren, I am choking.

Barabbas [*to* THE WATCHER]. Can you see our comrade?

How can he still hold out? I would have coughed up my life long ago.

Lightning.

The Watcher. The crowd is coming down . . . breaking up. . . . Why?

Barabbas. Is he dying? Tell me. I am waiting. [*He jumps down from the steps.*]

The First Apostle. What is to be done? He is going to die. Apostles?

The Second Apostle. I don't want to know the moment when our Master passes away.

The Third Apostle. And do you see that his anger may burst forth in his death? And that he may destroy the city that has seen his torture? Oh, what a hellish sky!

The First Apostle. Won't you reply? What is to be done?

Rumblings of a storm.

Barabbas [*to* THE APOSTLES]. What is to be done? I'm going to tell you.

Surprise. The dark lanterns go out suddenly.

The Second Apostle. Barabbas! The robber!

Barabbas. I know what is to be done. It is time for it. . . .

The lightning becomes tinged with red.

The Watcher. Calvary is struck with dread and its old graveyards of horror chatter their teeth.

Barabbas. In the first place, where is your leader?

The First Apostle. Our leader? He is weeping? We are forsaken.

The Second Apostle. No leader . . . no Master . . . nothing but wretches!

Barabbas. Where is he who used a sword in the Garden of Olives?

The Second Apostle. Peter? You have been told: he is weeping.

PETER *enters.*

Peter. We must flee, brethren. They will take advantage of the panic to strike at us.

Barabbas [*to* PETER]. Flee? When the other is going to give up the ghost? And you are the leader?

Peter. No, I am only a runaway. The other, I betrayed him. What do you want?

Barabbas. Are you a man?

Peter. I am forever he who denied.

Barabbas. Where is your sword?

Peter. Jesus said to me, "Put up your sword."

Barabbas. You are lying.

The Watcher [*covering his head with a cowl*]. What is now happening can no longer be gazed upon.

The tocsin begins to ring. An outcry starts in the distance.

Peter. You do not know Jesus.

Barabbas. He's a pal. I was in prison with him.

The Second Apostle. Leave this robber, Peter. He's a simple soul.

Peter. He is a rebel. Yes, you are a rebel. It's not that. . . . You, the pariah, must have hope and you shall be saved.

Barabbas. It's not a matter of saving my skin, as you are doing. Pariah, yes indeed. And as such I tell you I hunger after Justice. What did Jesus promise those who hunger and thirst after Justice?

Peter. Be quiet! You are drunk, Barabbas. You smell of wine.

Barabbas. But I'm not trembling. I'm not hiding myself. Like you who haven't been drinking but who smell of fear. I came to you to protect you, to defend you: so much did your cowardice move me to pity. I shall act without you. For my thirst for Justice is inexpressibly aggravated to the extent that the blood of Jesus flows. [*Sudden exit of* BARABBAS.]

The First Apostle. This robber is strange, Peter. Do we know God's designs?

Peter. God no longer reveals His designs to me, the renegade.

The Watcher. Truly, truly, it is better that man is not witness of these things.

Hue and cry.

The Second Apostle. Peter, what are the wild beasts that are weeping on the skyline?

The Third Apostle. Peter, among the crowd of the living there are ghosts that guide it.

The First Apostle. Peter, a hand of flame is descending on the Temple.

Peter. I can no longer see Calvary. O God, poor God, die, that our distress may be complete! That we may be drenched in bitterness! That we may return to the oblivion whence you drew us forth!

The First Apostle. Jesus dying! But what death? Is it dying?

The Second Apostle. Our kingdom destroyed? But if this kingdom were beginning?

The Third Apostle. I implore you . . . In this moment at least, let us think of him, for it is of us that he is thinking as he dies.

The uproar does not stop growing.

Peter. Jesus, have pity on us who can no longer do anything, neither pray nor weep, who can no longer do anything other than quake and watch you dying; us who are lost, bewildered, on the fringe of the crowd, us who are lightheaded and bemused from grief, but who remain your apostles for all that, us who can never efface the seal with which you marked us, us who can never forget you, nor live without your haunting memory. O Jesus, our poor Master, our poor King! Our poor God! [*Weeping, he falls to his knees.*]

A disheveled woman, MAGDALENE, *leaps toward* THE APOSTLES.

Magdalene. Ah, let the crime finish! He has shed more blood than the heart of the whole world contains.

The Apostles. Magdalene! Where have you come from? Is he dead? Sister!

The clamor grows.

Peter. Magdalene, have you come from Calvary? Jesus?

Magdalene [*who has fallen to her knees among* THE APOSTLES]. Jesus? I saw his wounds blazing and, one by one, the twitches of his agony. Death is climbing up his cross. Wait yet. Endure yet. He is going to die . . . soon . . . I feel it . . . I shall tell you . . .

The Apostles. Magdalene . . . say nothing.

Magdalene [*clairvoyant*]. What he is enduring cannot be understood by our intellects, nor felt by our flesh. A

God alone suffers and dies in such a way. Wait yet,
brethren. Death seizes him by the throat. He is hardly
breathing any more. I am close to him, against him.
Coldness ascends his limbs. His glassy eyes are filled with a
horrible ecstasy. The cross trembles. The infinite is
expanding.

The Apostles [*hiding their faces*]. Magdalene! Magdalene!

Magdalene. It is the struggle of God against death.
And death is carrying him off. He is opening his mouth.
He is going to cry out. Stop your ears. He is crying out.
[*She lies on the ground.*] His head has fallen. All is ac-
complished!

Formidable thunderclap. THE APOSTLES *throw themselves
to the ground.*

The Watcher. It is finished! The Crucified is dead!
SILENCE!

*And, as if the city and the sky heard this command, all
comes to a standstill, storm, tocsin, hue and cry. It is an
opaque, lethargic silence that seems to last an eternity,
beneath a wan light that also seems to last forever. Only
a voice, very far away, howls.*

The Voice. We . . . have . . . killed . . . a . . . holy
. . . man!

And everything begins again. The tocsin rings wildly. THE
CROWD *howls. The trumpets sound the alarm. The storm
rages in the void. The gesticulating* APOSTLES *are on their
feet.*

Peter. Jesus . . . dead! Thou . . . dead . . . dead!

Magdalene. Living in love! Sweet death! Enchanted
corpse!

The Apostles. Jesus . . . finished! Peter . . . flee! And
the body?

Magdalene. His kingdom?

The Apostles. Flee. The crowd is coming running. Take
command of us, Peter!

Peter. Come! The crowd will trample us down. Christ
is dead. Come, Magdalene, Christ is dead. . . .

Magdalene. He will rise again.

The Apostles. Dead . . . Flee . . . Lost . . . [*They are
going, shouting incoherent words.*]

The Watcher. The world is not destroyed. But it is unrecognizable. The world ceases to be and starts again. [*He makes off.*]

At the moment when THE APOSTLES, *led by* PETER, *are going, a violent laugh rings out.* BARABBAS *pushes* THE APOSTLES *back.*

Barabbas. Stop!

He is followed by BEGGARS *who are carrying torches.*

A Beggar. Long live Barabbas!
Barabbas. Get back, apostles! To work! The festival of the Crucified! Be with us! It is the hour of Justice. Long live the beggars, the humble, the lowest of men! It is the hour of the beggars, the oppressed, the scorned. It is the hour of Christ. It is the hour of convicts and slaves.
The Apostles [*fleeing in all directions*]. No, neither violence nor hatred. He alone . . . Justice . . .
Barabbas. Cowards! I am your leader. Where are you going? It is too late. The riot has begun. The city is ours. On, to the attack of Calvary! We must parade the corpse in the streets, in front of the palaces. There must be blood, fire. They shall pay!
The Beggars [*surrounding* BARABBAS]. Long live Barabbas! Vengeance!
Barabbas. Comrades, they have killed the one who wanted to upset everything. He loved the people, whose rebellion he embodied. He died for ideas that are our own. He died for the people and for all peoples. It is for us to make his cause triumph. Down with the priests, the judges, the rich, the sensualists, the exploiters! Down with bondage! Down with falsehood! Pull down that old shanty, the Temple! I, the robber, I tell you, and I swear it before these crosses, time is fulfilled! We are new men! Forward, comrades! Open the doors of the prisons. There won't be any more poor. You shall eat your fill. You shall speak your language. You shall live as you wish. And the Crucified will come back among us in three days. He shall be our king. Come on! Long live anarchy!
The Beggars [*at the acme of exaltation*]. Long live Barabbas! Anarchy! Jesus! The beggars! [*Yelling with joy, they rush in all directions.*]

BARABBAS *is following them, but* MAGDALENE *has gotten up and catches hold of him.*

Magdalene. Barabbas, my brother!

Barabbas. Come, woman! He is dead. Come quickly!

Magdalene. Where? Why?

Barabbas. To do Justice. To avenge the one who has been murdered. The beggars are avenging him. He was the king of the beggars. He loved us, eh?

Magdalene. He loves us. But he isn't dead. You can't kill love.

Barabbas. I love him too. He too came from the people. He knew the truth, he did. He will understand me. Come!

Magdalene [*restraining* BARABBAS]. No! Don't kill! There's enough with his blood, with his sacrifice. [*Sudden change.*] Avenge his suffering and mine, avenge them! No, I am wandering. Don't listen to me! Or else . . . Do Justice and kill, yes, and then . . . and then kill the hatred in your heart.

The men in black have come into view. MAGDALENE *sees them.*

Magdalene [*very quickly*]. Flee, brother! [*She indicates the men.*] They are seeking you!

Barabbas [*drawing his dagger*]. The pigs! Go away, woman! Go to the others. Encourage them. I shall defend myself alone. It is time to scatter these night birds.

BARABBAS *pushes* MAGDALENE *away. She makes off like a sleepwalker.* BARABBAS *gathers himself together, ready for combat.*

One of the Men. Barabbas!

Barabbas. Here I am, cops! Barabbas and his knife! On guard!

THE CLOWN *appears on the debris of the booth. Brief fight. The men in black withdraw.*

The Clown. What did he say?

Supple and silent, THE CLOWN *hops behind* BARABBAS *and thrusts a knife in his back. Then he disappears with a high-pitched laugh. The men in black immediately disappear.*

Barabbas. Eh? [*He staggers.*] They've got the better of me. And from behind? A fine bit of work! [*He falls to his knees like an ox.*] No, no, they haven't got the better of me yet. First, to work . . . [*He gets up painfully and shouts hoarsely.*] Bear up, beggars! I'm coming. [*But he falls to his knees again.*] You'll do all right without me. Yes, they've got the better of me. So what? I was condemned to death. . . . It's all the same to me. I'm no longer afraid. And I'm bleeding. Hey! Jesus! I too am bleeding. Sacrificed the same day. . . . [*He collapses to the ground and half raises himself.*] But you died for something. I am dying for nothing. Nevertheless it's because of you . . . for you . . . Jesus. If you want . . . And if I could give you my hand . . . and see you smile . . . Jesus. . . . My brother. . . . [*He collapses finally, rolls over, and dies looking toward Calvary.*]

THREE ACTORS AND THEIR DRAMA
(*Trois Acteurs, un Drame*)

A Dramatic Comedy in One Act
(1926)

Translated by Geᴏʀɢᴇ Hᴀᴜɢᴇʀ

INTRODUCTORY NOTE

I have only known Pirandello—through translations of his works—for a few years, and if there is any resemblance, there is no need for me to trouble myself about it. Does the fact of placing the beginning of a play on the bare stage of a theatre, for example, prove that one has undergone the influence of that work entitled *Six Characters in Search of an Author?* In the past there is no lack of plays that begin on a bare stage. I could cite some that go back to the nineteenth century. And I myself wrote, in 1926, a play in one act called *Three Actors and Their Drama.* It's the business of the double identity of the actor, who plays a part on the stage and plays a part in life, and who, finishing up by confusing his two identities, will conduct himself on the stage as in life. In writing this piece at a time when I was completely unaware of Pirandello, I did no more than take up an old idea that I was familiar with from parodies. Actors begin to perform a play seriously, but they are a little merry, a little drunk, and they make their tragedy degenerate into farce. The public accepts it, and the evening sinks into buffoonery— to the detriment of the poor devil of an author, who talks about hanging himself. That was Pirandello in anticipation, if you like; in any event, Pirandello had no part in it—no more did I.

From *The Ostend Interviews*

CHARACTERS

THE AUTHOR
THE INGENUE
THE JUVENILE LEAD
THE HEAVY LEAD
THE PROMPTER

THREE ACTORS AND THEIR DRAMA

PROLOGUE

SCENE—*The curtain is down. The feeble light one sees immediately before a play spills from a batten. The familiar sounds of scene shifting are heard.* THE AUTHOR *enters along the footlights. He is followed by three actors in their everyday clothes. All four are pale and make pitiful silhouettes in the semidarkness.*

THE AUTHOR. Well then! You've not got to lose heart tonight. What are you risking? You are actors and you are earning your bread and butter, while I, the author, am risking my reputation. You will be paid. I'm expecting a check from my brother.

The Heavy Lead. Wasn't it from your mother?

The Author. Well, from my family! . . . Is that any concern of yours? Ah, money! That's something else that's nagging at me! I'll have put all I possess into this wretched business. Have I achieved fame? Nothing like it! You can see well enough that fame isn't to be bought. . . . [*Excited.*] Is my play good theatre or is it not? You tell me, you who are in the business!

The Juvenile Lead. Your play's splendid, but the public won't bite. Why? It's baffling. It's been seen before, even with masterpieces.

The Author. I won't say that you're not doing your utmost. What I have noticed is that there is no heart in it. I assure you, if there was heart in it . . .

The Juvenile Lead. We do our job. That's enough— and it's a great deal for what we're paid. If there's no heart in it, it's because we haven't any to put in it.

The Heavy Lead. Besides, why did you choose us in particular?

The Author. Because there were three of you, as though

129

by chance, and because you had the faces that were needed.

The Ingenue. As far as our faces are concerned, you can say they are the real ones. No one has ever looked more like the part. . . . [*She shivers.*] I'd like to go to bed. Couldn't you write a play where the actors go to bed?

The Heavy Lead. Rather than one where the audience goes to sleep? . . .

The Author. All right! . . . Destroy my illusions. Not about art, about those who live on it.

The Ingenue. Live on it? Is this your idea of a joke?

The Author. I have no desire to laugh, my dear.

The Juvenile Lead. Nor have we, nor have the spectators. And so . . . You are responsible for your failure. Is this dismal thing supposed to be a play? There are three people in it, and it's because there isn't a fourth that only three people die! Something cheerful is what's wanted. . . .

The Heavy Lead. The Middle Ages weren't cheerful. I suggested bringing the comic element into your tragedy, to balance it. Then it would have been different, because we three, we're cheerful types. . . .

The Author. I don't doubt it. [*Nervously.*] That's not the point. By letting me down, you've missed the chance of extricating yourselves from the second-rate. Have you ever studied your parts? How do you spend your time? You, the heavy lead, in fighting with your wife. . . .

The Ingenue. I say! . . .

The Author. And you, in sniveling and drinking! . . . And you, the juvenile lead . . .

The Juvenile Lead. My dear sir, our private life—

The Author. Exactly. You play tragedy in your private lives, while on the stage you only bungle around. I've had enough of it. I'm not a barnstormer, I'm a poet! Anyway, it's going to stop. . . . Tonight is the last time we're going to play. I've brought you to this town on purpose, a county town where, it seems, there is an elite. I've seen to the hired applause and had a drink with the critics. There will be a full house. Let's not argue any more. I ask you to make an effort, to have a little professional conscientiousness, for once. . . . Do it for dramatic art, if you don't want to do it for me!

The Juvenile Lead. It's a difficult business.

The Author. And is writing plays easy? Do you at least understand what I have written?

The Juvenile Lead. The unfortunate thing is that we understand too well. . . . No, it will never work. To safeguard your play you should have chosen three actors who didn't look like us and who didn't know each other.

The Author. What's this got to do with it?

The Juvenile Lead. Because we knew your script before you did!

The Heavy Lead. We've been acting your play for years!

The Author. I swear I plagiarized no one!

The Heavy Lead. Don't get alarmed. We'll act your play; but for the very last time. That settles the matter.

The Author. Unless it catches on, you mean?

The Heavy Lead. The very last time!

The Author [*bewildered*]. Then . . . thank you. So it's the last time you'll play it? Well, for myself, there's a chance that I may never pick up a pen again, that this dramatic poet may disappear forever. [*Pause.*] Go and get ready. I'm going to the bar. Look, it's making me tremble. . . . [*He goes, but turns and makes a despondent gesture with his hand.*] Act like artists! [*Goes out.*]

The Heavy Lead. Artists? We are, old chap, day and night. That's what's doing for us! . . .

Long pause. The noises behind the curtain have stopped. The three actors stand still and seem to be waiting for one of their number to speak, but no one finds anything to say, and suddenly THE INGENUE *starts to sob without restraint.*

The Heavy Lead. Now what's the matter? . . .

The Ingenue. Nothing!

The Juvenile Lead. She's got the wind up. . . . It's only natural!

The Ingenue. I don't want to think about it, but all the same I am thinking about it!

The Heavy Lead. Pah! . . . You've only got to stick to your part and do what's needed at the right moment. . . . It's the same for you as for us.

The Juvenile Lead. And everything will work out as we decided last night. We'll finish up really well!

The Ingenue. I shan't have the courage. . . .

The Juvenile Lead. Can we find the courage to live?

The Ingenue. If one of us had thought of going, we shouldn't have gotten to this pass. . . .

The Heavy Lead. Going wouldn't have solved anything. I'm a fatalist. There's nothing like action. Let's take advantage of the opportunity this play offers. . . .

The Ingenue. I'm frightened.

The Juvenile Lead. Don't act like a child. It's as simple as A B C. It doesn't need thinking about. The play does the acting for us and dictates our moves. Does the author suspect the good turn he's doing us? . . . It will bring him publicity, won't it?

The Ingenue. I'm frightened. . . .

The Heavy Lead. But, my dear, it was you who had the idea. . . .

The Ingenue. I wasn't thinking of my mother . . . or of my first communion!

The Juvenile Lead. I too have made my first communion, but I'm not in a funk.

The Heavy Lead. And I've gotten past the age . . .

The Ingenue. Everyone always says they're not frightened. One of us will get run in, you'll see.

The Juvenile Lead. Impossible! The daggers have been changed for revolvers.

Pause. A warning bell rings backstage.

The Heavy Lead. You're not still weeping, Mariette?

The Ingenue. No. It's not worth the bother. The audience can do the weeping. . . .

The Heavy Lead. What a good joke we're playing on the public!

The Juvenile Lead. D'you think they'll really be fed up with the theatre, after this?

The bell rings again.

The Heavy Lead. It's time. As agreed, eh? Real tragedy!

The Juvenile Lead. All the same, we can say good-by, can't we? Good-by, Mariette!

The Ingenue. Good-by, Raoul!

The Heavy Lead. Good-by, Mariette! Forgive me. . . .

The Ingenue. If you will forgive me. . . .

The Juvenile Lead. Good-by, Albert. It's a bad memory to keep. . . .

The Heavy Lead. Our life was a bad play. . . . And we were rotten actors. . . .

They shake hands, then go out slowly and uncertainly.

THE PLAY

After a time, the knocking for curtain rise is heard. The footlights come on. THE PROMPTER is in his place, from which he comes into view, from the waist upward, from time to time during the play. In the wings, a phonograph begins to play the great melody from Tosca—to create atmosphere, no doubt. When the melody is finished, there are the three knocks, and the curtain goes up. Shabby painted scenery, with braced sidepieces. The back cloth depicts a Gothic crypt, the sidepieces a drawing room of the Empire period. The furniture is in the Louis XVI style. An elaborately engraved suit of armor stands in a recess. Everything is bathed in moonlight.

THE DUKE, *in a costume of the Valois period, is turning over the pages of a folio volume. Eleven o'clock strikes in a distant clock tower.*

THE DUKE. Eleven o'clock! When midnight shall sound, I will conjure up the spirit of Evil. Yet it is but eleven o'clock by the vast night that swamps the world! And what am I, in the depths of this darkness? A humble mortal ravaged by the pursuit of happiness. . . . Happiness? Elusive chimera! . . . And here I am old. Have I known happiness? No, I have been unable to overtake that shadow, more unreal than the phantoms that haunt this manor. How heavy is the night, to me! . . . [*A trumpet rings out.*] Watchman, in your high tower, leave men to their nightmares. And if you discern comets in the sky, fiery swords, or other terrible signs heralding the world's end, give me notice of them by a lively flourish. [*He gets up and walks about ceremoniously.*] I no longer believe in God, horrible as that may seem. I believe in the devil, even though he is not very obliging. To him I have surrendered my soul and my body, worn out by debauchery and adventures, and I shall join him again in his Hell at the moment I myself have chosen. Has not astrology foretold me of this tragic fate which feeling condemns, but which reason approves? . . . And, in truth, how could one not end tragically in a manor such as this? . . . [*He stops, trying to remember what follows.*]

The Voice of the Prompter. . . . my death . . .

The Duke. Do these bells ring a prelude to my death? . . . [*He listens. The bells ring late.*] So be it! My will is made. To the devil, I leave my bones. To the knight who is my vassal, I leave my manor and the mortgages that encumber it. To my young wife, I leave my treasures and her liberty. . . . [*He sighs, then swaggers.*] No weakness! . . . With me there is extinguished a gallant and accursed race. I was at the last crusade, Od's blood! It was the sensuous Orient that undid me. I want the echoes of this castle to repeat that it was not to slaughter the Turk nor to free the Sepulcher that I went to the Holy Land. No! I was dazzled by the houris' sensual delights. Why did I not stay with them? Why did I not abjure the religion of my fathers for that of Mahomet? I came back from Byzantium weary and prematurely aged. [*He sits down.*]

Voice of the Prompter. . . . last mistake . . .

The Duke. It was then I made a last mistake. . . . I believed I had become wise, moral, and paternal, as is befitting when one is past fifty years. Alas! I chanced upon this young girl! . . . I was too fond of life. I was too fond of love. . . .

Voice of the Prompter. . . . artless gaze . . .

The Duke. This maiden with the artless gaze I made my wife. There happened to me what is fated to happen to presumptuous old men. I was . . . Let me hide my grief, I hear her fairylike tread.

THE INGENUE *appears in a Burgundian dress and wearing a hennin.*

The Duchess. O husband, how ominous it is in this place! What gloomy thoughts were yours?

The Duke [*kissing her on the forehead*]. My child, I was indulging in the study of forbidden arts. It is my refuge. . . . Is not my age that of meditation? Yours is that of dreams, of love . . .

The Duchess. I dream, perhaps, but not of love. Am I not the faithful wife cited as example?

The Duke [*after starting with surprise*]. Then what does a young wife dream of, if not of love? I shall not harbor resentment against you for it. It is essential that you find happiness; that is the wish I ordain. . . .

The Duchess. Thanks, my lord! But whence this anxious mien?

The Duke. From studying the future. It is written that our fates shall be at variance, that you will live a better life. . . .

The Duchess. I do not complain of the way I live, except that this manor is a little damp. . . .

The Duke. You do not complain because you are well-bred. But why do you sigh unceasingly? I do not wish to know. . . . Did I not tell you on the morrow of our marriage that I resigned myself to being your father?

The Duchess. Why not have left me my virginity and my innocence?

The Duke. At the touch of your youth I had faith in myself! As for your virginity, let us talk of other things, my child.

The Duchess. I shall make no reply. Have we not said all that we had to say to each other on that matter? . . . [*Pause.*]

Voice of the Prompter. . . . moonlight . . .

The Duke [*picking up the prompt*]. Why do you gaze on the moonlight?

The Duchess. I was thinking it was time for sleep. [*A cracking noise.*] There are mysterious sounds tonight. . . .

The Duke. It is midnight drawing nigh.

The Duchess. I am sensible of the mark of misfortune everywhere. . . .

The Duke. Misfortune never wanders far. . . . What does it matter to you, if it doesn't overtake you?

Voice of the Prompter. . . . equivocal . . .

The Duchess. How equivocal your words, my lord!

The Duke. Equivocal? [*He is obviously going wrong.*] Like our position! But I alone support the burden of our fate. [*As though lost, he is on the lookout for* THE PROMPTER.] I am going up on the keep to be engulfed by the heavenly bodies. And I shall consult your delightful star. As for mine, it rises bloody. Do you tremble?

The Duchess. Are you quite sure that the stars do not lie?

The Duke. How should I know? What in the universe

is not untrue? Can it be that the world is the handiwork of a perverse god?

Dignified and fated, he goes out. THE INGENUE *is left standing, dejected. She looks about the place, then takes a note from her bodice.*

Voice of the Prompter. . . . matchless mistress . . .

The Duchess [*reading*]. "Matchless mistress, I shall come. Seek not to know which way or how. This night shall be decisive. Either you will belong to me, or our romance will end in blood. If you will not accept my freeing you from this unseasonable old man, I shall transfix my heart at your feet. . . ."

Voice of the Prompter. . . . O Tristan . . .

The Duchess. Tristan, my knight, why this painful dilemma? . . . Is it not simpler secretly to have a passionate fondness for each other, while my crumbling husband gives himself up to the occult sciences? You overstate, as always. . . . What is going to come of it? I am thinking aloud, Tristan, and perhaps you are listening! Come! Will this night end without drama?

Voice of Tristan. I stand in awe . . .

The Duchess. He spoke! Is it you? Tristan, where are you?

Voice of Tristan. I am nowhere, if I am not in your heart!

The Duchess. I am afraid! Tristan, I wish to be in your arms. . . .

Voice of Tristan. They are here!

The suit of armor begins to walk with arms outstretched.

The Duchess. Sublime stratagem! [*In the arms of the armor.*] I love you, my knight!

The Knight. I love you, my Duchess! [*He lifts the vizor of his helmet. Like the juvenile lead that he is,* THE KNIGHT *gives* THE INGENUE *an interminable kiss.*]

Voice of the Prompter. . . . this night, spring . . .

The Duchess [*stammering*]. This night, spring . . . You have never kissed me that way before, Raoul! . . . [*She corrects herself.*] Tristan! . . . This spring night . . . a night for living. . . .

The Knight. For dying . . .

The Duchess. Of delight . . .

The Prompter [*anxious, he has put his head out of his*

box]. The flowers are fragrant . . . the stars are glittering . . .

The Knight. The flowers are glittering, the stars are fragrant. . . . You are lovely!

The Duchess. Clasp me so tight that it bruises me. . . .

The Prompter. No one sees us. . . .

The Knight. Let them see us! Though a thunderbolt fall, I shall not let you go!

The Prompter. Midnight will strike. What are you going to do?

The Duchess. What are you going to do? . . . [*Noise of footsteps in the wings.*] The Duke! Do not destroy us!

THE KNIGHT *goes and takes up his first position.* THE DUCHESS *hides her face.* THE DUKE *enters.*

The Duke. What the stars have told me I shall not reveal. . . . Poor woman! Your bosom heaves! [*He searches about the room.*] I heard voices.

The Duchess. That is impossible!

The Duke. Let us assume so. . . . [*He sits down.*] I am weary of astrology. It is an illusion like all the rest. Courage fails me. One thing remained to me, you!

The Duchess. Do I not remain to you?

The Duke. You are pretty in your paleness. Is it for me? I doubt it. You are transfigured by love. I undergo a thousand deaths from it, but it is my expiation.

The Duchess. What are you seeking with your sidelong glances?

The Duke. The shadow of misfortune! Misfortune has entered this manor. . . . It draws nigh. And midnight is about to strike. . . .

The Duchess. You frighten me out of my wits! What do you mean?

The Duke. The hour for returning to oblivion. Have no fear, my will is made [*he lights a cigarette*] . . . and I have left a letter for the police.

The Prompter. The memory of me . . .

The Duke. The memory of me? I don't give a hang. . . . I leave the memory of a blunderer, a mug, a failure. . . . There are crowds of fellows like me. . . .

The Prompter. . . . ask of you a last mercy . . .

The Duke. And now I ask you for a last kiss, a real one. . . .

The Duchess [*weeping*]. You don't mean it! [*She kisses him.*]

The Duke. Tears, and not stage tears! I am grateful to you for them.

The Duchess. You won't do it!

The Duke. I shall play my part to the bitter end. Now that I have had this kiss, I ask you again to believe that I wasn't fooled by you. I pretended not to be aware because I loved you. And I suffered in silence.

The Prompter. My nobility . . .

The Duke. I was a deceived husband, but I knew it, I winked at it. . . . Is that immoral? Didn't I have the excuse of a ridiculous and burning love?

The Prompter. My nobility . . . oh, heavens! . . . my nobility!

The Duke. And so I don't reproach you at all. You have my pity, and so has your lover who is listening to me. You loved each other, so much the better. . . . I was deceived, so much the worse. . . . This is the ransom for that. . . .

The Prompter. My nobility . . .

The Duke. It couldn't last, you understand, Mariette. If you'd given me the go-by at the beginning, it would have been simple. But you had scruples. I am touched by that. And now allow the old fool to quit the boards. I shall play it first-rate, as in my job. And tell your lover, who is moreover my friend, to play it as I am. That's all. . . .

The Duchess [*throwing herself at* THE DUKE]. Bertie!

The Prompter. My nobility! . . . for God's sake!

The Duke [*who has stood up, pushing* THE DUCHESS *away*]. No fuss. Good-by! [*He takes a revolver from his doublet.*] *Vive la France!* [*He turns away. A shot.* THE DUKE *slumps down.*]

The Prompter. Run! May Heaven help us. . . .

The suit of armor leaps toward THE DUCHESS, *who is standing open-mouthed, gasping.*

The Knight. Let's get out of here. . . . Heaven help . . .

The Duchess [*howling*]. No! He's dead!

The Knight. We are alive!

The Duchess. I want to die. . . .

The Knight. Death disgusts me. Are you coming?

The Duchess. No. He killed himself for me! I love him!

If you had killed him, I would have been your woman.
Go away!

The Knight. Mariette!

The Duchess. Mariette says to hell with you! I'm going
to die. . . .

The Knight. We shall see. . . .

The Duchess. I'm the one who has the floor! Have you
your revolver? Here's mine. [*She takes out her weapon.*]

The Knight. You're trembling. Stage fright?

The Duchess. I have; but I'm still playing. . . . [*She
turns away.*] Good-by, handsome! . . . [*A shot. She
falls.*]

The Prompter. The only thing left for me to do is to
enter a monastery . . . a monastery, you wretched actors!

The Knight [*bewildered*]. A monastery . . . Mariette!
. . . Bertie! . . . I didn't think that you . . . I can't live
without you, Mariette! I shall rejoin you in eternity. . . .
[*He takes out a revolver, puts the barrel in his mouth, and
fires. He utters a cry of despair and falls.*]

*The strokes of midnight sound. In the wings, the phono-
graph takes up again the great melody from* Tosca. The
Prompter *wrings his hands and throws the sheets of his
script at the corpses.*

The Prompter. Deadheads! . . . Pack of swine! . . .
Gang of brutes!

And the curtain comes slowly down on the carnage.

EPILOGUE

Scene—*But the curtain goes up again, as usual. One of the
suicides stirs: it is* The Heavy Lead. *He gets up, comes to
the footlights, and bows. The curtain comes down again
behind him. And* The Heavy Lead *makes hypocritically
for the wings. But before he gets there, the curtain allows*
The Juvenile Lead *through. He comes down and bows
in his turn. The pair catch sight of each other and start
with surprise.*

The Juvenile Lead. What? Grandpa!

The Heavy Lead. You? Not dead?

The Juvenile Lead. I aimed badly. Where are you going?

The Heavy Lead. To the police, to report Mariette's death. And you?

The Juvenile Lead. Me? I'm going to commit suicide.

The Heavy Lead. It's difficult, my boy. You get too used to dying on the stage.

The curtain parts again and allows THE INGENUE *to come through.*

The Ingenue. You two? . . . [*She is on her way out.*]

The Juvenile Lead [*bringing her back*]. Where were you going?

The Ingenue. To the morgue, to inquire about you.

The Heavy Lead. Did you bungle, Mariette?

The Ingenue. Not at all. I fell down dead, I swear it!

They gaze at each other, perplexed.

The Juvenile Lead. What are we going to do?

The Heavy Lead. Carry on with it.

The Ingenue. Commit suicide again?

The Heavy Lead. No. . . . Carry on with it as we did yesterday, as always. What has altered? There are still three of us, as in the plays, so let's carry on acting. . . . [*He laughs.*]

The Ingenue. Who are you making fun of?

The Heavy Lead. No one. I'm laughing because I'm glad! We ought to be dead and we are alive! You get it?

The Juvenile Lead. I get it. [*He laughs.*]

The Ingenue. It's stupid! [*She laughs.*]

The Heavy Lead. Come on! Things are going to work out. I'm going to open a pub. And you two? I haven't the heart to separate you. You shall play together: you shall tour the provinces.

The Juvenile Lead. You're a brick!

The Heavy Lead. A father, boy. I know how to behave. Kiss Mariette. That no longer makes any difference to me. [THE JUVENILE LEAD *kisses* THE INGENUE.] I've played old men's parts so often. . . .

A shot in the wings. The actors start, then stand nonplused. Noises behind the curtain, running, calling.

The Ingenue. Don't get excited! Shots—we are familiar enough with them. Something must be going on. Listen!

The Juvenile Lead. If it's a suicide, he'll come and bow.

The Ingenue [*bursting out with a hysterical laugh*]. The author!

The Heavy Lead. Good God! He's not an actor, he isn't!

The Juvenile Lead. The author?

The horrified face of THE PROMPTER *appears in the gap in the curtains.*

The Prompter. The author! . . . Yes, indeed!

The three actors, scared and gesticulating, dash toward the wings yelling.

The Actors. The author? . . . The author?

And it's all over!

PANTAGLEIZE

A Farce to Make You Sad in Three Acts,
Nine Scenes, and an Epilogue

(1929)

Translated by GEORGE HAUGER

EPITAPH FOR PANTAGLEIZE *

Who was Pantagleize? or, rather, *Who is he?* for nothing proves that he is dead when the curtain falls—the fall of the curtain in the theatre never having killed anyone, except the authors of wretched plays! Well then, am I Pantagleize? Such has been claimed. I insist with absolute conviction that I am not he—not I, although there are peculiar affinities between the character and his author which, after all, mean nothing; but they do exist. Let us say that Pantagleize is like an older and more knowing brother who left me in the happy days of childhood, in those days of Eden when the animals are guardian spirits, and when all is lovely—life—and when all is good—man! . . . A brother who left me, and whom, bearing names not his own, I meet now and then in monstrous cities where life is not lovely and where man is not at all good; and who, poor shamefaced fellow, or poor failure, hides himself, after giving a glance that is beyond words.

What would be the good of pursuing him? I realized that he no longer existed as an individual, but that he had a powerful existence as a mythical character—and one no more goes after myths than after chimeras: one watches them go by, one recognizes their immortality, and, in the face of it, one thinks on one's own impermanence. This older brother is, in a word, the Poet, the incarnation of the poet, unfit for anything except love, friendship, and ardor—a failure, therefore, in our utilitarian age, which pushes out onto the fringe everything that is unproductive, that does not pay dividends! A useless mouth to feed! A man overboard! And it is well that it is so!

If he has, by his profession, become a myth, he has not done so deliberately. Pantagleize never does anything de-

---

* *Pantagleize* became the first of Ghelderode's plays to be seen publicly in England when the Proscenium Players gave a series of performances of the present translation during October, 1957. The author wrote the *Epitaph* specially for this occasion. It has never before been published. [Translator's note.]

liberately, not even make poems, for he never writes, or scarcely, and if he has talent, or if he touches us, it is not his fault. He is a determinist, a fatalist, if you prefer it, and he believes in the Fate of ancient times just as he does in the penny horoscope that has revealed his destiny to him. Yes, he has become a myth because of the theatre.

Between ourselves, the theatre is still a strange and doubtful business, in spite of appearances of modernity. There is over and over again a bit of witchcraft about it —and it is not so long since actors had to live and die outside the Church. Still, the Church does nothing without reason, and remembers that the adepts of that magician, that caster of spells called Orpheus, are in possession of dangerous powers, and that they are able, like the devil, to assume a thousand and one shapes, to have ten souls, to live a hundred lives and die a hundred times! The marvels of the theatre have allowed Pantagleize to slip through the wings and wander around (in what dimension?) and make himself invisible in order to materialize somewhere else. This nice but touchy fellow escaped from me. I had written about him in a story, in 1925, before putting him in a play, in 1929, for a young Flemish actor, Renaat Verheyen, who realized him wonderfully in 1930, and died shortly afterward at the age of twenty-six. He was not shot by hideous, repressive soldiery, but, as Cocteau said when speaking of Radiguet, he was "shot by the angels."

I very much want to say good-by at this depressing juncture: that would be wise. But it must go on record that Pantagleize, who has been shot many a time on many a stage in Europe, is hard to kill. Here he is now in Leeds, in that fine country of England that, through the centuries, has been the home of the most tremendous nation of the theatre. I am both proud and uneasy about it. Still, in addition to the theatre, this fine England loves eccentrics, individuals, characters, and it is the last place, or soon will be the last place, where a man has the right to be himself, whether he is an eccentric, a ghost, or a poet. Consequently, I have faith that the audience will not drive my Pantagleize away; and who knows if they won't claim him as somewhat English—in origin, at least? A mime, a clown—the poet is a bit of these as well! Yes, Pantagleize is a distant relative of the great circus, invented and codified by England, a fugitive from that circus which gave the world that other poet of actions called Chaplin. It is not so far from Chaplin to Pantagleize, and since Chaplin was himself born of the prodigious poetic discipline of Little Tich,* who brought happiness to my young days, the English audience can say that Pantagleize is probably Anglo-Saxon by his descending, in moral genealogy, from Little Tich through Chaplin! Moreover, my first meeting with the lunar individual whom I was to call Pantagleize was in 1919, in the Rhineland among the blood and fire of revolution, where in an occupied town the good Germans were fighting among themselves, under the quizzical gaze of soldiers—of whom I had the honor to be one. I was going back to my regiment and I came across this indescribable civilian, this Diogenes, who was reading a book as he nonchalantly crossed a public square which was swept by machine-gun fire. When he got to the center, he looked up at the sky and opened an umbrella that he had on his arm, then recommenced his poet's peregrination, reading—what? Heine, probably, or Rilke! The whole army burst into laughter, and so did the *schupos* and the *Spartakists* as well. The gods protected this apparition who, with his delicate profile and his air of detachment from all contingencies, could have been the incarnation of that well-known pacifist, the wise Erasmus, for he was not to be counted among the vanquished, the dead of that stupid day. Pantagleize was born! This was at the same moment as that other hero was born, that soldier-Chaplin who immortalized the trenches and who, in the most stupendous exploit of all, took prisoner the Kaiser himself! You know enough. . . .

Has this play *Pantagleize* any sort of a moral? Yes, if you want, although a moral is not necessary in the theatre: often it is even harmful. The moral of this sad story—and the story of man is always sad, absurd, and void of meaning, as Shakespeare wrote—is that in our atomic and auto-disintegrated age, this age from which dreams and dreamers are banished in favor of the scientific nightmare and the beneficiaries of the future horror,

---

* *Little Tich* was the stage name of Harry Relph (1868–1928), an English music-hall and pantomime comedian, famous for balancing on the tips of his comically exaggerated boots which were said to be as long as he was tall. [Translator's note.]

a fellow like Pantagleize remains an archetype, an exemplary man, and a fine example who has nothing to do with that dangerous thing, intelligence, and a great deal to do with that savior, instinct. He is human in an age when all is becoming dehumanized. He is the last poet, and the poet is he who believes in heavenly voices, in revelation, in our divine origin. He is the man who has kept the treasure of his childhood in his heart, and who passes through catastrophes in all artlessness. He is bound to Parsifal by purity, and to Don Quixote by courage and holy madness. And if he dies, it is because, particularly in our time, the Innocents must be slaughtered: that has been the law since the time of Jesus. Amen! . . .

CHARACTERS

PANTAGLEIZE, *esquire, the hero of the day*
RACHEL SILBERCHATZ, *a Jewess*
CREEP, *a policeman, thick but cunning*
BAMBOOLA, *a Negro*
INNOCENTI, *a waiter*
BANGER, *lame and bearded*
BLANK, *a wavy-haired stripling, a poet*
THE BALLADMONGER
MACBOOM, *a general*
THE BANK MANAGER
THE ASSISTANT BANK MANAGER
A SOLDIER
ANOTHER SOLDIER
FOUR WAITERS (*supers*)
THE DISTINGUISHED COUNSEL
SIX MILITARY JUDGES (*supers*)
THE GENERALISSIMO
THE OFFICER
SOLDIERS OF A PATROL (*supers*)
SENTRIES (*supers*)
THE CROWD (*off-stage*)

SCENE—In a city of Europe, on the morrow of one war
and the eve of another.

PANTAGLEIZE

ACT ONE

SCENE I—PANTAGLEIZE'S *room, a garret. Dingy early morning light.* PANTAGLEIZE *is asleep—that is, his bare feet are poking out of the bed. The bed is a sugar box. An open umbrella serves as canopy. No furniture. On the left of the stage, a huge calendar, which remains there until the end of the play.*

Silence. An alarm clock goes off somewhere. The Negro BAMBOOLA, *carrying a lighted candle, comes into the room. He is in his shirt sleeves. Yawning uncontrollably, he goes toward the bed and gazes at* PANTAGLEIZE'S *feet. He swings a feather duster in his right hand.*

BAMBOOLA. Boss? . . . [*The feet have heard and they quiver.*] He's asleep, yeah. [*Mournfully.*] I good nigger, get up six o'clock, work like a black, yeah, he bourgeois sleep. [*Furious.*] Boss? . . . It's six o'clock. [*The feet move. A great snore.*]

Pantagleize [*from the depths of his box*]. Ahrrrr. [*Then silence.*]

BAMBOOLA *is in distress. He puts down the candle, makes some movements with the feather duster, yawns, and sits on his behind, worn out already.*

Bamboola. Big night for niggers is coming. Good nigger, bad nigger, eat civilized folk, yeah, sleep twelve hours, and drink pale ale. All rotten, all blow up, yeah. [*He gets up and goes toward the box.*] Massa Pantagleize? Excuse me. . . . It's five past six! [*He gives the box a violent kick.*] Excuse me!

Pantagleize [*gives a toneless cry*]. Ouf! [*The feet move again.* PANTAGLEIZE *talks in his sleep.*] No, no, no, no. . . .

151

I do not like this violence. You want to cross the Atlantic?
Go on, then. We shall have a divorce. I am frightened of
water.

Bamboola. He dream? Boss, in the depths of your dream,
listen. [*He leaps about and sings in a falsetto voice, ac-
companying his singing with kicks on the box, in a mock-
jazz fashion.*]

> Patata golo bili patata
> Zoozoo pata bili pata
>
> [*The feet quiver.*]
>
> Booloo pata zizi pata
> Pototo gili bobo patata . . .

Pantagleize. Ah! Oh! Shipwreck! [*He gets out of his
box in a single bound.*]

Bamboola [*obsequiously*]. Boss, ten past six and not
raining.

PANTAGLEIZE *stretches himself. Flowery dressing gown,
trousers too short, seaman's white and blue sweater. He
is dazed.*

Pantagleize. I've been dreaming, that's certain. [*He
yawns.*] Ah, well, time to live? Brrr! what a morning for
an execution. [*He hums.*] Greetings, my ultimate morning!

Bamboola [*bows*]. Good morning, Boss!

Pantagleize. What's got hold of you?

Bamboola. I say, "Good morning, Boss!" In Africa,
polite people, in the morning, they say, "Good morning."

Pantagleize. Good morning, Bamboola, good morning!
[*He seizes* BAMBOOLA'S *hand.*] Have you slept well?

Bamboola. Not much.

Pantagleize. I have—much too much.

Bamboola [*sententiously*]. Big night coming when all
folk sleep same sleep.

Pantagleize. No doubt that will be tomorrow or the
day after.

Bamboola [*credulously*]. So soon?

Pantagleize. Or—who knows?—today.

Bamboola [*visibly moved*]. Boss, what you say?

Pantagleize [*amused*]. Don't get excited, Bamboola. If
it came to pass, as all things come to pass, you wouldn't
be any the less a Negro shoeblack nor I a philosopher, by
trade. Aren't these fine occupations?

Bamboola. Very beautiful.

Pantagleize. Well, now . . . how many pairs of shoes do you shine a day? And after that, what do you do? You go and play poker with the taxi drivers. After that? You dance and pick up tips—when you don't pick up Madame's jewelry. After that? You sleep. Whereas with me, Pantagleize, my way of life is that of reflection. I confess to you that by dint of reflective thinking, I no longer understand anything about anything. Well, I go for a walk. I read the manifestoes about art which tell you nothing at all, and I contribute to a fashion journal in which I sign myself "Ernestine"—even though I never look at women. My girl friend is a monkey at the Zoo. She is called Cleopatra, and has fleas, and eats half of my food every midday. In return, she grimaces abominably at me. And I love her. Still—if in the morning we have the big night, or if tonight we have the big morning—we shall both go on doing the same things; but we shall be compelled to do them. Thenceforth our trade will seem a burden to us: thenceforth will our slavery begin. . . . [*He blows out the candle. It has grown lighter.*]

Bamboola [*bursting with ideas*]. Boss! . . . m! . . . m!

Pantagleize. What? A speech? [*He gives his boots to* BAMBOOLA, *and after putting on his collar, combs his hair.*]

Bamboola. Yeah, Boss. I make speech very well. Listen, Boss? The Negroes will be made white. Poor pariahs of colonization. Still listen, Boss? Bamboola have beautiful destiny. I, child of nature, save mad old world. [*He throws down the boots, takes a pamphlet from his trousers' pocket, and reads emphatically.*] "Parliamentary rottenness," yeah. "When the exploited people . . ."

Pantagleize. I know that. [*He recites in an inspired fashion.*] "Reaction will tremble before its coffers, whence flows the blood of the enslaved plebeians. . . ." [*Confidentially.*] Yeah. I touched fifty francs for writing that pamphlet, but it was Whatshisnameski who put his name to it. One must live, Bamboola. You shine shoes. . . . [*Suddenly practical.*] Have you cleaned mine? You know very well that our fellows judge us by our feet.

Bamboola [*disturbed*]. Here, Boss.

Pantagleize [*putting on his boots*]. And you said it wasn't raining?

Bamboola. No, Boss.

Pantagleize. What century are we in?

Bamboola. The twentieth since the little child God, Boss. [*Inspired.*] But the weather . . .

Pantagleize. What's the date?

Bamboola [*wanly*]. The . . . the . . . the . . .

Pantagleize [*carrying on*]. Because I must hand in my fashion article. Women are going to be flat and spiritual. The line . . . What date did you say?

Bamboola. The . . . the . . . the . . . the . . .

Pantagleize. A Negro and a stammerer, that's the limit! And you want to save mankind? And you read pamphlets? I hired you to clean my boots, to tell me the time, the date, and the state of the weather. Nevertheless, you awakened me too late, and in an upleasant way. You told me it wasn't raining, and you hadn't even opened the window. You have cleaned my boots by spitting on them —and cleaned them badly. And you can't say what date it is? Shame on you, black man! What's the matter with you? Have you got a mouth made of wood, like the idols in your country?

Bamboola. Excuse, Boss.

Pantagleize. You wouldn't be in love, would you? Bamboola, that is a fatal mistake. Love your fellow man, love your country, love mankind—that doesn't commit you to anything. But don't love a woman, not one woman alone. That is the source of all evil, especially for an impressionable Negro. I shall look at the date for myself— though I don't give a rap for the year, the month, and the day. Am I not above contingencies? [*He goes to the great calendar hanging at the side of the stage and tears off a page. The date appears: May 1.* PANTAGLEIZE, *somewhat shortsighted, reads aloud.*] "Saint Vitus." A cookery recipe. "Serve hot." "Open the mouth and swallow." And on the back, a joke. "Charlie met . . ." This is going to be funny. [*He laughs.*] Ho! . . . Ho! . . . [*He gazes at the Negro and considers him attentively.*] Are you ill, Bamboola? You are very pale for a Negro. Is it because of this date? An unhappy memory, no doubt? Didn't you eat a missionary on this date?

Bamboola. Not ill, Boss. Never ill.

Pantagleize. All Negroes say that. Believe me, brother of the night, your race is degenerating.

BAMBOOLA *looks obstinately at the calendar and rolls the whites of his eyes. He wanders around, then suddenly seizes* PANTAGLEIZE'S *hand.*

Bamboola. Boss . . .

Pantagleize [suddenly understanding]. Thank you . . . thank you . . . I understand. I am very grateful. I really had forgotten. [*He points to the calendar.*] Today, Bamboola, today I am forty years old. You remembered? That's fine. [*One hand on his heart, he prepares to give forth his reflections.*]

Bamboola [vigorously]. No, Boss! . . . No! . . . No!

Pantagleize [imperiously]. Yes, Bamboola! Yes! . . . Yes! . . . Forty years old, I tell you. A sad day, eh? I always believed I would have a destiny, a wonderful destiny, and in this childish belief I was just like you. And, alas, now I have reached the age when one slips into the category of failures. What have I done on this planet—except to wonder what I was going to do? What am I? A philosopher? Not even that, since I grow sad at my lot even on my birthday. Ah, I who have dreamed of being a captain, an explorer, an aviator, a champion cyclist, a member of parliament, a prophet, an actor, a tenor, and a one-man band—I am forty years old, and my destiny has never begun. Will it begin? Or is it my destiny to have no destiny? I am growing old. Mankind, milling all around me, I understand less and less. I have neither vanity, nor pride, nor love, nor self-respect. I have nothing but my queer name, my crucial age, and an insufficient intellectual ballast, all completely out of date. If I were still a fine young fellow—like you, Bamboola! Is this a destiny, now!

Bamboola. Not sorrow, Boss. You no fine young fellow, but you little race apart. All change, Boss. Your destiny as well.

Pantagleize. Possible? After all? [*He searches in his pockets.*] I have kept a paper that Professor Estampa-Fakir sent me after seeing a specimen of my handwriting. You believe in magicians, Bamboola? Obviously. Here is my horoscope, appropriately vague and luminous. [*He unfolds the paper.*] "You, who are so far without a destiny, will find your destiny begin unexpectedly when you reach your fortieth year. So the stars foretell. Your destiny, suddenly aflame and as soon extinct—historic, perhaps—

will begin with the dawn and end with the evening. On what will befall, the stars maintain a diplomatic silence." [*He folds up the paper.*] All from a specimen of my handwriting. You see it's not a laughing matter. Hasn't anyone ever foretold your fate?

Bamboola. I foretell. Your Bamboola cabinet minister.

Pantagleize. I congratulate you. When you are a cabinet minister, remember me. Let us go on awaiting events. Nothing is as harmonious, regular, logical, and mathematically exact as events, once they have happened. What sort of things will they be? What does it matter? Already we know that it's not raining and that it's the first of May.

Bamboola [*hopping with excitement*]. Wah!

Pantagleize. All of which urges me to take a walk, since the day promises to be a lovely one.

Bamboola [*roars*]. Boss! You said?

Pantagleize. Take a shower, my boy.

Bamboola. Boss said . . . that it will be a lovely day? That's what he said?

Pantagleize. Oh . . . I said that. It was a feeling. Here we are in the month of May, merry May.

Bamboola [*jigging up and down nervously*]. Hi! . . . Hi! . . . Lovely day! . . . Hi! . . . Hi! . . . Wah! . . . Wah!

Pantagleize. Are you going mad?

Bamboola. Hurrah! Negro happy! [*Giving vent to roars of pleasure, he rushes at* PANTAGLEIZE.]

Pantagleize. Help! . . . Stop it, you brute! [*He falls under the impact.*]

Bamboola [*lifts him up and hugs him*]. Nice Boss, you not angry?

Pantagleize. Bamboola, your manners are not those of a future cabinet minister. You leap about, you roar like a wild beast from your native forests, and all because I say the day . . . Listen to me. I said there was a chance that the day would be lovely. I don't know. Every day when I go out, I decide to repeat to all the people I come across, to the innumerable ghosts who make up all the people in the street, some cheap, trite conventional phrase —one of those clichés which I offer at every turn, and which saves me the trouble of having to express anything intelligent. For example, I say, "Life is sweet." I get the reply, "Indeed." Or else I say, "The leaves are beginning to show." They answer, "Yes, that is true." So, my friend, each morning my great task is to find the appropriate phrase. Not always the same one, of course. Today, since it is not raining, I shall say that the day is lovely. You have got to be cunning, for if it rained and I said the day was lovely, I should be regarded as too witty; and you know that in this country they write off humorists. So I shall say, with an inspired, enraptured air, and in an assured voice, that shred of a lyric, "What a lovely day!" [BAMBOOLA *collapses*.] Eh?

Bamboola [*groaning*]. Oh . . . oh . . . oh! . . . Boss! . . . Oh! . . . Oh! . . . Oh!

Pantagleize [*standing him up*]. Come on, pull yourself together!

Bamboola [*on his feet, babbling as in a trance*]. Boss . . . he said . . . seriously . . . what . . . a . . . lovely . . .

Pantagleize [*with formal diction*]. Seriously, "What a lovely day!"

Bamboola [*in ecstasy*]. He said that . . . this morning? He is going to say that . . . today?

Pantagleize [*uneasy*]. Indeed! It's within my rights. I shall say that to no matter whom, presently, in the street, throughout the city.

Bamboola [*wild with delight*]. Dear Boss! Comrade!

Pantagleize [*drawing away*]. Back!

Bamboola [*frantic*]. And it's you? You say?

Pantagleize [*getting angry*]. Of course, you dusky idiot. I assure you that my saying won't be of any significance to normal folk, even if it does send you off your rocker.

Bamboola. Oh! Oh! You know. You act dumb.

Pantagleize [*uncertain*]. I give you my word! The philosopher, knowing all, has no wish to know anything. The philosopher looks at the sky and says, "What a lovely day!" It's not striking, but it's safe enough.

Bamboola [*hilarious*]. Safe enough! Hee, hee, hee! You make joke.

Pantagleize. Joke? Will you explain?

Bamboola. Explain? No more need explain. I warn quick. [*Admiringly.*] And it's you? Pantagleize! Oh, ho! [*He dances and gesticulates—a menacing war dance.*]

Pantagleize [*impressed*]. Yes, I, Pantagleize. [*Aside.*] Has all this something to do with my destiny? We shall see later.

Bamboola. Dance!

Pantagleize [*imitating the Negro and dancing*]. If it
will give you pleasure.

Bamboola [*suddenly bursts out sobbing*]. Too much,
unbelievable! I happy!

Pantagleize [*stopping his dancing and weeping in his
turn*]. I also happy! Dry your tears. We are going to try
to understand.

Bamboola. No time! You see. Tremendous event!
Wonderful destiny! Comrade, come to my Negro heart!
[*He hugs* PANTAGLEIZE *violently.*] And long live . . . long
live . . . the . . . [*His voice no longer comes. He makes
triumphant gestures and goes out quickly.*]

Pantagleize [*coming back to reality*]. Bamboola! Long
live what? Ah, you are going to make a laughingstock of
yourself, you impulsive creature. My hat? My jacket?
All because I said . . . "What a lovely day"? Any idiot
will tell you that. Bamboola, wait for me! My umbrella!
I announced a lovely day, but it could turn out a bad one.
[*Wearing a deerstalker and a checked jacket, and with his
umbrella under his arm, he dashes off in pursuit of the
Negro.*]

Blackout

SCENE II—*A café. At the back, a counter. Behind the
counter, a back cloth painted to represent mirrors. A figure
comes and goes. It is the waiter,* INNOCENTI, *who is clean-
ing up. Talking to himself all the time, he arranges seats,
tables, bottles, and so completes the setting of the rudi-
mentary scene.*

INNOCENTI. Not slept enough. Living in stench . . . Pah!
Filthy job. Serving, always serving. I am a slave in a
black coat. The slave of idiots who have a thirst. What
does humanity ask for? Something to drink! "Here's your
drink, sir!" Serving drinks to individuals who argue,
slaver, sing out of tune, and vomit in the toilet. Pah!
When I have a drink it's in the office, and the beer there is
bitter. Serving. Drudge! All your intelligence can rise
to is to serve a beer. For that, in order to do that, your
mother brought you forth in agony. Pah! I went to bed at
three o'clock. It's hardly seven. And there are people who
are sick because they sleep too much. [*He has finished
arranging the café. He puts his coat on and sits on a high*

stool, fed up.} Dawn follows dawn. Nothing ever changes. Presently the pigheaded customers come, with their wives who embalm themselves like corpses. Bloodsuckers, parasites . . . ugly . . . ugly! [*Falsetto.*] Waiter! [*Furious.*] Ah! I'd like to serve them . . . the damned . . .

A knock at the door of the café.

Voice of Blank. Open up!

Innocenti. Go hang yourself!

Voice of Blank. The long tongue is hung and with dragon's thirst the gullet of morning swallows the tramways the factories swagger the twilight hour melts in my eye sweet as your name Innocenti who open only to the angels.

Innocenti [*recognizing the voice of* BLANK]. All right, we can hear you. [*He opens the door.*] Up already or haven't you gone to bed yet?

Voice of Blank. There are crowds who stay awake. Beware the sleeper!

Innocenti. Poet! The last customer has gone away, hiccuping all the time. Who's going to offer you a drink in exchange for your dangerous fever, your poetic jargon? Are you looking for a bench to sleep on?

Enter BLANK, *man of the world, loosely tied bow, long hair. Very effeminate, with a high-pitched voice.*

Blank. Silence! I come, as I come each day, to trample on my heart. [*He takes a step and crushes an imaginary heart.*] To be cold and cruel. My friend, I laugh. [*He pretends to weep.*] And I weep. [*He laughs.*] And if I accept drinks from the bourgeois, that is because of my humility. Ah! I was asleep standing up and I had a nightmare. I was in a desert where a mirage appeared in the shape of a beer pump.

Innocenti [*rubbing the tables*]. And you are waiting for me to serve you. . . .

Blank [*reciting*]. We serve our passions, we serve our ideas. We serve to grow in stature and to be reborn and to prevail! One has these thoughts at seven in the morning, waiting for the miracle of a beefsteak.

Innocenti. Rub the tables down. You'll see your beefsteak come out of them.

Blank. Is this the cloth? [*He rubs the tables.*] Don't rub out my poems, the sky, love, and the rest. All is posthumous, like aperitifs drunk but a short while ago; but if you look into the depths of my eyes you will see that I come from the region of light.

Innocenti [*who has had enough*]. Shut up!

Blank [*throwing down his cloth*]. Mind your manners! [*Seriously.*] Waiter, if I were to tell you . . . what I am afraid to tell you.

Innocenti. What?

Blank [*in a voice from beyond the grave*]. That this is a serious moment!

Innocenti. It's the moment for you to go home. Go and sleep till midday, and come back when you're sober. Leave the workers to their work.

Blank. I, too, am a worker. I fashion chimeras. But that doesn't concern you. Tonight, perhaps, I shall throw away my poet's mask and be a man among the others.

Innocenti. And you will earn your bread? If you could only guess for a minute what reality is like!

Blank. Reality! I have touched it with my finger. The proof . . . Tell me, what is the date today?

Innocenti. I don't know. All days are the same. All days are days of loathing.

Blank. What date? There's a calendar on the wall. Go and see.

Innocenti [*going toward the calendar*]. You mustn't cross a madman. [*He stops.*] Oh . . . the . . . [*He suddenly shrinks—both face and hands.*]

Blank. The very same. This is why I spent a restless night, why I ramble more than usual. [*Seriously.*] Flaming red date! Figure of fire!

Innocenti [*feverishly*]. I had forgotten. Tell me, tell me again, what is happening?

Blank. Poor man! The sun is not yet risen, but without doubt it will light up stupendous happenings.

Innocenti. I thought that these . . . ordained events took place in epics.

Blank. In a fable, no, in an epic. It begins today.

Innocenti. It makes me tremble. Tell me about it, comrade.

Blank [*mysteriously*]. It is a huge and delicate plan. It is a piece of precision machinery. It is a work of art. It is a heroic thing, just, unescapable, mysterious. We obey invisible forces. Those who command this action are as though at the top of a lighthouse and see all the ocean.

As for us, we are on the ocean, in thick darkness, knowing nothing but the signal. Who will give it? No one knows.

Innocenti [in a dream]. The signal!

Blank [in a calm voice]. Well, there you are! Don't accuse me of night-roaming and sleepwalking again. This is not the moment for falling out, but for fighting against the most relentless power there is: man himself. [*He bows; speaks ironically.*] Blood, dynamite, elements of poetry, I break my mirror and sing for others. On this gala day, I shall be pure and lovely, a poet on the floor of the amphitheatre. . . . [*He blows his nose.*] Here, waiter, give me . . .

Innocenti [mechanically]. A beer?

Blank. A fraternal kiss.

Innocenti [moved]. Comrade! [*They embrace.*]

Terrible din: vociferous entry of BAMBOOLA, *wearing a gray bowler and yellow gloves. He is hilarious.*

Bamboola. Comrades! Bamboola happy! [*He jostles them.*] Dance cakewalk.

Blank [choking]. Tarantula, epileptic, wild Negro, on this morning when wisdom begins . . .

Bamboola. Yeah, scalp poetry! [*He gives a heavy blow of his fist to* BLANK, *who staggers.*] No more meeting, laugh! You happy quick, or else . . .

Blank. I laugh—under your discipline. [*He laughs.*]

Innocenti. I laugh too—from nerves. [*He laughs.*]

Bamboola. Hottentot dance!

BAMBOOLA *claps his hands and, in a sinister fashion, begins to dance.* BLANK *and* INNOCENTI, *unconscious of what they are doing, imitate him, clapping their hands and repeating with the Negro, "Aya! . . . Aya!" During the dance,* CREEP, *a policeman in plain clothes, comes in and secretly observes the scene.*

Creep. Danse macabre!

Bamboola [who has scented the enemy]. Stop! [*All are stock still.*] Sh! [*All three prick up their ears.*] Bamboola, child of the bush, scent wild beast. No matter. No more dance. Dance tonight when all finish.

Blank [in an easy manner]. So, you are in the know? And the cause of your joy?

Bamboola. Nigger's joy, ha, ha! I, inferior man, I know more than you.

Blank. You really mean the . . .

Bamboola. Ah! [*He drags them into a corner.*]

CREEP *gravely crosses the café and, all the time unnoticed, goes and sits on a high stool near the counter.*

Blank. Let us know, tell us exactly—first, the signal.

Bamboola. Not speak with words. Unwise. Code language. Two handkerchiefs, please?

BAMBOOLA *moves back a few steps and, a handkerchief in each hand, begins to signal in semaphore with his arms. The other two raise and lower their arms to indicate that they have understood.* CREEP *has taken a note of the signaling.*

Innocenti. But where is the signal coming from?

Bamboola. Listen. I use sea lion language. [*With unbelievable grimaces, he begins to give forth long and short sounds.*] Honk . . . honk . . . honk . . . honk . . . honk honk honk . . . dot dash . . .

Innocenti and Blank [*in acknowledgment*]. Honk!

CREEP *has noted the telegraphy.*

Blank. Fine! And the time, and all the considerations?

Bamboola. Here they are. The walls have ears, so I speak deaf-dumb. [*He goes into the matter with appropriate gestures of his hands. The others acknowledge likewise.*]

Innocenti. Wonderful! And the sequence of operations?

CREEP *takes notes all the time.*

Bamboola. What language I use, eh?

Blank. Modern verse.

Bamboola. Yeah. Listen, little modern poem. [*With tremendous speed, and quite without punctuation, he rattles off:—*] This is Radio roocoocoo hello hello Central telephoning Miss Kakakarak Number Two sector crack thousand million stars munition depot good evening station tutut sector three ministry and police I eat chocolate and drink whey bank Boss sector four come toy soldiers and nursemaids long live the proletata class soup at midday on the flank suppression without pain flash Harrys in columns of four tonight eternity begins. . . . Signed "Bamboola."

Blank. Pure poetry! Orpheus in the blacking tin! But who?

Innocenti. Yes, who is it, who . . . ?

Bamboola [*artlessly*]. It's not me.

Blank. Nor me.

Innocenti. And it's much less me.

Bamboola. Then it must be someone else. [*He smiles.*]

Blank. Do you know him?

Bamboola. I have that honor.

Innocenti. You're bluffing. No one knows him. What is this, treason?

Bamboola. No, chance.

Blank. Who is it?

Bamboola [*formally, artificially*]. An imbecile.

Innocenti [*alarmed*]. An imbecile? But he's going to cause a catastrophe.

Bamboola [*superciliously*]. Tell me, my friend, you think a revolution a picnic or a stage play?

Blank. Or a poem? [*Businesslike.*] Bamboola, since this person you talk of does exist, why isn't he here?

Bamboola. He in other place. Perhaps he come. Perhaps quite near.

Innocenti. Perhaps he's here without our knowing it? Who knows? Let's have a look: every minute is precious.

They search about the café—all the time without seeing the policeman. They search under the tables, behind the counter, and disappear crouching under the benches.

Finally, CREEP, *no longer seeing anyone, calls.*

Creep. Waiter!

A groan of fear goes up from the counter. Slowly the heads of INNOCENTI, BLANK, *and* BAMBOOLA *emerge gazing with stupefaction at* CREEP *on his high stool.*

Innocenti. God! [*He gets up and comes uncertainly toward* CREEP. *The other two, under the stress of emotion, flop into chairs.*] What would you like, sir?

Creep. A half of beer—carefully drawn.

Innocenti [*in a toneless voice*]. There you are!

Creep. I ask you for a beer and you give me a port? Never mind. Give it here. [*He scrutinizes* INNOCENTI.] You seem distracted.

Innocenti [*forcing himself to smile*]. A little off color, sir. Overwork. [*He breathes heavily.*] I hope you will excuse me for not having seen you right away. Have you been waiting long, sir?

Creep. Quarter of an hour.

Innocenti. Good Lord!

Bamboola [*muttering*]. I, child of black woman, scent wild beast.

Blank [*ditto*]. Queer face, this chap.

Creep [*drinks*]. I was watching you, and I said to myself, "This waiter and the customers seem excited, incoherent. What's going on?"

Innocenti. Nothing, sir, nothing at all.

Creep [*good-naturedly*]. You can confess freely. I'm curious. And it doesn't matter one way or the other to me. Besides, I'm well up with all the news. [*He pulls out a newspaper.*] I read the papers.

Blank [*in an undertone*]. Bamboola, is it him?

Bamboola. Good God, above all not him!

Creep [*benevolently*]. And I've come to town especially to see the event. It doesn't happen often, does it?

Innocenti [*ill at ease*]. Not often; but it happens.

Creep. It's my opinion that the world won't be destroyed today. There's nothing to be afraid of. Get rid of those medieval ideas.

Innocenti. Are you joking? You'd better explain yourself, sir. [*Annoyed.*]

Creep. Indeed? Are you a visitor from Mars?

Innocenti. That's it . . . from Mars.

Creep [*indignant*]. Well, it's all a matter of the sun.

Innocenti. I meant to say . . . the sun.

Creep. The sun has affected you, eh? After the eclipse you'll be completely off your head.

Innocenti [*at last realizing their cross-purposes*]. The eclipse? Of course, this morning, the big eclipse, the total eclipse.

Bamboola [*relieved*]. Eclipse. Yeah, Boss! Good nigger very afraid. All go black.

Blank [*pretending to be afraid*]. Yes, sir. I am so sensitive. Think of it, the death of light. . . . You spoke of medieval times? We live in them always. Terror is within us.

Creep [*paternally*]. Be calm! We are in the twentieth century. Science, gentlemen! Wait, I'll read the details in my paper. Waiter! A glass of port.

Innocenti. Certainly! [*He draws a glass of beer.*]

Creep. You give me a beer? I'll put that down to the eclipse. [*He unfolds his paper, which completely hides his face.*]

The trio wipe their foreheads, make signals calling for discretion, and indicate CREEP. BAMBOOLA *produces a knife and explains in signs that he is going to cut* CREEP'S *throat. The others calm him down. Pause. Outside, someone is heard walking with a peculiar gait. They listen.* BANGER *enters. He is a rough man, bearded and lame, and he carries with difficulty a heavy object wrapped in a cloth. He grunts. The trio get up and move several paces toward* BANGER, *who, stunned by this greeting, stays rooted to the spot.*

Banger. What? [*Standing in a straight line,* BAMBOOLA, BLANK, *and* INNOCENTI *all signal together—*BAMBOOLA, *with two handkerchiefs, in semaphore,* BLANK *in Morse, whistling the dots and dashes, and* INNOCENTI *in deaf-and-dumb language. At this display,* BANGER *bursts out laughing.*] Are you ill? [*He puts down his bundle.*] There's no point in acting the goat. You think that looks good from here? [*More signals to get him to keep quiet.*] Cut the comedy; there are such things as orders. [*More violent signals.*] And it's more than time that we knew zero hour and who's going to give . . . [*Threatening signals.*] That is if someone . . . [*Realizing the anger of the trio, he desists.*] I don't know; you're going on like a lot of toreadors. . . . Look! [*He pulls away the cloth covering the heavy object. It is a fully equipped machine gun. The trio retreat, arms flung in the air.*] There! Now we have a way of talking. [*He replaces the cloth.*] That will have its use, by and by. [*At last he sees* CREEP.] Who's he, that type there? [BAMBOOLA *stands in the middle of the café and imitates a policeman directing traffic.*] What? He's a . . .

Bamboola. Who's left his fancy dress at home, yeah.

Banger. You should have warned me. [*He hides his machine gun under a table; then, in gentlemanly fashion, aloud.*] And how are things?

Innocenti [*with mock politeness*]. As you see, sir, rather well.

Bamboola. Bamboola very well, very well, thank you.

Blank. Poetry is doing well, too, Mister Beard. I belong to the latest school. Lend me your ears. "Whom do the nations await in this astronomic darkness? elephant, chair-leg oculist? no! flower-beard! an imbecile it would appear! So it appears! And thus I the oracle reply to the questions which are unasked."

Banger. Very pretty, your poetry—a bit sugary, but one gets its meaning without understanding it. An imbecile, eh? How can you pick out an imbecile among the herd of humanity? He may be the first person to come in, the first one to cross the threshold of this café.

At these words, PANTAGLEIZE *comes in.*

Bamboola [*his throat parched*]. It's him!

Pantagleize [*to himself*]. Well! Is it my eyesight that's gone wrong? The people one comes across don't have their usual appearances at all. What does it mean? I step out of doors. Dazzling weather! Just right for walking a lot and thinking very little. Yet everything around seems unusual. Even the city has another aspect, another sound. What do I see? Processions forming, newsboys yelling incomprehensible words, curbside astronomers, military patrols. It's a holiday . . . and the day of the eclipse. The crowd is unbearable—as though it were being tormented by flies. The passers-by are all pale and wan. What an absurd idea to have a public holiday when there's an eclipse. [*Sighs.*] In an attempt to get away from this irritating mob, I bethink myself of a café which I visit on the thirty-sixth of every month. And what do I find here? A collection of shady individuals, who look at me as though I owed them money. Why are they staring at me? Can they read the signs of my destiny on my forehead? Well, let us rise above contingencies and have a drink while we wait for the eclipse and the procession. If you please, waiter! Would you be so kind as to allow me to trouble you?

Innocenti. Sir!

Pantagleize. A glass of water, aqua pura, without tadpoles.

Innocenti [*bringing a glass and a bottle of wine*]. Here we are, sir.

Pantagleize. Your hand is trembling, waiter. You must take care of yourself.

Innocenti. Later, sir. [*He gazes at* PANTAGLEIZE.]

Pantagleize [*drinking in little sips*]. This water has a capital taste. I shall drink it for the rest of my life. [*Addressing* INNOCENTI.] Why are you staring at me?

Innocenti [*in a low voice, but distinctly*]. So, you are the imbecile?

Pantagleize [*disconcerted*]. Perhaps I am the imbecile—one imbecile among all the rest. At least I allow myself to give that impression. Still, I confess ignorance of what I am. What is an imbecile?

Innocenti [*pointedly*]. Are you the imbecile?

Pantagleize. The imbecile? [*He scrutinizes the waiter.*] I daren't cross him. He's a madman. [*Firmly.*] Indeed, I am the imbecile—whatever it pleases you to see in me. [*Catching sight of* BAMBOOLA.] Bamboola! You can speak on my behalf, vouch for my imbecility, can't you?

Bamboola [*stammering*]. Yeah.

Pantagleize [*drinking*]. You haven't gotten over your trouble, then, Bamboola?

Bamboola. Boss knows these comrades?

Pantagleize. I don't know these comrades. I've no need to. I'm the fool and sufficient unto myself.

Blank [*joining in*]. Sometimes the imbecile wakes up a poet. That happened to me. Do you like poetry?

Pantagleize. Yours? Of course. I also used to be a poet not so long ago. In those days, the *avant-garde* only wrote about reinforced concrete and internal combustion engines. [*He drinks.*] I am listening—but you have already conquered me with your artlessness.

Blank. Pighead or pinhead sweet fool from your wooden head comes forth the electric word oh ravisher of eclipses and merchant of processions the constellations and howitzers make Confucius laugh.

Pantagleize [*nods and carries on in the same vein*]. Confucius stuffed with straw is ancient history you are as handsome whippersnapper as a hairdresser whom a pipe makes ill climb up the ladder quickly and go see on Olympus if I am not to be found there.

Blank. Remarkable! You are . . . you are clever.

Pantagleize. You find me somewhat confused.

Blank [*touchingly*]. You are a poet without realizing it! Agreed? Then, agreeing that, and since you have so many gifts, such inspiration, I conjure you to reveal to us elliptically some precise, urgent, cardinal word. In the face of poetry, in the face of the whole world which is listening to you, speak—and prodigies shall spring therefrom.

Pantagleize. If it will give you pleasure. . . . One moment. . . . [*He takes out a little notebook. Silence. He*

gets to his feet and takes up the stance of a heavy father.]
I speak! . . . "What a lovely day!" [*He sits.*] I have
spoken! [*All are bowled over. Panic.*]

The Four Revolutionaries [*all together*]. It's him. The
signal! Bliss! The die is cast! I happy! What did he say?
Does he know? Be calm! To work! All is accomplished!

Pantagleize [*amazed*]. What now? Do they find it so
good?

Innocenti [*very quickly*]. Comrade . . . Was that what
you meant to say?

Pantagleize. That and nothing else.

Innocenti. When? Where?

Pantagleize. Now, presently, when it pleases me, everywhere, on the avenues, on the promenade where I shall go
to see the eclipse and the procession. It will be understood
well enough.

BANGER *seizes the machine gun. The Negro puts on his
hat and yellow gloves.* INNOCENTI *makes wild gestures.*

Banger. I'm going back to my post. Look sharp! [*He
goes out with his gun.*]

Pantagleize [*wide-eyed, trying to restore order*]. I beg
your pardon. I didn't mean to disturb you. It was just a
saying like any other. If I had had any idea . . . Gentlemen . . . You are mistaken to work yourselves up in this
way. And on a holiday!

Blank [*going out*]. Good luck!

Bamboola [*raving*]. Pantagleize! Boss! . . . So long!
. . . at the Pantheon! . . . In the infinite! [*He goes.*]

Innocenti [*wearing a cap*]. Gladness on earth! Slaves,
arise! The day of justice is here! [*He goes.*]

Pantagleize. This is very fine All poets! What have they
been drinking? Where are they going? What are they
going to do? Or perhaps I'm the victim of a hallucination.
[*He wants to leave.*] Waiter! Waiter!

Creep. Waiter! Waiter!

Pantagleize. We are calling in vain, sir. I think I saw the
waiter go out. I think he was a little unsettled, like the
others.

Creep. It's the approach of the eclipse, sir. The slightest
thing bowls them over. For example, this phrase you read
to them a moment ago. What does it mean?

Pantagleize. That phrase, sir, is an exceedingly commonplace one. It means, in other words, what fine weather we're having today.

Creep. I thought as much. Yes. This phrase did exist, but it had to be thought of. I am delighted to meet an intellectual. Without being offensive, what is your name, sir?

Pantagleize. Pantagleize.

Creep. Most enchanting! And are you going to see the eclipse?

Pantagleize. At once. It would be wrong to stay in a café on such a lovely day.

Creep. Indeed so. A thousand thanks, sir.

Pantagleize. A thousand pleasures, sir.

They salute ceremoniously. PANTAGLEIZE *goes out dignifiedly—without forgetting his umbrella. At once,* CREEP *leaps from his stool and seizes the telephone.*

Creep. Hello! . . . 1324 . . . Police headquarters! . . . [*Pause.*] This is Chief Inspector . . .

RACHEL SILBERCHATZ *bounds into the café.*

Creep. Well! . . . The Jewess?

RACHEL SILBERCHATZ *has snatched up a stool which she flings at the policeman's head.* CREEP *collapses, knocked out.*

Rachel. Son of a bitch! [*She goes out very quickly.*]

Blackout.

SCENE III—*The promenade. A wall. A street lamp. At the back, skyscrapers and towers are seen rising up. Incessant din. Broad daylight. The sun is already high.* THE BALLAD-MONGER *rushes to accost someone.*

THE BALLADMONGER. Thirty-two choruses for a franc, all the latest successes! Here you are, sir!

Enter PANTAGLEIZE *reading a newspaper.*

Pantagleize. Ha, ha! These daily papers! I used to think that they spread good sense and morality at six sous; but I'm beginning to think they're put together by practical jokers. What business have these journalists to conjure up the terrors of the year 1000 A.D.? It makes you die with laughing. True enough, in the year 1000 you would have died of fright. [*He bumps into* THE BALLADMONGER.] Songs, madame? Do you know the one my mother—even though she was an unmarried mother—used to sing? [*He sings in a high-pitched voice.*]

> Sleep, my cupid,
> Sleep, my stupid.
> Your mummy so gay
> Made a slip one day,
> And Fortune turned that
> Into you, you brat.

The Balladmonger. That song moves me to the depths of my soul. I should say that you're a man of the people.

Pantagleize. A bastard, madame. A love child.

The Balladmonger. A man of the people. . . . Buy this song, now. No! I'll give you it—"The International."

Pantagleize [*taking it*]. What is it?

The Balladmonger [*impassioned*]. The last struggle of all. . . .

Pantagleize. Struggle? Why? What for?

The Balladmonger. For liberty . . . for . . .

Pantagleize. Lofty intentions! Thank you—though I'm not fond of romances. [*He puts the song in his pocket.*] Let's talk about something else—the weather, if you like. What a lovely day, isn't it?

The Balladmonger. Wh—wha—what did he say? [*She rushes headlong from the stage.*]

Pantagleize [*watching her rush away*]. And I was going to buy thirty-two from you for a franc, madame. [*He pauses, baffled, for a moment, then opens his newspaper.*] Who would have thought that this celestial phenomenon would have turned people's brains like this! What will it be like, Jehovah, when the sun changes color? At present, it's still light, and already people look as though they had escaped from madhouses. Soon they'll be at least coming back from the dead. [*He looks at the sky and hails it.*] Good day to you, sun! Classic star! Beneficent star! The world doesn't bother about you except by reason of its fear of darkness. The world, believing it is going to die, will be uneasy about you for ten minutes. And if men scattered about this terrestrial globe do not clash cymbals and shoot arrows toward your disc, it is only for fear of ridicule. [*He goes back to his paper.*] A serious and profitable occupation, reading the papers. It removes

everything abnormal from your make-up, everything that
doesn't conform to accepted ideas. It teaches you to reason
as well as the next person. It gives you irrefutable and
generally admitted opinions on all events. This morning,
now, I throw in my lot with the ideas of this gazette; and
what do I read? Let's only read the headlines. "Great
popular procession!" Well, it's a good thing for the people
to take a walk. I shan't go in this procession; but I shall
watch it go past, because if everybody went in the procession, there would be nobody left to watch it, and
hence there would be no point in having a procession.
Reciprocity is a great truth. If no one went in the procession and everyone watched it go past . . . [*He reads.*]
Ah! The great eclipse! "The importance and the rarity
of this phenomenon will not escape . . ." no doubt. I
wonder if they announce the end of the world. It's not
usual to do that only once. Here it is—the terrors of the
year 1000, the distinguished prophets, how our ancestors
conducted themselves on occasions of eclipse. Ho, ho! A
fine article! And to think that my destiny is beginning on
the day of the great eclipse. That is no doubt significant.
[*He reads.*] What more is there to read? "The terror of
the ages, plague, cholera, the sea serpent." I've got goose
flesh! But, you stupid devil of a journalist, if you had my
power of observation and if you had studied the public,
instead of rifling the encyclopedia, you would have written
that the crowds of today are as terrified as those of the
Middle Ages. And I go further. If people go in processions on eclipse days, it's to reassure themselves. What
have I seen since this morning? Epileptics, madmen, bab-
blers, dreamers. I bet that the first passer-by who . . .

RACHEL *suddenly appears and stops in front of* PANTA-
GLEIZE.

  Rachel [*very quickly*]. Comrade, what do you think of
today?
  Pantagleize [*at a loss*]. I think . . . miss . . . I think it
will be a lovely day.
  Rachel. Stop! Stand fast! [*She rushes out.*]
  Pantagleize [*beside himself*]. There's the proof—this
woman who asks me such a stupid question. It's very dis-
heartening in an informed and educated age. And these
journalists who complicate things with their horrific
conjurings. [*He becomes furious.*] If I were editor of this

paper . . . No, I take it upon me to hearten poor mortals
with the weak voice of a philosopher. I was indeed inspired this morning when I chose the announcement of
a lovely day as the phrase for all occasions. Everyone
will realize the profound truth of what I say when it is
fine and clear after the eclipse. And superstitions will
have gone back into the void. [*Assured, he looks at the
sky.*] Sun, little sun, you are going to turn a somersault.
Be careful; they may construe your antics very badly.
[*Resigned.*] And if it should be the end of the world, it
would be all the same. We would perish singing hymns,
we should perish with a stoic gesture. Farewell, illusory
earth! Ah! Little sun, little eclipse! When all is said and
done, it has a certain effect on one.

*Enter an astronomer wearing a robe, pointed hat, and
false beard. He sets up his telescope and directs it toward
the sky. It is* BAMBOOLA *on detached service. He watches*
PANTAGLEIZE *and makes signs to unseen people over the
wall of the promenade. Then he takes out his dark glasses
and unrolls a picture of the eclipse, which he waves.*

Bamboola. Eclipse, Boss! You see eclipse, 'clipse, 'clipse,
fifty centimes. Authentic eclipse. I only true eclipse, all
others imitation.

Pantagleize [*examining the astronomer*]. Oh, what a
disguise! Tell me, mountebank, what's the reason for this
historical reconstruction?

Bamboola. Boss, the public like mountebank's costume
and claptrap.

Pantagleize. Bravo, Nostradamus! You are selling the
eclipse? And glasses to see life darkly? I want to see life
a soft blue. It's a lovely day today, and I have a destiny.
This morning, my dear Nostradamus, I was born under
the sign of the eclipse. What do you think of that, dunce
cap? Aren't you really one of the Wise Men? [*He puts a
pair of dark glasses on.*] Good Lord, anyone would take
you for a Negro! The sky has a prehistoric look about it.
[*He takes the glasses off.*] Foretell the events, please. Is the
world going to end?

Bamboola. Don't know, Boss. Either all fine or all
wretched.

Pantagleize. That's a slender prediction. Aren't you
selling programs of the procession as well? No? What is
this procession?

Bamboola. Proletariat, Boss, oppressed sovereign people. Men on march.

Pantagleize. Of course. A procession is men on the march. No doubt they will be going around the city?

Bamboola. No. On march in history, across centuries, toward ideal of brotherhood.

Pantagleize. That's a noble idea. I prefer the eclipse. The sun, now, he also is on the march in the universe, and he always comes back to the same place. We put dark glasses on to look at him. I think that on this particular day all humanity is wearing glasses, isn't it?

Bamboola. Boss, he have pessimist irony? And yet you announce lovely day.

Pantagleize. To all and in the face of all, or may the devil break my bones. [*Sadly.*] I have no luck. All these astronomers and astrologers, and not one farsighted enough to tell me my future.

Bamboola. Yes . . . authentic . . . made in the observatory . . . [*Taking up his patter again and waving the picture.*] With wonderful calculations, for fifty centimes. Ladies, gentlemen, the eclipse . . . 'clipse . . . 'clipse . . . 'clipse!

Voice of Creep. 'Clipse . . . 'clipse . . . 'clipse . . . forty-five centimes. Beware of imitations. The official eclipse. To try one is to buy one.

BAMBOOLA *is taken aback. Enter* CREEP, *grotesquely dressed up as an astronomer. He has a top hat and wears dark glasses which make him unrecognizable. He sets up his telescope on the other side of the promenade.*

Creep. The wonders of the sky, sir. . . .
Bamboola. For fifty centimes.
Creep. For forty-five centimes.
Bamboola. Guaranteed, the authentic eclipse!
Creep. Here is the true, the only eclipse!

PANTAGLEIZE *looks at both of them, while in the distance, music sounds.*

Pantagleize. A second Nostradamus? It's the other one's brother. [*To* CREEP.] Here's forty-five centimes to tell me if we're going to have the end of the world.

Creep. No, monsieur, for the world has taken its precautions.

Pantagleize. Thank you. You reassure me. And this music, is it in honor of the sun?

Creep. No, monsieur, it is the proletariat manifesting its joy.

Pantagleize. What joy?

Creep. The joy of work.

Pantagleize. If I understand you, they march about because they are happy to work? The people are very deep. Work is fine. I understand the people so much better than I understand myself that I march about all the time. [*He goes to* BAMBOOLA, *who during this conversation has been examining the new astronomer through his telescope.*] Your colleague seems to me to be a rum character. The way he speaks . . .

Bamboola. Look out! He not come to sell eclipse; but he know happenings very well, yeah. And he get my telescope on skull.

Enter a woman in dark glasses. It is RACHEL.

Pantagleize [*addressing the woman*]. Madame, are you looking for the eclipse? I offer it to you.

Rachel. What there is to see is not in the sky, but in the street. [*To* BAMBOOLA.] What time is the eclipse?

Bamboola. In five minutes thirteen seconds.

Creep [*intervening*]. Thirty seconds.

Rachel. I wasn't asking *you* anything.

Pantagleize [*worried*]. Have I offended you, madame? What pretty eyes you must have behind those glasses. I would so much have liked to say something gallant to you.

Rachel. Say again what you said just now about the weather. What did you say?

Pantagleize. I said, "What a lovely day!" . . . without thinking I was saying so well.

Rachel. Your words are golden. Salute! Greetings! [*She goes out.*]

PANTAGLEIZE *is crestfallen. The music is heard mingled with distant singing.*

Pantagleize. This lady is a little offhand with you. I was right in maintaining that eclipses are no good for the calm of nations. We must fear dreadful mishaps.

Creep. We must fear, indeed.

Pantagleize. Then they do well to play music. That will restore spirits. There will be dancing in the darkness. Above all, we must set an example of self-possession. [*He dances a step or two.*] Like this, gentlemen. Why don't they improvise choruses on simple words? For example: "Life is sweet"; "The day likewise"; "Good health"; "Much good may it do you" . . .

Bamboola [*annoyed by this foolishness*]. Boss, the eclipse going to come.

Pantagleize. I am depending on it. Besides, I shall not watch it through your telescopes. No, no! [*He climbs on the wall closing in the promenade. The two telescopes are focused on him.*] Oh! The vastness, the procession, the flags! It's capital, this view! And what a magnificent thing is the people on the march. [*He leans against the street lamp.*] What a crowd! What a mass! You would think it was an army. Hey! On the move, milling about! Bravissimo, good folk! [*Rumbling in* THE CROWD.] Look at that! But . . . but . . . I came here to watch, and you would think that it was me that everyone was watching. It couldn't be that I am the eclipse? [*He is uncertain.*] And this crowd, it's singing. . . . And it doesn't sound joyful. It seems to be snarling like a pack of hounds, when it ought to be manifesting its happiness. Come along, gentlemen of the proletariat, smile! But . . . but . . . the flags! They are not gaily colored: they are black. It's funereal. Is it to harmonize with the light of the eclipse?

The light grows dimmer.

Confused Voices in the Crowd. The man! You! There! On the wall! Him! Yes, it's him!

Pantagleize. Are they calling to me? It's strange how I've become suddenly popular. You find a stupid phrase, launch it, and become a celebrated author. [*To the invisible crowd.*] Indeed. Yes, it's me, friends. I am very well, thank you. The man? This is the man. I mean, here I am. . . . [*He looks at the sky.*] It wasn't a joke. The sun's giving out. [*The muttering grows.*] They should put the searchlights on. What do I see? An airplane circling the sun? What a strange bird! A good sign or a bad one? [*The music strikes up again.*] They'll play any amount of music. It will be a procession of shadows that goes by. Oh, how pale these crowds are. Where are they coming from? They are waiting. They are marking time. What

are they waiting for? They are going to overwhelm everything. [*He turns around.*] I'm going somewhere else.

Bamboola [*breathlessly*]. Stay! The eclipse!

The light grows dimmer.

Pantagleize. Oh, I'm not afraid. But the crowds are.
You can see it. And indeed one has the feeling that the
world might well come to an end. Everything is growing
dark. Someone must have the heart to reassure these good
folk, to give the lie to what the papers say on the one
occasion when they seem to be telling the truth. I can
always show the public that I don't give a rap for them.
Why not? [*The music comes closer.* PANTAGLEIZE *begins
to dance.*] Look how I don't give a rap for the eclipse!
I dance! Dance, good people! [*Black flags go slowly past
on the other side of the promenade wall. Cries, laughs,
threats, jeers.*] Ha, ha! Come on, then, frightened crowds.
Don't look at the comatose sky. It will recover from its
heart attack all right. This eclipse is a stunt arranged by
the journalists to force up circulation. The end of the
world? And so . . . ? How simple you are! Here you
are, gathered in thousands, and you are afraid? The sky
won't fall in: I'll answer for that. [*To the astronomers.*]
It's working. I'm as good as an orator. They're listening to
me. The multitude has turned to me. Success, gentlemen!
I must go on, trot out choice phrases to them, hold them
breathless. And this is my destiny! I am he who shall give
heart to humanity on the fateful day. [*Proudly, he makes
gestures toward the crowd. Darkness closes in rapidly.*
PANTAGLEIZE *gesticulates like a scarecrow.*] I shall speak.
I shall speak in all altruism. [*He hugs the street lamp.*]
And here is my platform!

Bamboola. Speak!

RACHEL SILBERCHATZ *enters, pretending to be an onlooker.*

Pantagleize [*clinging to his lamp*]. The eclipse? To hell
with it, citizens! It's all sham. And if the sky *is* black, it's
only a magic-lantern effect. Gentlemen of the proletariat,
I am not a cheapjack. I won't sell you rabbit droppings.
But, loving my brother, passionately, I gaze on you and
admire you, grains of sand, fleas, midgets. What are you
afraid of? I tell you truly, this darkness is a trick. It's a
theatrical effect. The Antichrist has been dispensed with.
The sun is sound at heart. It's not going to happen this

time. No more can the people perish. I have written so
in those pamphlets you are so fond of. And so, comrades,
let the bands play. Sing! March! *Qu'un sang impur
abreuve vos sillons.* After all, this is your day. Beat down
lies! Boil the journalists! Enjoy yourselves. It isn't midnight yet. It's . . . never mind what time it is. It's the
hour of the good man. And I declare to you what I shall
not cease to declare: Long live the sun! Shame on the
eclipse! It's the loveliest day there could be! In all truth,
what a lovely day!

PANTAGLEIZE *has scarcely shouted this phrase before the
darkness becomes total. A shot smashes the street lamp.*
PANTAGLEIZE *rolls on the promenade. There is a flash.*

Pantagleize [*on his behind*]. It's the . . . end . . . of
. . . the world. And . . . and . . . what's happened? I
brought it about! [*He weeps bitterly.*]

*Explosions in the distance. The crowd yells. Revolutionary
song. Flags go by. Red light. Incessant shots. There is
fighting behind the promenade.*

Bamboola [*getting rid of his robe and beard*]. To arms,
comrades! [*He rushes toward* PANTAGLEIZE.] Go!
Creep [*in his turn, getting rid of his rig-out*]. Stop!
Pantagleize. Nostradamus? It wasn't me, I swear it.

BAMBOOLA *seizes* CREEP *around the waist and flings him
over the wall.*

Pantagleize. What's happening, Negro?
Bamboola [*leaping on the wall*]. Resurrection! Revolution! [*He yells indistinguishable words.*]
Pantagleize. What? And the eclipse? My destiny is
having a rough time.

*Other silhouettes rise on the wall—*BLANK, INNOCENTI, *and*
BANGER, *waving flags. They shout to* THE CROWD.

The Revolutionaries [*on the wall*]. Long live . . . For-
ward . . . Death to . . . The last struggle.
Pantagleize. The last struggle?
Rachel [*running to* PANTAGLEIZE]. Come!
Pantagleize. Excuse me, miss, I am innocent.
Rachel. Come! You are a superman. You are great. You
are wonderful! [*She hugs him, kisses him on the mouth,
and begins to drag him along.*]

Pantagleize. Really?
Rachel [*deliriously*]. I love you!
Pantagleize [*allowing himself to be dragged*]. Miss? You love me? You mustn't joke. . . .

They go out. The curtain comes down on the red and black picture of the revolutionaries waving their flags and embracing one another among the shouts and the din of the shooting.

ACT TWO

SCENE IV—RACHEL SILBERCHATZ's *room. Darkness. The eclipse is still taking place. At the back, curtains open onto nothing. Little by little, light will filter weakly through this opening. A table, an armchair, a reading lamp. The curtain rises on complete darkness. No one on the stage. Voices are heard on the stairs.*

VOICE OF RACHEL. Come along.
  Voice of Pantagleize. Where?
  Voice of Rachel. Here.
  Voice of Pantagleize. Yes.
  Voice of Rachel. Can you see?
  Voice of Pantagleize. No.
  Voice of Rachel. Look out.
  Voice of Pantagleize. What for?
  Voice of Rachel. For that.
  Voice of Pantagleize. Yes. [*Noise of someone falling on the stairs.*]
  Voice of Rachel. Fool!

Silence. They are in the room. RACHEL *switches on the lamp. Huge fantastic shadows. An explosion in the distance.*

Pantagleize. Oh!
Rachel. That's the arsenal going up.
Pantagleize. There'll be trouble.
Rachel [*in a very loud voice*]. Ass!
Pantagleize [*haughtily*]. The moment we can speak aloud, I shall ask you for a little more light. It's gloomy.
Rachel. Lower your voice.
Pantagleize. And why?

Rachel. Do as you're told!

Pantagleize. Never.

Rachel. One!

Pantagleize. I shall answer you with the word . . .

Rachel. Two!

Pantagleize. . . . that a general at Waterloo . . .

Rachel. Three. . . . [*She staggers.*] Ah! [*Sobs.* PAN-
TAGLEIZE *holds her up.*]

Pantagleize. Miss? What is the matter? Would you like
some smelling salts?

Rachel. It's going. Nerves on edge. [*She frees herself.*]

Pantagleize. It's the eclipse that's causing it.

Rachel [*laughing violently*]. The eclipse? Ah! this
eclipse! It is very fine!

Pantagleize. Yes, indeed. [*He laughs.*]

Rachel [*seriously*]. Why are you laughing?

Pantagleize. Reaction.

Rachel. You are pale.

Pantagleize. Do you think so?

Rachel. Are you ill?

Pantagleize [*swooning in his turn*]. A little hazy.

Rachel [*holding him up*]. Smelling salts?

Pantagleize [*coming to himself*]. Whisky.

Rachel [*gives him a bottle*]. Here.

Pantagleize. Thank you. [*He drinks.*]

RACHEL *takes the bottle from him and drinks in turn.
Then she gazes at* PANTAGLEIZE *attentively.*

Rachel. I don't know you!

Pantagleize. No?

Rachel. You are . . .

Pantagleize. Yes.

Rachel. . . . the one who . . .

Pantagleize. Which one?

Rachel [*commandingly*]. Who are you?

Pantagleize. I . . .

Rachel [*bewildered*]. It doesn't matter much.

Pantagleize. To be sure.

Rachel. For the irrevocable has been accomplished, and
it was by you that the irrevocable was accomplished.
Whoever you are [*highly wrought*] . . . you have saved
humanity with a phrase. That alone is what matters. And
I, a humble woman, have saved your life. I am proud of
it. You have done your duty.

Pantagleize. Indeed?

Rachel. But this is not the time to be sentimental. To be brief, let me tell you . . .

Pantagleize. What?

Rachel. That I love you.

Pantagleize. Really?

Rachel. Yes. And do you love me?

Pantagleize. I . . .

Rachel. Yes, you love me. We all love each other, for we are entering an epoch of love.

Pantagleize. Shall we go to bed, then?

Rachel. The love of man for man, the great brotherhood of humanity. [*Distant explosion.*] And this love will be born of blood and ruin. The ruin of the old corrupt world, the blood of men without love. New Eden. New World. New Heaven. I shall be Eve. . . .

Pantagleize. I'll be Adam.

Rachel. And we shall go toward the promised land flowing with milk and honey.

Pantagleize. Where is it?

Rachel. Everywhere, everywhere that flesh suffered and the soul cried out. Through the continents and the seas. Like a cyclone, the revolution overthrows, annihilates, submerges, delivers.

Pantagleize. Revolution?

Rachel. Yes. [*Explosion.*] And it is your splendid, immortal work!

Pantagleize. What!

Rachel. You are an idol, a savior, an apostle!

Pantagleize [*moved*]. My destiny. I am . . .

Rachel. You are a brother. Come to my arms. [*She throws herself on* PANTAGLEIZE *and hugs him frenziedly.*]

Pantagleize. Darling!

The telephone rings. RACHEL *frees herself.*

Rachel. I'm aflame when there's something to be done. [*Takes up the telephone.*] Hello. Hello? Yes. [*She puts her hand on her heart.*] What ecstasy! [*She puts down the telephone.*]

Pantagleize. Good!

Rachel. Good, yes! When the eclipse is over, the capital will be in our hands.

Pantagleize. Bravo!

Rachel. There's no time for dreaming. Everyone to his

job. Look at the map. [*Their faces are lit up as they lean over the map.*] Here is zone eight—done with. Strategic road—we're blocking it. Airfield—we're blocking that. Look outside. There's a tower. Do you see a white light on the tower?

Pantagleize [*going to the curtains at the back*]. Yes.

Rachel. Good! Another triumph! [*Telephone bell.*] Hello? . . . The Government in flight. Fine. We are the Government! [*She gaily puts down the telephone.*] Smoke, fire, and away it goes! [*Lyrically.*] O race of Israel, your day is come! Persecuted people, you shall command the nations and you shall persecute in your turn! Oh, my ancestors, despised of the ghettos, may the Eternal give strength to my arm! [*Suddenly cool.*] To work! Write a short note for the Committee.

Pantagleize. For the . . . ?

Rachel. No, I'll do it. You shall go . . . [*She looks at him.*]

Pantagleize. Rachel . . . Work? You were talking of love.

Rachel. You call me Rachel? That is my name. And you are . . . ?

Pantagleize [*moved*]. Pan—Pan—Pantagleize.

Rachel. Pan—Pan—Pantagleize? Don't know him. But through this day of liberation, we all know one another. [*She is doubtful.*] Sit down. [*Ambiguously.*] Where were you last night?

Pantagleize. At home.

Rachel. Whom did you see this morning?

Pantagleize. A Negro.

Rachel. Who else?

Pantagleize. A poet, a barman, and a lame chap.

Rachel. And how did you know?

Pantagleize. I didn't know anything.

Telephone bell.

Rachel. Hello? . . . Better and better. [*She puts down the telephone.*] Well, comrade, I don't understand anything—nothing at all.

Pantagleize. Nor do I.

Rachel. We mustn't try to understand. First the events, the comments afterward. I obey, as you obey.

Pantagleize. Whom? Do you know?

Rachel. It is forbidden to know. After the eclipse, when

the game is played and won. But what disturbed me,
alarmed me, was the dreadful night of waiting. Horrible!
For everyone, for all the comrades. The revolution was
ripe, worked out in every detail. What a night! Everything was set for this morning, under the cover of the
crowds. All our formations assembled, drawn up, as
manageable as battalions. New methods. Everyone at his
post. Everyone determined. But it was inconceivable. No
order during the night, either of attack or of postpone-
ment. Nothing. You had to wait. All that you knew was
that we were done for, our plans were known. Spies. To
prove it, the patrols, the mobilization of the army. Bad!
Bad! Where was the unknown man, the special messenger
who was going to give or not going to give the signal?

Pantagleize. How thrilling!

Rachel. And the time came, the appointed hour. It was
then that the word suddenly flashed out like lightning.
The man had come, the mysterious comrade. My task was
to follow you and protect you. There are police everywhere. I didn't meet you at the frontier. We were not
to know how you were to come to us. You were there.
I recognized you by your appearance. You were too
natural, too naïve, too stupid. You played your part
marvelously. You are still playing it. You are acting
surprised. Yes, you are very capable. And you are modest.
You don't want to admit to yourself the greatness of your
destiny. [*She is greatly excited.*]

Pantagleize [*choking with delight*]. Yes . . . but . . .
my dear girl, I'll tell you something in my turn. It's un-
imaginable!

Rachel [*firmly*]. Be quiet! We are wasting time. Look
at the tower. How many beacons?

Pantagleize [*goes to the curtains*]. Two.

Rachel. To work. Nothing but action.

Pantagleize. Action! [*He drinks.*]

Rachel. I shall stay here and keep my ears open. You
take this revolver. [*She hands him a revolver.*]

Pantagleize [*taking it*]. Ha ha!

Rachel. You will go.

Pantagleize. I shall go.

Rachel. Have you had instructions about the treasure?

Pantagleize. The treasure? That's you.

Rachel. Fathead! Now, here are the instructions. If you
don't get a move on, I have orders to do you in.

Pantagleize. And you love me?

Rachel. Before anything else, I love humanity. Listen. You will go to the State Bank. It is guarded. There are soldiers inside, outside, and on top.

Pantagleize. Is that all?

Rachel. But you are a superior being. You have genius. I don't know the password that gives access to the safe. Find out. It's vital that you get into this stronghold of capitalism.

Pantagleize. I have genius.

Rachel. If necessary, you will kill—or be killed. You will seize the imperial treasure and bring it, within forty-five minutes at the most, to the Objective Bar where the Committee is sitting. Understood? Be off—and if you fail, good-by.

Pantagleize [*moved*]. Rachel!

Rachel [*sharply*]. No emotion. Good-by. The treasure. Besides, you are a first-rater, a splendid chap, underneath these stupid antics, and I am well aware of it.

Pantagleize. Delighted!

Rachel. That's all. Good-by for now—or forever: that's a matter of little importance.

Pantagleize. Not the least. [*He puts his hat on, and goes, casting entreating glances at* RACHEL, *who pretends not to see. With a sigh.*] Good-by. I feel I shall never see you again.

Alone, RACHEL *gives a dull laugh. She takes up the telephone.*

Rachel. Hello? Objective Bar? Where am I? At home. The man? At the bank. Is he really an imbecile? In any case, he's the chosen one. What? I'm being shadowed? Who? I'll look out. I'll stay here. Alone. No. I'm not being watched any more. All quiet. Courage, comrades! [*She puts the telephone down and looks about her uneasily. A noise.*]

Voice of Creep. Rachel Silberchatz?

RACHEL *puts out the light the moment the curtain moves.* RACHEL *shoots. In the pale light, a man leaps out. Short hand-to-hand struggle. Silence. A gruff voice laughs in short bursts.*

Blackout

SCENE V—*In the central tower of the State Bank. Two grilles at the back. Center, a huge safe. Gates to left and right. A* SENTRY *before each gate. Two civilians are at the grilles. Distant cannon are heard.* GENERAL MACBOOM, *trailing a huge saber, seems to be in the grip of fierce terror.*

MACBOOM. Cannon? Cannon indeed; unless I'm all at sea. Would you believe it? I've been a soldier for fifty years and this is the first time that cannon have been fired outside of maneuvers. I'll bet they're firing at us, and at me in particular. Gentlemen, let us prepare to die in this bank. This safe will be our field of honor. Soldiers, you are going to die.

The Two Sentries. At your command, sir.

Macboom. For duty, for liberty, for justice, for the well-being of humanity! And should one of you survive this dreadful slaughter, let him go to Eugenie. She is my wife. Let him go to her and say—with the respect due to her rank and to her sorrow—that I died for her . . . for her who is at once . . . duty and liberty. [*He weeps. The two bankers weep also. Cannon. The general pulls himself together.*] You heard? They dare to fire cannon! So, these revolutionaries are gunners? They understand military theory? By the batteries! If they had stuck me on the barricades instead of putting me in front of this treasure, I would have ground them to pieces. [*Cannon.*] We are dead! [*He staggers.*]

The First Sentry [*holding him up*]. Not yet, General. Don't be afraid.

Macboom. Afraid? To your post, soldier. I am seventy years old and have fifty years' service. You understand? Cannon shots have nothing to do with soldiers of my rank. [*He wipes his forehead.*] What are they up to, these revolutionaries?

The Second Sentry. Firing cannon, sir.

Macboom. That's what I was thinking. But by the blunderbuss, why don't they leave that to the regular artillery?

The Bank Manager. General, I think they are after our money.

Macboom. In that case, the order is not to let them have it. [*He waves his saber.*] Let 'em come!

The Bank Manager and the Assistant Manager. Bravo, General!

Macboom. The loyalty of your sentiments touches me, gentlemen. [*Cannon.*] If I allow myself to be guided by my long experience, the battle draws near. That's a barrage. They can bring up their cannon, these ragtime artillerymen; by my badges of rank, I'll make mincemeat of them! Look! [*He performs exercises with his saber.* THE SOLDIERS *draw back. The bankers hide.*]

The Bank Manager and the Assistant Manager. Bravo, General!

Cannon. The general shudders.

Macboom. They were aiming at the safe that time. See that your hearts are in the right place. Posterity will remember us in its orations. Prepare for the fray. In extended order, forward! [*The two* SOLDIERS *lie on the floor.*] State of siege! By the brigade group, I'll kick these civilians outside!

The Bank Manager. Orders, General! The governor of the bank has ordered us to guard the treasure, and he has sworn to have anyone who fails in his duty shot.

Macboom. What does this beastly civvy of a governor think he's meddling with? First of all, gentlemen, shooting is a matter for the military. And I, damme, have had orders from the Minister of War to shoot all the skunks of civvies I find in the way, by my busby!

The Bank Manager and the Assistant Manager. Mercy, General! Have pity!

Macboom. Make your choice. Either die at your posts or die out here, fighting to the death. What can you do?

The Bank Manager. I am the manager, General.

Macboom. Then you know how to read and write? Well, you dog of a civilian, you are going to write my report and describe the tragic hours we pass in this casemate. You, civvy number two, will correct what the other writes. Military style, like this, eh? "I have the honor to bring to your notice . . ." [*The two bankers write. Three cannon shots.*] By my breechblock! Three cannon firing at once. Soldiers, we shall perish because of the ceiling. These stupid pigs of financiers haven't strengthened their bank there, by the barrack gate!

The First Sentry. It's all bombproof, the ceiling and the rest of it.

Macboom. Yes; but I'm not bombproof. The treasure is better off in that respect. It's in the safe. Do you think there would be a little space left? I'm not very much at ease here. [*Cannon.*] A little funny in the intestines.

The Assistant Manager. Me too, General.

Macboom. And the orders are such that if I leave this place to go to a smaller place, I am obliged to have myself shot. [*He listens.*] No more firing? The revolutionaries are all slaughtered. Well done! With me, it wouldn't have taken so long. I would teach them to bother the army! Tell me, soldiers, what are these fellows, these revolutionaries?

The Second Sentry. People who fire cannon and who want to pocket the State's cash.

The First Sentry. Probably discontented people as well.

Macboom. Discontented? By my . . . ! And do you think I am content? Those who are not shot out of the guns ought to be impaled on the noses of the shells! You are going to see my report to the Minister. What have you written, civilian?

The Bank Manager. That I have the honor, General, to bring to your notice that the cannon shots fired by pieces of artillery manifestly aimed at the bank where the troop is installed with the general, at two forty-nine, in field marching order.

Macboom. It's obvious that you've been educated. Continue, and try to write a good round hand. And put at the head, Fourth Division, and the password. I've forgotten the password. Soldier, do you know the password?

The First Sentry. Go to the devil!

Macboom. You insult me in the face of the enemy? I'll have you shot with ignominy at once, in a fortified enclosure, notwithstanding your previous record.

The Second Sentry. That's the password, sir.

Macboom. That, the password? [*He thinks.*] That's right. I remember. I pardon you, soldier, and compliment you on your memory. But, by my bandoleer, what was the Minister of War's idea in manufacturing so unmilitary a password? Still, the Minister is more intelligent than I am, for his rank is higher than mine. Soldiers, I am wholly satisfied with you, with your good conduct under fire. Civilian, put that in the report.

The Bank Manager. And the civilians, General?

Macboom. Put, for their honor and their advancement,

that they were moving in their spirit of sacrifice and their high morale. Civilians, I am satisfied with you. I have an idea that something else is going to happen. The artillery has shifted. See if our sentries still know the password. [*He goes to one of the gates.*] Sentry Number Ten, give the password to Number Nine, who will give it to Number Eight, and so on. Off!

Voice of Sentry No. 10. Go to the devil!

Voice of Sentry No. 9. Go to the devil! [*The voices die away. It sounds like an argument.*]

Macboom [*coming away from the gate*]. You'd think that the army was sending me to the devil. [*To* THE SENTRIES.] Soldiers, does a revolution last long?

The First Sentry. That depends on the gunners, sir. If the revolutionaries fire well, it's soon over. And if the troops fire better, it's soon over just the same.

Macboom. You are intelligent, soldier. If I'd had anything to do with it, the revolution would never have begun.

Voice of Sentry No. 8. Go to the devil!

Voice of Sentry No. 9. Go to the devil!

Macboom. What? The password coming back? It's the enemy. Soldiers, 'shun! My saber! You hear? They're shouting the password. It's the Minister—or else it's the new revolutionary Minister.

The Second Sentry. Fire on him?

Macboom. Wretch! Salute him!

Voice of Sentry No. 10. Go to the devil!

Macboom [*losing his head*]. Civilians, stand up! Company, shoulder arms! Present arms!

The soldiers present arms. The general salutes with his saber. Enter PANTAGLEIZE.

Pantagleize [*dumbfounded*]. More soldiers? I'll never get out of this cavern alive. Still, they don't seem to be taking me for a . . . I've seen a hundred and fifty sentries who've asked me the password.

Macboom. My respects, Excellency. Look, the treasure is being guarded according to regulations.

Pantagleize [*coolly*]. I compliment you.

Macboom. Thank you, Excellency. Soldiers, His Excellency compliments us. And will His Excellency allow us to ask him the password, according to orders?

Pantagleize. I reply with what I have said to your

sentries. I say without ceremony, "Go to the devil, General!"

Macboom. I'm going, Excellency.

Pantagleize. There's no hurry. [*Aside.*] By God, would that be the password? I send everyone to the devil and they let me pass. [*Aloud.*] Strange password, isn't it? [*He looks around.*] Your soldiers are well trained. Don't let them tire themselves out needlessly. Order arms! At ease! Easy! [THE SOLDIERS *obey.*] You do me too much honor, General. Who told you I was an Excellency?

Macboom. There's no doubt that Your Excellency is an Excellency, or something of the kind. I'm not making a mistake over that, you know. You are certainly here on a mission.

Pantagleize [*uneasy*]. Indeed, on a forced mission.

Macboom [*shrewdly*]. About the treasure?

Pantagleize. Exactly, the treasure. [*He takes out a revolver and counts the people.*]

Macboom. Ah, Excellency, that object is a firearm. When you know how to use it, you kill people—and when you don't know how to use it, you still kill people.

The bankers hide. The general is not at all easy.

Pantagleize. A precautionary measure. With these battles in the streets, these rioters . . .

Macboom. Especially when one is on a mission. [PANTAGLEIZE *puts his revolver in his pocket.*] Well, at your service, Excellency! Have you orders with regard to the treasure?

Pantagleize [*unconcernedly*]. Yes, I'm going to take it away.

Macboom. Good. That is wise, now. It's no longer in safety here. What a responsibility I've had, Excellency! Why wasn't this thought of sooner? They'll take the bank by storm. They'll trample us down. It is written! . . .

Cannon. The bankers make desperate signals to the general.

Pantagleize. Hurry up, General, the treasure.

Macboom [*officiously*]. What a release! Quick, civilians, the combination of the safe. Open it, by my bullet case, or I'll have you under arrest.

The Bank Manager [*going to the safe*]. We should have confirmation, General.

Macboom. Who is in command here? [*Telephone*

rings.] There is your confirmation. [*He rushes to the telephone.* PANTAGLEIZE *half takes out his revolver.*] Hello? . . . The general . . . Yes . . . The bank . . . Yes . . . The treasure . . . Yes. I understand, Colonel. I understand everything. I'll see to it. No need to explain. I am master of the situation. At your service! [*He puts down the telephone. Cannon.*] You hear? Firing into us. The safe, gentlemen. It's high time.

THE BANK MANAGER, *very disturbed, opens the safe and takes out the case containing the treasure.*

Pantagleize. Take it easy. Here we are.

Macboom [*giving him the case*]. There, Excellency, intact. That's worth three thousand millions.

Pantagleize. I know.

Macboom. The crown diamonds. Where are you going to take them?

Pantagleize. That's a secret. Thank you, General. I shall draw attention to your great courtesy. Would you like a receipt?

Macboom. Don't bother. [*Cannon.*] How is it going outside?

Pantagleize. Famously—shooting, smashing. It will no doubt finish by ending. [*Telephone rings.*] I'm not bothered about that. I only know my orders, just as you only know yours. Good-by, General. I'll go out the same way.

Macboom. Delighted! Civilian, show His Excellency out. Soldiers, 'shun! Slope arms! Good day, Excellency. Look out for bullets!

PANTAGLEIZE *goes, followed by* THE BANK MANAGER. *The general salutes. Cannon. The telephone rings insistently.*

Voices of Sentries [*dying away*]. Go to the devil! Go to the devil!

Macboom. Good riddance! Civilian, put in your report . . . [*Smiling with relief, he picks up the telephone.*] Hello? Yes. The general. But . . . [*Silence.*] You have already telephoned me on that matter. Yes. I'm listening. The treasure? Someone's coming? For the treasure? But it's over. He's been.

THE BANK MANAGER *comes back.*

Macboom. Hello? What? [*He staggers.* THE BANK

MANAGER *holds him up.*] . . . that a person was coming . . . a re-vo-lu-tion-ary? [*He breaks down.*] Help! Stop, thief! They . . . will . . . shoot . . . me! Eu . . . ge . . . nie!

The two bankers yell with terror. The two SOLDIERS *are seized with helpless laughter. The general sobs. Tremendous noise of cannon. Cracking sounds. All goes black.*

SCENE VI—*The Objective Bar. Heavy curtains and a big palm. The outline of a double bass. Green light. Boisterous entry of the four revolutionaries who dispose themselves around a table.*

INNOCENTI. Comrades, the Provisional Committee, possessing full powers, is now in session, and provides, first of all, that . . .

Bamboola. First of all, comrade, let's have a chair.

Banger. Then let's have a drink, comrade.

Blank. And, finally, let's put on airs, like Comrade Innocenti.

Innocenti. What do you mean, dimwit?

Blank. Only that no one here has the right to speak in the name of the people and of the revolution. It's as easy as that.

Banger. That's right. Waiter!

Blank. Better call him "comrade waiter." There are no longer any servants.

Innocenti. I was a waiter, and that's what I remain. [*Ironically.*] It will be a pleasure to serve you, comrades. What will you have?

Bamboola. I, good nigger, will have the presidency.

Banger. Why?

Bamboola. Because I good nigger.

Blank. Bravo! Blackness was born of the eclipse. This blackness is red, and I maintain it won't turn out white. Drink! Comrades, the revolution was the work of the poets.

A WAITER *comes, stiff and formal.*

Waiter. What would the comrades like?

Bamboola. Bourgeois champagne, please, and me to take the floor.

Innocenti. Take the floor? What for? Speeches are

made to cause revolutions, and revolutions are caused to make speeches, eh?

Bamboola. Yeah. I cleaned boots. Now good nigger big chief. I clean universe.

Banger. Go on, let's hear.

Bamboola. I proclaim martial state and law of siege. *Fini.* Shoot all imbeciles.

Blank. I protest. The revolution . . .

Innocenti. Yes, if we were talking about the revolution.

Bamboola. Finished, comrade. No more talk about it.

Innocenti. What? And what's going to happen to the people?

Blank. Indeed, the people! But . . . the people are sovereign. They are moving toward their deliverance. We shall lecture them tonight. [*He drinks.*]

Bamboola. Yeah. Organize, distribute powers, ceremonial.

Banger. Prestige, that's what's needed. Here goes! [*He drinks.*]

Bamboola. Me Minister of War, for example. [*He drinks.*]

Blank. I agree, modestly, to being Minister of Arts and Sciences.

Banger. I'm Finance . . . But where's the money?

Bamboola. No more capital or capitalists.

Banger. Then Minister of the People's Inviolable Cash.

Bamboola. And you, Innocenti?

Innocenti. To hell with it! The talk of a pack of drunkards in a little café.

Bamboola. Treason! You going to leave us?

Innocenti. Humbugs! Throwing in your hand already? And what's going to happen to the others, if you please? Those who are stopping the bullets? Those who have blind faith in your speeches? You have watched the revolution from the top of an observatory. You have directed it on the strength of boy-scout signals. Here are the bulletins—incoherent, contradictory. The shooting is still going on. Flames are roaring. And we talk! Drink, Ministers! I'm going somewhere else. [*He is about to go. Amazement of the others.*] Moreover . . . You are really too stupid. This is not the revolution that was called for —like something in a film studio. How the police must be laughing! [*He goes toward the door.*]

Bamboola. You not said everything. Speak!

Innocenti. Where do you get this right of command? [*He spits toward the Negro.*] No, I haven't said everything. What you don't know, gentlemen, is that we are victims of a dreadful misunderstanding.

Blank. Just say that the cops caused the revolution to land us in the cart, and take to your heels, you tinpot apostle.

Innocenti [*very calmly*]. No, it's more terrible than a betrayal. Listen to this. . . . [*Pause.*] The revolution shouldn't have broken out this morning.

Banger. What does it matter, if it's been successful?

Innocenti. I repeat that there has been a tragic misunderstanding. We have been under an illusion, all of us, and we have hallucinated the masses. There was this eclipse atmosphere . . . and God knows what mumbo jumbo.

Banger. You're seeing things—or else you want to queer the pitch. Everything's going all right; it's in the bag. And you want to announce calamity. Get a hold of yourself.

Innocenti. You're a lot of amateurs.

Blank. Eh? Out the door!

Innocenti. Illusionists, drunkards, irresponsibles, readers of pamphlets. Your revolution? . . . It belongs to the music hall.

Blank. Traitor!

Innocenti. Repeat that! [*He strikes* BLANK *who returns the blow. They are separated.*]

Bamboola. Hey, comrades . . . this reign of brotherhood. Everyone embrace.

Banger. Come on, have a drink! Let's conclude a peace. The quarreling can come later.

Annoyed and angry, they drink. Silence.

Innocenti. You agree, then, that there's work to be done?

The Rest. Yes . . . Yes . . .

Innocenti. Come on, then. [*He folds his arms. They all look at him. Shrugging his shoulders,* INNOCENTI *takes up the telephone.*]

Innocenti. Rachel Silberchatz doesn't answer. [*He reads the bulletins.*] Three o'clock . . . a quarter past three . . . Yes, if one were to believe these papers . . . You've got to take enthusiasm and interceptions into account. All right—but Rachel doesn't answer. [*He puts down the telephone.*] The line is cut. [*Pause.*] What time is it? And still no report. Who is going to keep us in touch with outside? [*Pause.*] And what's happened to that fellow, the funny chap, the special messenger who gave the signal? He should know more about it than us.

Noise of voices outside. A SOLDIER *comes in.*

The Soldier. There's a queer type out there, comrades. . . .

PANTAGLEIZE *comes in, carrying the case.* THE SOLDIER *goes out.*

Pantagleize [*raising his hat*]. The Objective Bar? This is it? Pardon me. I've just come to have a drink. [*He is taken aback.*] Eh? What's this, an old boys' reunion? They told me I would find the Revolutionary Committee here.

Innocenti. It is here. Are you trying to be funny?

All Except Innocenti. Hurrah!

Bamboola [*hugging him*]. Pantagleize! You good fellow. Man of the day.

Pantagleize. Good lord, it's Bamboola! What's happened to you?

Bamboola. Me? President of the Republic. Have a drink?

Pantagleize. Anything! Would you think I'd just sneaked this little packet from under the nose of a general?

Innocenti. The revolution has nothing to do with the imperial treasure. Who told you to do this?

Pantagleize. I beg your pardon. This action was pure gallantry. But what is this treasure against the eyes of the beauty who asked me for it? [*Recognizing* INNOCENTI.] Ah! It was you who served me with the water that tasted so good. Well, waiter—or, no doubt, Minister —you may know that I laid hold of this treasure to please a young lady—a bit Jewish.

Innocenti. Rachel? You've seen her?

Pantagleize [*smiling*]. She even told me she loved me. Then, after a touching farewell, she ordered me to bring you the treasure at this objective place. Here I am. [*He bows.*] My name is Pantagleize!

All Except Innocenti. Hurrah! Bravo, Pantagleize!

Innocenti. Be quiet! [*To* PANTAGLEIZE.] Tell us, now,

man, where you came from this morning; the signal . . .
the phrase . . . ?

Pantagleize. That was whispered to me by . . . my sub-
conscious.

Innocenti. Are you acting like an imbecile, or are you
an imbecile?

Pantagleize. This morning you were unanimous in declaring me an imbecile. Am I still one, now that I have
been smart enough to make off with the swag? Even
though only imbeciles can bring off such things. Have I
done well? And this saying, "What a lovely day!" Was
that the thing to say? [*He drinks.*] That won't happen
again. Just a simple phrase! Tum-tum-titum! I don't give
a damn for it. Hasn't my destiny begun? Yours too,
gentlemen comrades. Already Bamboola sees himself
President of the Republic.

Innocenti. Pantagleize, I beseech you, who mentioned
this phrase to you?

Pantagleize. You are going to worry me to the finish?
I swear to you it was . . . occult.

Innocenti [*shaken*]. Occult? Yes . . . you mean it came
to you through secret channels?

Pantagleize. The occult always comes secretly. This
very day has been occult because of the eclipse. You must
admit that this has been a fine eclipse, as eclipses go. The
whole of bourgeois society has been eclipsed.

Innocenti. Explain yourself.

Pantagleize. Well, my friend . . . [*He sits down.*] I
meant the bourgeois, pouf! evaporated—all these mas-
queraders, these animals, these insects that swarmed in the
thoroughfares. Vanished. It's magic. The city has been
swept clean.

Blank. You see, Bamboola, all the fools are dead.

Pantagleize. There's still one left, because I'm here. But,
young man, you who speak with such an air, could you
wage a revolution without fools?

All Except Innocenti. Oho! Oho! Oho! [*They drink.*]

Innocenti. Quiet! And what have you seen in the streets?
What is happening?

Pantagleize. Magisterial happenings. People . . . everywhere . . . dead . . . living . . . and some more dead
than alive. Funk . . . heroism . . . plenty of scoundrels
. . . police. Revolvers . . . bang bang . . . machine guns
. . . crack crack crack. Patrols . . . pursuits . . . hand-

to-hand   fighting . . . skedaddling . . . proletarians . . .
songs . . . Taking of the Bastille . . . black flags on the
buildings . . . And the sun, recovered from its eclipse,
shining on a wonderful scene of ruination, ashes of
Babylon! [*He takes a breath.*] Ouf! Comrades, it is indeed a lovely day.

All Except Innocenti. Hurrah! Victory!

Innocenti. Shut up! [*To* PANTAGLEIZE.] Why are these
happenings no longer communicated to us, us who are
supposed to control them?

Pantagleize [*pityingly*]. My dear fellow, you don't
know the people. They inform you of nothing because
they are drinking—and what better could they do? They
are looting the shops and restaurants. Haven't they en-
dured hunger and thirst long enough? Remember the
revolution of ninety-three, my friend. It's the same thing,
without the guillotine. There should be a guillotine—it's
so decorative.

All Except Innocenti. Bravo! A guillotine!

Pantagleize. And let us guillotine the art critics, the
property owners, and the chiropodists. We'll strip all the
rest naked and give them the same costume. After that,
they'll do gymnastic exercises, collective movements, to
regenerate them: one . . . two . . . three . . . one . . .
two . . . three.

Bamboola. Genius. You a Minister.

Pantagleize. Of what?

Bamboola. Of gymnastics.

Pantagleize. What an honor! What will my fiancée,
Rachel, say?

Innocenti. This Rachel, was there no one with her,
about the house, when you left her?

Pantagleize. Suppose you were to call me Excellency?
When I left her she was crying out . . . [*Imitating a Jew
at prayer.*] God of Israel, Thy people persecute their
persecutors. The Philistines grovel in the mud. The Ark
of the Covenant shines above the nations. [*In his own
voice.*] If there was anyone there, I didn't know. But I
was hardly on the stairs when I heard the noise of a
violent quarrel. [INNOCENTI *picks up the telephone. Nothing.*] What does it matter, dear friends? It's time to
celebrate this lovely day to which, you claim, I have
modestly contributed. Yes, the cause has succeeded. Was
it a good cause or a bad cause? All successful causes are

good causes. So let us drink! Waiter! Serve all these
Excellencies, and that includes me.

Two WAITERS *rush in, serve, then station themselves behind the Ministers' chairs, as at a big function.*

Banger. Better and better! And . . . is the Provisional
Committee going to sit any more today?
Blank. Please, the Council of Ministers.

INNOCENTI, *in despair, holds his head in his hands.*

Bamboola. It is in session. Waiter, cigars!

A third WAITER *rushes in, serves, and stations himself
behind* BAMBOOLA.

Pantagleize. Wonderful, this new society! Champagne
and cigars! I beg leave to take the floor.
Blank. Me first.
Bamboola. I speak good Negro.
All Except Innocenti. Bravo! Good Negro!

The telephone rings. INNOCENTI *listens, starts, controls
himself, and puts down the telephone.*

Banger. What was that?
Innocenti [*pale*]. Nothing. Everything's all right. [*He
laughs unpleasantly, then, in a forced voice.*] Long live
the revo . . .
Blank. As you say. . . . That's the first intelligent
phrase he's uttered. Carry on! Comrades, I drink to pros-
perity. . . .
Innocenti [*to* PANTAGLEIZE]. Clear out, friend, it's high
time.
Pantagleize. Why? It's nice here.
Bamboola. I call on Minister Pantagleize who I have
cleaned his boots.
Pantagleize [*on his feet*]. Gladly.
Blank. First of all, let me congratulate you. [*Inspired.*]
Adventurer errand boy and bottle stopper glow equally
on your forehead you dance on a rope and say "Rats!"
to the archangel it is ten to four and the laurel consumes
itself diffuses your delight leaves Hell complaining. [*He
applauds himself. The others laugh coarsely.*]
Pantagleize [*drinks and climbs up on the table; he
staggers a bit*]. It would be a good thing to guillotine the

poets as well. Waiter, more light! We are not just any-
body. We know how to live.

A fourth WAITER *rushes in, turns the lights up brighter,
then stations himself behind* INNOCENTI'S *chair.*

Pantagleize. Send for orchestras, harps, and cymbals.
Give me a trident and the tables of the Law—and a crown
into the bargain. Tonight I shall do strange things, even
marvels. Look at the marvel of my equilibrium. When
the country sways . . . The people shall see. . . . To begin with, citizens, it will be necessary to invent the people. We shall destroy the only true God and set up idols
in rubber and triplex. I am for the false gods. Now then,
comrades . . . Angels of Shrove Tuesday, I bless you in
your suppurating charity and praise you in the anticipation of a joyful explosion and a glorious immortality in
the glass cases of a museum. Happenings are at a discount,
I say! Ho! History at bargain prices! I have seen the
plague sufferers and bogy men as commanders in chief of
the legions of the proletariat who were wearing sauce-
pans and chamber pots on their heads. Legions of im-
pertinent skeletons whose actions were stupid and woebegone. For liberty, comrades! Liberty to spit on the
ceiling and empty your bowels on days of rejoicing. But
remember you must give the earth to the beasts and to
man his misery. Thus we shall order actions which are
so preposterous that they will be irreparable throughout
eternity. Well, then! What is left that is reasonable?
Living? You are too swinish—and too ill to die. So you
will become statues. Is it too late to talk about them—the
people? No. When they have been invented and when
we have tasted their resistance to dynamite and to our
speeches, we shall give them pajamas, motorcycles, and
three pounds of international sausage per head. The rest
is our business. The rest? The deluge, humanity! Ah, dear
Ministers, humanity was ugly and passionate. It was wise
and foolish. It used to become madly delirious. I propose . . .

Bamboola [*half rising*]. The publication of your speech.
[THE WAITER *behind him fells him with a sharp blow
from a blackjack. Without a sound or a gesture,* BAM-
BOOLA *sits in his chair, knocked out. No one has noticed
anything.*]

Blank. Errors, of course, excepted. Would you like . . .

[*He half rises. Same business.* BLANK *is discreetly knocked out. The other* WAITERS *do not move a muscle.*]

Pantagleize [*lightheaded*]. Would I like? I would like . . . the way out. May Jupiter guide me to a South Sea island, where I shall be taboo, where I shall edit an artistic review with the Crown's ha'pennies.

Banger. First you've got to lay in gherkins, caramels, and toothpicks. . . . [*Same business.* BANGER *is carefully put to sleep.*]

Pantagleize. We shall lay in crutches and eyecups, stretchers and shrouds; we shall lay in intelligence and all the writings of the sociologists. Then we shall make pneumatic hearts, automatic brains, and backsides with springs to receive the boots of the new masters. Do everything for the best. I shall requisition eclipses.

Innocenti [*getting up*]. What muck! Shut your mouth . . . or I'll knock you down! [*Same business.* INNOCENTI *is felled in silence.*]

Pantagleize. You don't have the floor, impudence! [*He looks at his companions and is surprised at their appearance, understanding nothing.*] Eh? Are you asleep? [*Annoyed.*] That's the last time I make a speech, d'you hear? [*The four* WAITERS *remain motionless.*] Sleeping when the revolution swells up, mounts to its zenith. Waiters, carry these people to their beds. [*Whistle. The four* WAITERS *each grab a man and drag him out.*] I am the master here. [*He looks at the empty room.*] Am I dreaming, or am I not dreaming? Oblivion, what have you done with those puppets? [*Outside, orders are given. He grows sad.*] What happenings! And what might they all mean? Ah! If I'd stayed in my room . . . [*He jumps down from the table and drinks champagne.*] My health! Not worth while going on with this speech—I would be the only one to applaud.

The palm tree moves and places itself behind PANTAGLEIZE. *It is* CREEP, *disguised as a palm tree.*

Pantagleize. What? [*He sees the palm.*] Do they grow in bars, these animals? [*He bows to the palm.*] Tell me, palm tree of the desert—stricken with thirst, no doubt— what does a palm tree feel when it sees someone drinking champagne?

Palm-Creep. It feels the satisfaction of a task accom-

plished. But this satisfaction will not be complete, my
dear sir, until the handcuffs are on you.

Pantagleize [picking up his case]. A reply like that deserves that I uproot you. *[He knocks the palm over.
CREEP blows his whistle.]*

Palm-Creep [on the floor]. I'll get you.

Pantagleize. See you at the next eclipse! *[He rushes into
a corridor and disappears.]*

THE WAITERS *come back.*

Palm-Creep. Quick, to the left! *[Two WAITERS rush off.
The other two stand CREEP up again.]*

A Waiter. What about the Ministers?

Palm-Creep. In the cooler! Quick!

One of the Waiters [coming back]. He got away in the
street.

Palm-Creep. Get him, dead or alive!

Shots outside. Cries. Oaths.

Blackout

SCENE VII—RACHEL SILBERCHATZ's *room, as at the beginning of the act. The curtains allow the light of late afternoon to filter through. In the room, all has been turned
upside down. Maps and papers on the floor. RACHEL is in
the armchair, apparently asleep with her eyes open. Someone is coming up the stairs.*

VOICE OF PANTAGLEIZE. Fine pearls, jewels, gold, platinum,
diamonds, radium, and I don't know what—millions. Em-
eralds, rubies, tiaras, necklaces. And for you, you daughter
of kings and prophets.

PANTAGLEIZE *comes in, disheveled but happy, carrying the
case. He is obviously drunk.*

Pantagleize. Oh, Rachel! I find you again, white and
lovely, far from the tumult. *[He looks at her.]* Asleep?
Yes, one should sleep after such a day. I shall keep watch.
You will hear me from the depths of limbo where your
soul wanders. Besides, what I have to tell you is like a story
such as you might hear in a dream. Fabulous, the treasure,
the Golden Fleece, conquered for you, and I place it at
your feet. There's enough of it for anyone to be able to
live on the interest. But what is this treasure worth against

the pearls and jewels of my love! [*He opens the case and inspects the jewels.*] Vanity! So contemptible! I would much rather have brought you rarer things, a moonbeam, a necklace of dew, the secret of perpetual motion; but you don't find these things in the safes in banks. [*He shuts the case and sits close to* RACHEL.] My child, my sister, I am shattered. I, too, must sleep. I would already be on a comfortable express, but I had to see you again. I'll run away presently, with you. All the countries we shall go to are beautiful. Countries where there are no revolutions, of course. [*He holds his head.*] Where have I got to? Let's sort out today's wanderings. Early this morning there was a calendar, a Negro, then a street lamp, an eclipse, yelling dervishes and clay-pigeon shooters at a fair. And you, Rachel, who saved my life. My destiny pursued its course. Then the theft of the treasure. Shortly after that I became Minister of something or other. Then a palm tree that talked. Then running away. Running away!— that's the least mad thing in all this. What part have I played? Is it over? I bet it will finish in a marriage. Let's draw up the terms of this equation: eclipse, woman, treasure. It's so odd. And am I still a minister? What a responsibility! And the revolution, wasn't it my duty to make it my business? What should one do in such a situation? Make a speech or fire a revolver? It's not important. I resign as Minister. [*He gets up.*] Minister! When it's so easy to be rich and in love beside a sleeping beauty. [*He tiptoes around the armchair. He stops, a little uneasy.*] How white she is. You would think she was wax. What sort of sleep is she sleeping? She sleeps like an invalid. Poor woman! May the guardian spirits of night surround you and drive off the bats of nightmare! [*He sighs.*] Such a contrast! Recently you were agitated, you were like a goat or a dancer; and here you are, silent as a statue, quiet as a picture. [*He snorts.*] I am rich, famous, and in possession of a destiny. Yet here I am, quite without desires. I have no wish other than to be drowned in sleep, anonymous in the dark, without memory, without thoughts, without past, without future. I am weary, without hunger, without thirst. [*He drinks from the whisky bottle.*] I am waiting for nothing but Rachel's awakening. The strange sleeper who listens to me and pretends not to see or hear me. Sleep. When one is asleep, one does nothing stupid. [*He treads on the maps, picks them up, and folds*

them.] Papers? Maps? What was she doing? Order is
what is needed. Ah, Rachel, you have such qualities! You
are gifted, capable, practical, modern, eh? Your room is
like a business office. What a life! But what place have
you given to love? Is it really a woman's job to bother
with all this? A revolution? The revolution is in our hearts,
darling. The other is a joke, and papers are all that remain of it. I don't want to see these papers any more. You
shan't keep them. [*He puts them in the case.*] Be a woman.
I who have won you have completely different ideals—a
little romantic, but one comes back to that. And then, at
forty, your soul rediscovers a kind of ingenuity, a sort of
childishness. Rachel, we shall go and live in nature with
the birds and little beasts, far from the barbarous cities
and the conflicts of humanity. I shall shear sheep and you
shall make butter, listening to the songs of savages pad-
dling on the twilit river. [*Firmly.*] I can't bear strong
feelings. Nor can you. For proof, look at you! [*He drinks.*]
Dear and lovely one, I have been excited all day long; but
things are better this evening. I am forgetting everything
except that my destiny revealed you to me, and that all
this revolution had only one end—that we should meet.
It's too much happiness for me! [*He weeps.*] And here I
am weeping, foolish clod! This, from a former Minister!
[*He pulls himself together.*] Be a man! I've got to accomplish the imperative task of taking the express with
this creature. Let's get rid of the melodramatic atmosphere.
She's got to know that I'm here and that I bring her a
fortune and my love in this case. [*He makes a noise,
searches for the electric lamp, throws it down.*] Lamp
smashed? This candle will do the job. [*He lights the
candle and puts it on the table.*] What a silence! [*Gra-
ciously.*] Rachel, my love! Cuckoo! [*Silence.*] Rachel!
Miss Rachel! Comrade! [*He rolls his frightened eyes.*]
What a sleep! I'd better use stronger measures. No. I'll
place the butterfly of my kiss on the flower of her brow.
Like this. [*He goes to her and kisses her, then draws back
at once, wiping his mouth.*] Bah! What a sensation! Rachel!
[*He wanders around.*] No, no, I don't want to get
panicky. Rachel, it's not nice. [*He lifts his feet.*] My
feet are sticking to the floor. I'm walking on flypaper. [*He
sniffs.*] Bah! There's a smell . . . a smell like a butcher's
shop! What's smelling like that? What is there in this
room? I'm not afraid; but I like clear situations. [*He goes

to RACHEL *and takes hold of her.*] Get up, come along,
are you ill? [*He lets her fall back.*] My betrothed! She's
had an accident. She has. [*He catches sight of a paper on
the table.*] A note with blood on it? It's for me. [*Terrified,
he reads it.*] "They've murdered me . . . the re . . . vo
. . . lu . . . tion . . . is . . ." [*He lets the note drop.*]
Oh! I beg your pardon. [*He draws back, embarrassed,
looking at his feet.*] Like that, is it? Murdered? [*He draws
farther back.*] Excuse me, Rachel. My deepest sympathy.
[*He takes his case and babbles.*] Good-by . . . I hope we
shall . . . meet again! [*And he goes out quickly, without
looking again at the corpse.*]

ACT THREE

SCENE VIII—*A street. Debris. Light from fires and searchlights. The sound of someone running. Enter* PANTAGLEIZE.
*He is still holding onto his case. A body lies face down-
ward in the middle of the stage.* PANTAGLEIZE *runs round
and round the body, talking all the time.*

PANTAGLEIZE. One, two. One, two. I'm running. I'm
flying. Where am I? Where am I going? My destiny is to
gallop. I'm breaking records. One, two, one, two. And
this on my birthday. Running is tiring. So is having a
destiny. Bang! [*He jumps.*] They are still shooting. Is
shooting so jolly, then? Bang! Shooting all the time. If
only my destiny could guide me to a place where there
is no shooting. One, two, one, two. [*He stumbles against
the body.*] I beg your pardon! No doubt you are dead?
Of course—they're shooting. That's all they've done since
this morning. Lovely day! You must confess, sir, that
these happenings are regrettable. The result: here you
are, dead, sir. Isn't luck fantastic? Here we are, you
compelled to be dead and I to be rich. But you can lie
at peace, and I have to flee, to run without stopping, even
though I'm asthmatic and my fortune is enough to let me
ride about in a carriage. I'll tell you something in confidence—but wait till I go and have a look at the skyline
to see there are no patrols or armored cars. [*He goes to
the left.*] Bang! Only bullets. [*The corpse profits from this
activity to sit up and take a look at* PANTAGLEIZE. *Suddenly
it lies down again.* PANTAGLEIZE *goes to the right.*] Bang!
Bullets again. [*He comes back.*] If they hit you, sir, you'll

only be more dead. And if they hit me, it will be because
my destiny has sent them. In that case, I shall be dead like
you, and there will be a perfect brotherhood between us.
[*He sits on the body.*] It was very much in spite of myself,
sir, that I got mixed up in today's goings on. Who profits
from these events? Pantagleize, sir. Oh, I'm not a bourgeois.
If I have become rich, it's only been so as to be pleasing
to a woman. You understand? No. No more do I. There
is nothing to understand. For example, do you know why
you are dead? It must have a funny effect on you. Being
alive has a funny effect too—when they are shooting. It's
not that I put a high price on life [*shots*] but this treasure
. . . It's scarcely a few hours since I found myself rich,
and it's a sweet sensation to feel yourself a multimillionaire.
Perhaps waggish destiny will soon rob me of it all. [*He
thinks.*] I fear today hasn't been a lovely one, except for
me. I've experienced all the surprises, all the thrills, all the
feelings, even that of my own superiority. I'm a film star,
but I'm completely ignorant of the screenplay. I was a
Minister, when nothing had pointed me out for that
career. It should have ended in a marriage; but the marriage didn't happen. I'm like a widower. It's a pity. She
was dead, sir, or she acted like it; but I believe she was
dead, because she listened without laughing to the poetic
nonsense I told her without blushing. Why didn't I die
with her? Everyone is dead today—so much so that it's
almost indecent to be still alive. And my friends the
Ministers, are they dead too, sir? Yes, it's heartbreaking.
It would be better to leave this restless old world. I'm
going to gather together all those who are not yet dead
and go with them to an island. I shall become a philan-
thropist, a patriarch. I shall lay out my treasure to elevate
the thoughts of these wretches, and my reward will be
to see again, shining in my sleep, the eyes of this woman,
who dreamed of a universal love. No doubt, sir, mine was
not enough for her. [*He holds his head in his hands. The
approach of a patrol is heard.* PANTAGLEIZE *jumps.*] Act
dead! That doesn't commit you to anything. [*He lies
still, face downward.*]

    Voice of Macboom. In extended order, forward! The
lamppost as reference point. Halt! Fall in again! There's
nothing but corpses. Order reigns. Soldiers, once more I
am satisfied with you. [*The footsteps come nearer.*]

    Pantagleize [*raising his head*]. I am satisfied with the

fine fellows who fired bullets without hitting me. [*He
lies down again.*]

Enter the patrol followed by a breathless GENERAL MAC-
BOOM. *It marches around the stage.*

Macboom. Left wheel! Company, halt! [*The patrol
halts.*] Soldiers, take a breather. Damme, what an epic!
The god of the military is with us, there's no mistake.
No wound, no effective loss, nothing but victories! What
a mopping-up, eh? You admired my tactics, eh? As for
the revolutionaries, they can't do better than children,
that lot. By Heaven, here are two more. It's my work,
by my bayonet!

A Soldier. We can always fire on them to see, sir.

Macboom. No my friend, I don't want a homicide on
my conscience. Those fellows are the gravediggers' concern. All right? [*He mops himself.*] At last, a bit of calm!
It seems to me that it's all over. [*Distant shouts, scuffling,
shooting.*] By the barrack gate, did you hear that? Duty,
soldiers! To the attack! [*He brandishes his saber.*] Be
careful. I shall bring up the rear. No, wait. [*He uses his
field glasses.*] Don't bother. The police are rushing to the
scene. We are not going to spoil their strategy. We shall
go back where we came from. Company, about turn! At
the double, forward!

The patrol goes out—followed by GENERAL MACBOOM—
by the same route it took in coming. PANTAGLEIZE *gets up
and goes to the right—the direction of the scuffling.*

Pantagleize. Courage! It's a fine thing, is courage. [*He
gazes into the distance and follows the course of the scuffle.
The corpse gets up, rubs its back, and posts itself behind*
PANTAGLEIZE.] I've always admired the army. No, they're
getting all the knocks. But . . . it's the police! It's not
the army. In that case, well done! Down with the police!

Creep. What have the police done to you?

Pantagleize [*turning around, frightened*]. Nothing. . . .
There was a corpse here.

Creep. Well, now! What has happened to it?

Pantagleize. No doubt it's gone somewhere else. It's not
safe here. But wasn't it you, that great corpse?

Creep. Don't worry yourself. It was me. You see, I'm
resurrected.

Pantagleize. My congratulations. [*He shakes* CREEP's

hand.] You are not unknown to me. It was this morning in a little café. How are you coming along?

Creep. Not badly—in spite of the fact that in the course of my duty I received such a blow on the head that I was left for dead.

Pantagleize. Oh, the wicked fellows!

Creep. And how are you, my dear sir?

Pantagleize. Well, I would be happy if it weren't for the bullets. How can I tell you how I've spent my day? The fact of it remains, I am rich.

Creep. Oho! are we going to share?

Pantagleize [*offended*]. Not likely!

Creep. You are not for sharing? Nevertheless, you were . . .

Pantagleize. I still am Pantagleize. And you?

Creep. I am Creep. I have had occasion to meet you several times during the course of today, which some people declare lovely. I saw you on a street lamp. I saw you go into a bank. I saw you making a speech in a bar where the Revolutionary Committee was sitting. And I believe you went up to a Jewess' room.

Pantagleize [*surprised*]. Indeed! I don't remember anything. You are remarkable, sir. Was I so occupied? But can you tell me why I did all this?

Creep. No, my dear sir.

Pantagleize. I did all this because I am forty and my destiny began today. Strange, eh? And my destiny isn't finished yet—no more than this day is.

Creep. I believe that, willingly.

Pantagleize. I have difficulty in thinking that all that has happened was real. Wasn't it a dream?

Creep. It was only a revolution, sir.

Pantagleize. A real one?

Creep. Near enough. I must tell you, sir, that you showed great courage.

Pantagleize [*delighted*]. Honored, my dear sir.

Creep. And I have only one regret. It is that your destiny is going to separate us. If it weren't for that, with your face and your capacity I might have made something of you . . . in the police.

Pantagleize. You do me honor.

Creep. You have everything that's necessary, even the umbrella. Where is your umbrella, by the way?

Pantagleize [*holding onto his case*]. Here it is.

Creep. That? That's a case. [PANTAGLEIZE *is worried.*]
What's in it, may I ask?

Pantagleize. A bit of jewelry.

Creep. What! Haven't you a chew of tobacco?

Pantagleize [*disturbed*]. No; but if you would like to
come with me to the island of my dreams, we shall smoke
Oriental pipes and chew plants that make you sleep.

Creep. Good. I'll come with you. Let's go.

Pantagleize. We'd better arrange to meet.

Creep. No, I won't leave you.

Pantagleize. Please. I shall go alone to begin with. [*He
walks around the stage.* CREEP *follows on his heels.*]

Creep. I am very happy in your company. [PANTAGLEIZE
quickens his pace. Soon, he is running. CREEP *does the
same.*]

Pantagleize. Don't be so insistent, sir.

Creep. I don't want to leave a man who has a destiny
like yours, at any price.

Pantagleize. You're after my case. You shan't have it.

Creep. Don't misunderstand my intentions, sir. A policeman is an honest man—now and again.

PANTAGLEIZE *makes off to the right. A burst of firing stops
him. A flash.*

Pantagleize. Ah! Bullets! They're seeking me out. [*He
runs to the left.*]

Creep. You draw them toward you.

Pantagleize. There are other streets and I have long legs.
[*When he gets to the left, there is another burst and a
flash.*] Ah! these fusiliers are not very nice. [*He comes
back to the center.* CREEP *also. They bump into each other.
Shooting from all sides.*] We are risking our lives, sir.

Creep. True. Let's be careful.

Pantagleize. Help each other in danger. Be brothers.
There's been a lot of talk about brotherhood today. I'll
hide behind you. [*He tries to disappear behind* CREEP.]

Creep. Is that what you understand by brotherhood?

The shooting is redoubled.

Pantagleize. I wouldn't like anything unfortunate to
happen to you.

Creep. Too late, sir. [*He gives him a blow on the back
of the neck.*]

Pantagleize [*staggering*]. Or to me! [CREEP *takes the case*

and drags along PANTAGLEIZE, *who allows him to do it—as
though he were drunk.*] Ah, sir! Don't lose me on the way.
It was a lovely day. Watch how it will finish beautifully.

   Creep. Count on me.

   Pantagleize. Look at all the stars! No, the world has
turned upside down. It's my diamonds that have rolled
into the sky! [*They go out.*]

Blackout

SCENE IX—*A bare room. At the back, a table, at which the
War Council will sit. Two* SOLDIERS *march around in front
of the table, their paths crossing from time to time. They
sing as they march.*

THE FIRST SOLDIER. A soldier boy we knew,
   The Second Soldier. He loved a girl we know,
   The First Soldier. And when the bugles blew,
   The Second Soldier. She wept to see him go.
                    [*They halt and face the audience.*]
   Both Soldiers. Won't you come back, my love so true,
             And cuddle me as you used to do?
                    [*They set off marching again.*]
   The First Soldier. This soldier boy we knew,
   The Second Soldier. Struck terror in the foe . . .

Outside, a bugle call: the attention. The two SOLDIERS *take
up their posts at each end of the tribunal. A light from
above lights up the table. The* DISTINGUISHED COUNSEL
arrives like a ballet dancer.

   The Distinguished Counsel. Order, order! Will this
evening's hearing be over by midnight? They're expecting
me at the club. I've already done two barracks. Tell me,
what was that attractive thing you were singing? "This
soldier boy we knew, Struck terror in the foe . . ."
Go on.

   The First Soldier. And as was his due,
   The Second Soldier. He rose from rank so low.
   Two Soldiers and Counsel [*in chorus*]. Won't you come
        back, my love so true,
      And cuddle me as you used to do?

*A stroke on a gong. They stop. A back cloth behind
the table opens and reveals six members of the Council of
War who are seen from the waist upward, like figures in*

*an Aunt Sally. They are all masked with identical masks.
There is a vacant place in the center of their row.*

The Distinguished Counsel [*bowing very low*]. Gentlemen of the jury, my humblest respects. This is the third
time, and I hope the last, on which we sit to judge these
scoundrels. An unpleasant task, gentlemen! But society
must be cleansed, and we shall not succeed in doing so
tonight, despite our zeal. Nevertheless, gentlemen, we are
witnesses of the triumph of right over might. We must
congratulate ourselves on that. [*The six* COUNCILORS *nod
approval, rise and, two by two, shake hands, then sit again.*
THE COUNSEL *shakes hands with the two* SOLDIERS.] How
gloomy this place is! How can you win a case in a place
like this? Let's liven ourselves up, gentlemen! The very
thing! These fine fellows were singing a most amusing
song. [*To* THE SOLDIERS.] You said, "He rose from rank
so low. . . . ?

The First Soldier. This soldier boy we knew
The Second Soldier. Grew very sad, and so
The First Soldier. He wrote a letter to
The Second Soldier. This pretty girl we know.
Soldiers, Counsel, and Councilors [*in chorus*]. Won't
     you come back, my love so true,
     And cuddle me as you used to do?

Stroke on gong. They stop. Silence. THE GENERALISSIMO
*in black and silver, with an outrageously plumed medieval
helmet, rises in the vacant place behind the table as
though he were growing out of the ground. On his appearance,* THE COUNCILORS *sink back, and* THE COUNSEL *lies flat
on his belly.* THE GENERALISSIMO *raises his arm. All resume
their positions. Drum roll.*

The Generalissimo. They should be playing a funeral
march, gentlemen. Never mind. The Council sits. I ask,
as I have done twice before this evening, for the full rigor
of the law—
The Distinguished Counsel [*interrupting*]. This is intol-
erable! In that case, what is the point of this jury and my
appearance as counsel?
The Generalissimo. This jury and yourself are the pomp
and the prestige and the decorum and the decoration of
this ceremony. [THE COUNSEL *clicks his heels*.] Gentlemen,
I now appeal to your noble sentiments. We must act

quickly. Our sentences must be passed and carried out by midnight. The first!

Enter GENERAL MACBOOM, *panting.* THE COUNSEL *rushes to support him. The general salutes and painfully takes up position.*

The Generalissimo [*familiarly*]. General Macboom, you do not appear before the War Council as an offender, but as a man of honor. You had a lapse. Your vigilance was surprised when you were guarding the treasure. Is that not so?

Macboom [*with a sigh*]. Alas, Your Honor!

The Generalissimo. Why haven't you committed suicide?

Macboom. Because the regulations don't say . . . that a defaulting soldier . . . is bound to commit suicide, Your Honor.

The Generalissimo. Perfectly right. What have you to put forward in your defense, General? Speak freely. You are among soldiers.

Macboom [*pulls himself together and sticks out his chest*]. By gad! . . . by gad! . . . I have this to say, damme! It was the fault of those blasted civvies, by the battery! For myself, I would have put my foot behind them, because when the military is there, there's no place for civilians, by my billycan! For fifty years now I've asked for the suppression of civilians. If they'd listened to me, by the battle group, there'd be none of these sneaking tales that the civilians use to sabotage the military. And, by the bedbugs, if there had been no one but troops posted in that rathole of those skunks of bankers, everything would have gone according to plan, by my backsight! In short, and with due respect, I was mucked about and counter-mucked about by these dirty dogs of civilians who had lost their leading man, while we, the military, unflinching under the bombardment, risked death rather than dishonor, obeying orders. At your command! [*He clicks his heels and stands motionless.*]

The Generalissimo. That was to be expected. Counsel, you may speak, and remember that the case you are defending is that of a noble servant of the nation.

The Distinguished Counsel. Generals! [*He clicks his heels.*] It is my opinion that General Macboom has been the victim of unfortunate circumstances. Yes, the victim.

And how many victims will there not be on this day of calamities? Is the general guilty? No! Look at these white hairs that have never flinched, this tunic under which there beats a heart of iron! Who is guilty? The High Command! For thirty-five years, General Macboom has commanded the C.D.I.M.—the Central Depot for the Issue of Mess tins—with success, initiative and skill. Why, then, without warning, entrust the defense of a bank to him? Inconceivable blunder! It springs to mind at once that the contents of a bank and of a mess-tin depot are utterly different. Ah, gentlemen, haven't we here one of those underhanded maneuvers directed at his rank and at his enviable reputation? Aren't the Freemasons behind this? And what is the general accused of? Of having allowed the treasure to be taken? Was that a default? Scarcely. The treasure was an imitation. The real treasure is lodged abroad. But, gentlemen, if the general had not been there galvanizing the troops, it wouldn't have been the treasure that was stolen, but the bank itself! Now, on the other hand, what has happened at the Mess-tin Depot, during the General's absence? It is beyond words! A hundred and seventy-two mess tins have disappeared! And who will pay for them? The taxpayer! So, I demand that the High Command be blamed, and that my client, General Macboom, be mentioned in the Nation's dispatches. I have finished.

The Generalissimo. General, on behalf of the Empire, I congratulate you. You are one of the great defenders of our sacred institutions. Fall out!

Macboom [staggering with elation]. Thank you, Your Honor! Gentlemen!

The Distinguished Counsel [helping him out]. And thus is the soldier's valor rewarded.

The Generalissimo. Next!

BLANK *is flung in.*

Blank [white with fear and whimpering in a high-pitched voice]. Mercy! I won't do it again!

The Distinguished Counsel [arranging the poet's cravat]. Gentlemen of the jury, we are not the juvenile court. Send this lad back to his mother.

The Generalissimo. Silence, lawyer! You will busy yourself on behalf of this guttersnipe when the time arrives. [*To* BLANK.] Tell me, young hooligan, what do you do in life?

Blank [*bewildered*]. I—I—I—am a poet. A modern poet. [*General laughter.*]

The Generalissimo [*furious*]. A poet! Of course! More than that, modern! Not content with living like a parasite and spreading the demoralizing example of sloth and immodesty, you dare to claim to be modern! Not content with overthrowing society, you must overthrow syntax into the bargain and sow confusion in healthy brains. Recite one of your poems and let us see.

Blank [*in one breath*]. Sip on the crater is the first confession of the chilled pumpkin losing all its stuffed marrow the lovely child sucking the mauve star the Arab had melted the worm lonely and blue . . .

The Generalissimo [*bellowing*]. Enough! You make the dignity of the tribunal blush! That, my lad, is not poetry. Here is some poetry. [*Reciting.*]

> Across the sky, the storm clouds' wrack,
> The trumpet calls, "Attack! Attack!"
> And then the soldier bold in heart,
> ti-tum, ti-tum, ti-tum, ti-tum . . .

[*Approval of Council.*]

What you write is in code, to undermine military security. This Arab and the lonely worm, they stand for something, don't they, now? You are in a fine mess, especially as you were not a purveyor of poems, but of firearms, and you were mixed up in the Provisional Committee. Defend yourself!

The Distinguished Counsel. Your Honor, Generalissimo, you too have been young.

The Generalissimo. At his age I was learning trigonometry. Let him defend himself!

Blank. I didn't believe it was serious, sir. I—I only wanted to amuse myself.

The Generalissimo. Strange amusement! Defend him, lawyer. As a poet, he's got too much gift of the gab.

The Distinguished Counsel [*taking out a handkerchief and pretending to weep*]. Gentlemen, my heart is chilled. Look at this youth. You will never make me believe that this is a revolutionary. He has only assumed the airs of one, that's all. He is a child of our time, too intelligent, badly influenced by evil reading, and, like all his generation, the victim of a morbid need to show off. Send him

back home. He will be good. I do not say that he merits
a great deal of consideration, for a well-brought-up young
man does not have shady associates. But has he not sinned
in innocence? I ask for a conditional good hiding for this
delinquent—and the confiscation of his poetic genius.

The Generalissimo. I reply that a charge remains. This
young man has tried to revolt against the State. The proof
—these proclamations signed in his hand. Administer the
punishment laid down.

Blank. What? What punishment? Don't punish me at
all—not even with a flower!

The Distinguished Counsel [*consoling him*]. No, my
little chap, they won't do it with a flower. Be brave! Be a
man! Your poetry will live after you.

Blank [*realizing the situation*]. Help! They are going
to . . . [*One of the* SOLDIERS *seizes him and flings him
outside. Voices. Orders in the corridors.*]

The Generalissimo. Next! Hurry up!

BAMBOOLA *rolls onto the stage. He gets up and rushes
toward the table, intending to climb on it.* THE COUNSEL
holds him back by his trousers.

Bamboola. Boss, you going to know. I good nigger.

The Distinguished Counsel. But . . . it's a savage! There
has been a mistake. Negroes don't cause revolutions.

The Generalissimo. Get rid of your illusions, lawyer.
This dusky fellow appears in another light with respect to
his record. Fraud, white slavery, counterfeiting, black-
mail, drug trafficking, criminal assault . . . I pass over
the rest.

Bamboola. Boss, that not me. That other nigger. He also
called Bamboola. I good Bamboola. He bad.

The Generalissimo. What has the good Bamboola done
since this morning?

Bamboola. Nothing, Boss. I go for walk, see in city,
bands, procession.

The Generalissimo. And at the Objective Bar, please?

Bamboola. I engaged to dance and get drink. I not know
folks. [*Noise of a volley.* BLANK *has just been executed.*
BAMBOOLA *falls to his knees.*] Not die. Always happy. I
not revolution. Good nigger know nothing.

The Generalissimo. It's a pity that you are such a col-
lector. What a fine collection of weapons they found in

your hovel—a hundred and forty-seven rifles, forty-eight revolvers, twelve machine guns!

Bamboola [losing his head]. Not mine. They other Bamboola. He came hide. [*He beats his head in despair.*]

The Generalissimo. Enough! You have a weakness for ammunition. You are going to get some. What have you to say in your defense?

Bamboola. Mercy! I denounce comrades! I join police! You kind, Boss!

The Generalissimo. Lawyer!

The Distinguished Counsel. Well, now! . . . He good nigger. And you kind Boss. He done nothing, seen nothing. He know nothing. However, rather than try to whitewash this black offender, I shall crave the indulgence of this tribunal, convinced that we are really concerned with a good nigger, for did you ever see a nigger who wasn't a good nigger? I have finished.

The Generalissimo. The legal penalty! [*The two* SOLDIERS *overcome the Negro and drag him yelling outside. Shouts, orders in the corridors.*] Next!

BANGER *comes in. He is wild. His shoulders are hunched aggressively.*

The Generalissimo. Another Minister? What a lame government we should have had with this one! [*Laughter.*]

Banger. To Hell!

The Generalissimo. And you too! You acknowledge taking part in . . .

Banger. To Hell!

The Generalissimo [furious]. What have you to say in your defense?

Banger. To Hell! And once again, to Hell!

The Generalissimo. That's not much. Lawyer, can you . . .

The Distinguished Counsel [to BANGER]. What am I to say in your defense, comrade?

Banger. Why, what I keep on saying.

The Distinguished Counsel [woebegone]. See, gentlemen, he doesn't know anything but his destination. I beg that you put no obstacle in his way.

Volley outside.

The Generalissimo. To the wall!

Banger [*thunderously*]. To Hell! [*He goes out laughing coarsely.*]

The Generalissimo. Stop that! Are there any more?

Enter calmly INNOCENTI.

The Generalissimo. Come here, man. Name? Profession?

Innocenti. Innocenti, waiter.

Confabulation between the GENERALISSIMO *and a member of the Council.*

The Generalissimo. Is that a false name?

Innocenti. Let us say so.

The Generalissimo. And you are not a waiter. You are a doctor of law and of the political and social sciences, and more than that, a former professor at the University. What the devil brings you before this tribunal, mixed up with these criminals and ignoramuses?

Innocenti. My convictions.

The Generalissimo. What! An intelligent man doesn't have such convictions. It's not credible. You are a revolutionary, then?

Innocenti [*unaffectedly*]. Yes, in the old style, in the style of those who have seen.

The Generalissimo. Don't speak like that. You worsen your case. [*Volley.*]

Innocenti [*shrugging his shoulders*]. My case is simple. There is no point in discussing it, Your Honor. You are on that side of the tribunal and I am on this. Nothing will make us change places. I don't want to take up your time. Do your job.

The Generalissimo. You are not serious, my friend. Do you really maintain that you were mixed up in this revolution?

Innocenti [*with dignity*]. I was involved in this revolution on principle, and because revolution is my sole ideal. I don't disguise the fact that I found it hateful and ridiculous. This revolution miscarried, as it was doomed to, and that has been a good thing for the revolutionary ideal. All that remains for me is to share the fate of my comrades—whom I despise a little, while still loving them a lot. Grant me their fate, Your Honor.

The Generalissimo [*disturbed*]. You are asking for death?

Innocenti. It will save me from the degrading act of

suicide. It is logical that I should die. Filled with hatred,
I should damage your society, in spite of everything.
Filled with hatred, I am unworthy to work for the ideal
revolution. It is better that I disappear with my hatred,
since from this hatred only hateful work can come, inhuman and destructive revolution. The triumph of noble
minds will never come. I am sure of that. Let it pass.

The Generalissimo. And . . . is that all? Think. Have
you nothing to ask?

Innocenti. Give me a cigarette.

The Generalissimo [*holding out his cigarette case*]. Here
you are. Lawyer, offer your services to this gentleman,
please.

Innocenti [*smoking, to the lawyer*]. Don't trouble yourself for me. Just tell me where I must report . . . to have
an operation for this illness. [*He taps his forehead.*]

The Distinguished Counsel [*bewildered*]. To the left,
sir.

Innocenti. Thank you. [*Cold and distant, he goes out.
There is a moment of troubled silence.*]

The Generalissimo. Painful. [*He sighs.*] The session is
concluded, gentlemen. [*The members of the Council stand
up.*] What can you expect? It's the same as in surgery:
when a limb is diseased . . . [*They all nod their heads and
make vague gestures.*] Gentlemen, it gives me great
pleasure to thank you. And you, lawyer, sir, have used
eloquence as discerning as it was choice—as the occasion
demanded of you.

The Distinguished Counsel [*bowing*]. I have done my
duty.

The Council is already dispersing when PANTAGLEIZE
comes in, led by CREEP, *who carries an umbrella, the case,
and the street lamp from Scene III. Bustle and curiosity.*

The Distinguished Counsel. It's all over. They're not
trying any more. You can see that.

Creep. We're set down for this session.

The Generalissimo. More? Couldn't you get here
earlier? Take your places again, gentlemen, and let us be
quick. [*The Council sits down again.*] What's this fellow?

Creep. A rare bird, Your Honor. It's Creep that says
it, and I've seen a few.

The Generalissimo. Ah, you are the famous Creep? My
congratulations. It seems that your conduct has been

superb. [*Flattering "Bravos" from the Council.* CREEP *bows.*] Let's look closer at your client. Creep, you must have made a mistake. It's a clown!

Creep [*offended*]. Tremble, Your Honor! You have before you the most dangerous person that there could be. Examine him well, full face, three-quarter view, and profile. [*Mysteriously.*] It was he who gave the signal for the revolution. [*Amazement of the tribunal.*]

Pantagleize. The revolution? But that's not going on now. It's over. [*The tribunal laughs.*]

The Generalissimo. Explain, Creep.

Creep [*in police fashion*]. Pantagleize! [*He sets up the street lamp.*] Do you recognize this illuminating device? Yes. Did you climb on it? Yes. And what did you say to the crowd from up on this street lamp?

Pantagleize. I said, "What a lovely day!" [*Sensation.*]

Creep. Afterward you received orders from a Jewess whom I had the pleasure of executing. You went to the bank.

Pantagleize. That's quite right. Will you give me my case back?

Creep. Then from the bank to the Revolutionary Committee. You were appointed Minister, and you made a speech.

Pantagleize. A remarkable speech. What has happened to my colleagues the Ministers, please?

Creep. Having been able to get away, you returned to the Jewess' where you laid hold of plans for the revolution. Here they are!

Pantagleize. I recognize those papers. They're of no interest.

The Generalissimo. You recognize them? It's really you?

Pantagleize. Why not? It's the truth. Certainly it's me. [*He feels himself.*] Is it really me? You make me doubt. Yes, it's me and no mistake.

Creep. It's you. Do you recognize this object? [*He waves the umbrella that* PANTAGLEIZE *lost in the morning, during the scuffle on the promenade.*]

Pantagleize. My dear umbrella! Where did I leave it? My most grateful thanks! [*He takes the umbrella and presses it to him. The tribunal is puzzled.*]

The Generalissimo. Baffling! Our records don't say anything about this man. [*Worried.*] Pantagleize, are you a revolutionary?

Pantagleize. No, Your Honor. I write for a fashion magazine.

The Generalissimo. Then . . . explain. . . . What have you done? What do you know?

Pantagleize [*having rubbed his eyes*]. What have I done? I wonder. Have we time to wonder what we do? Does anyone really know what he does here? What do I know? I know that I know nothing. And when you know, do you know whether what you know is what you need to know? [*He laughs.*] What I know is that it's time to go to bed. It was this gentleman [*indicates* CREEP] who so much wanted you to know me. Since we are here, I shall make you some confessions. I am distressed. Distressed at having such a complicated destiny. Put a stupid phrase, an eclipse, a woman, and some treasure into a sack, shake them up, and out comes my destiny. I feel shrunk. I have left my philosophical heights. I used to fly very high, and here I am floundering on the common road. My noble philosopher's cloak is splashed with blood. Ah, gentlemen! [*Volley.*] You hear that noise? That's how people amuse themselves [*yawns*] on such a peaceful night!

The Generalissimo. Good, good! Now, to go back. You used this phrase? Did you know what it signified?

Pantagleize. It didn't signify anything at all to me. That's why I said it. It's my custom to be witty, rather than to say commonplace things.

The Distinguished Counsel. This can't go on. You have a lunatic before you, gentlemen.

The Generalissimo. You think so? For myself, I find him quite sound, even formidable.

The Distinguished Counsel. Let us avoid a judicial error. This man doesn't understand anything. He is the plaything of really terrible coincidences. A degree of innocence . . .

Pantagleize [*to the lawyer*]. You seem to be saying that I'm an imbecile.

The Distinguished Counsel. The word is an overstatement. A little simple, rather.

The Generalissimo. These lawyers! Pleading absence of responsibility! That's easy. But at that rate we have been trying nothing but irresponsibles.

The Distinguished Counsel. I say that this individual is stupid.

The Generalissimo. I maintain that this individual is acting stupidly.

Pantagleize. I am going to reconcile you. What is the issue? Being stupid, or acting as though stupid? Everything is relative. You can't see yourself, and you can't make yourself either. I am Pantagleize. What is Pantagleize? According to some, a qualified imbecile, according to others, a superman. And what do I think of myself? Philosopher, journalist, lover, rioter, robber, minister, multimillionaire? I am what? An imbecile? No. A failure —because love is missing! She is dead. Gentlemen, she is all twisted up and bleeding. And young girls should not die that way.

The Distinguished Counsel. You see! I demand to be heard!

The Generalissimo. Enough! You are trying to mislead us. The best jokes are the shortest. Pantagleize, we think that society wouldn't lose much if it lost you.

Pantagleize. Society, gentlemen! I was going to bid it farewell, without any thought of returning.

The Generalissimo. Then . . . bon voyage! [*He laughs mockingly and stands up.*] I think, gentlemen, the prescribed . . . [*His voice trails away. The members of the Council rise and, following their president, disappear behind the table.*]

Pantagleize [*standing crestfallen*]. They have a way of dropping the conversation. Will someone explain?

The Distinguished Counsel [*to* PANTAGLEIZE]. My dear client . . . you said very appropriately, "Everything is relative." [*He shakes his hand.*]

Pantagleize [*smiling*]. Which is the way out?

Creep [*pushing him to the left*]. That way. Haven't you anything else to ask?

Pantagleize. The time.

Creep [*takes out his watch*]. A quarter to midnight.

Pantagleize. Thank you. We certainly jostled each other a bit, but we're still good friends, aren't we? [*He shakes* CREEP's *hand.*] Good-by. I'll send you a post card. The way out? [*One of the* SOLDIERS *pushes him to the left.*] Good-by, gentlemen. [*He disappears.*]

CREEP *and the lawyer look at each other, tap their foreheads with their forefingers and burst out laughing.*

The Distinguished Counsel [*putting his hat on*]. Well,

that's the day over. Lovely day! Hey, soldier! Duty finished! That song, how did it go again?

The First Soldier [*singing*].

This soldier boy we knew

The Second Soldier.

Wrote to this girl we know,

The First Soldier.

"I'm coming back to you,

The Second Soldier.

No more to war I'll go."

Soldiers, Counsel and Creep [*going out*].

Won't you come back, my love so true,
And cuddle me as you used to do?

All goes black as the volley from the firing squad rings out.

EPILOGUE
[ad libitum]

A barrack yard. Night. A wall. Above the wall, a luminous mist rising from the town. Two hanging lanterns throw a sinister light on the ground. Four bodies lie against the wall. They look like fallen scarecrows. THE OFFICER, wrapped in a long cloak and carrying a lantern, moves about among the bodies, momentarily lighting each one up. A shadow glides in. It is THE GENERALISSIMO. THE OFFICER starts.

THE GENERALISSIMO. Lieutenant!

The Officer. Who goes there?

The Generalissimo. Come here.

The Officer [*comes*]. General!

The Generalissimo. They have been executed?

The Officer. Here they are. [*He indicates the wall.*]

The Generalissimo. How did they die?

The Officer [*with a high-pitched laugh*]. It was comical to see, sir. You would have thought they were puppets on strings. They moved about like dancers or sleep-walkers. Oh, a man's soon done for! And here they are, dead in the cause of . . .

The Generalissimo. I do not require you to supply an epitaph.

The Officer [*with a sickly smile*]. At your command, sir!

The Generalissimo. Where is your squad?

The Officer. Dismissed. I thought it was over for to-night.

The Generalissimo. Get them back.

The Officer [*shouting*]. Sound the fall in!

Voice of a Soldier. Bugler, the fall in!

THE GENERALISSIMO *goes out. A distant bugle sounds the fall in. A* SOLDIER *comes in on the right.*

The Officer. Where's the man?

The Soldier. Behind me.

The Officer. Wait for the squad. I'll be back. [*He goes out.*]

Pause. THE SOLDIER *yawns.*

Voice of Pantagleize. This way? You can hardly see. I can see less and less. Soldier, which is the way out?

The Soldier. Come along, friend. It's not far.

Voice of Pantagleize. I'm cold. It's a lovely night, but it's frosty.

The Soldier. Are you frightened of getting cold? [*He laughs at his joke.*] Walk around a bit.

PANTAGLEIZE *comes in, armed with his umbrella.*

Pantagleize. That's good advice. Walking makes you warm. When am I going to get out of this maze? Yes, I'll walk around. It's good in the open air. Which way did my friends go out, soldier? That way?

The Soldier. Yes. Go on. You'll meet them. [THE SOLDIER *moves away.*]

Pantagleize [*advances with his arms out, like a blind man*]. How black it is. How can you find your way out in this darkness? I feel as though I'm shut up, and yet I'm free. By God, I'm cold! [*He turns up his collar.*] Even though I'm sweating! And what a smell there is here! The same smell I've noticed before. [*He rubs his eyes.*] And how I want to sleep! It's overwhelming, having a destiny: it weighs heavy. Still, courage! Especially now that I'm going to take a long journey, far away. Not a honeymoon, eh? One of these journeys you only make once: where the land you discover is so wonderful that it is no longer possible to come back. I've completely made up my mind. You won't see me again. This is my last night in Europe. Afterward, the ocean, the infinite, another world, another Heaven, another earth. Rest, yes, on a peaceful island like an old cemetery with birds and crumbling monuments. [*He bumps against a body.*] Who's there? [*He leans down.*] Ho! Men? It's you, my friends! What? Asleep? Collapsed like exhausted beasts! Yes. After today! I am going to sleep like you. No. I shan't do like you. Sleep. I must go. I shall leave you. I asked you to follow me. You are not men of good will; but I love you. I still love you in spite of your weakness. I won't forget you. [*He walks around among the bodies, stepping over them.*] What are you dreaming of in your sleep? You would think you were fighting, making gestures of fear and repulsion. Do you hate each other? The fight is over, friends. All is finished. . . . [*He looks at them.*] At least for you who have arrived at the end of your journey. What was the goal? This wall? Aren't you going any farther? Aren't you going to get up again? My poor friends, it wasn't worth dreaming such things and uttering such fine words. Here you are, done for. What was the good? I'm almost tempted to stay with you, to sleep your absurd sleep with you, lost in the equalitarian darkness. [*He moves away from the bodies.*] We must part. It smells evil here. It smells of warm meat. I don't want to live with these memories any longer, with these sleeping men . . . and Rachel. No. I'm going. [*The approaching march of the squad is heard.*] I shall never again say that the day is lovely. I shall never again bother myself with eclipses, or with my destiny. . . .

A Voice. Squad, halt!

Pantagleize. All that remains is for me to find the way out—or to get over the wall. Someone's coming! [*He listens.*] Soldiers! [*He goes to the wall and scrambles up on it.*]

THE OFFICER *has come in and has seen him.*

The Officer. Well, my friend!

Pantagleize [*on the wall*]. I beg your pardon?

The Officer. You've dropped your umbrella.

Pantagleize [*pleased*]. Have I, indeed? [*He jumps from the wall and grabs his umbrella.*] Thank you, officer. How absent-minded one can get! Since you are so obliging, could you show me a more practical way out?

The Officer [*laughing*]. Certainly! Right in front of you!

Pantagleize [*bowing*]. Thank you. I don't see it. There's only a wall.

The Officer. It's there. Feel for it. [*Harshly.*] Squad, present!

Pantagleize [*turning around*]. What? Guns? [*He runs to* THE OFFICER.] Are you going to hurt my friends? [*He sinks down, crushed with emotion.*]

The Officer. Fire! [*Discharge. Flash. Silence.*] Order arms! [*Noise of rifle butts on the ground.*] Fall out! [*Laughter. Noise of the squad breaking away.* THE OFFICER *looks at* PANTAGLEIZE.] Twelve of them! And as for his wits, I don't think he had five of them, poor devil! [*He lights a cigarette, walks around, then suddenly stops, attentive.*]

Pantagleize [*in a choking voice*]. Oh! Oh! The sky has fallen on my head! [*He supports himself on his elbows.*] I've been damaged somewhere. Friends, that's decided it. I'll stay and go to sleep near you. [*He tries to drag himself toward the bodies, but falls.*]

The Officer [*leaning over* PANTAGLEIZE]. You not dead?

Pantagleize. Who's speaking? Good evening, sir. I am Pantagleize. I've been injured a bit, you see. Miss Rachel Silber . . . whatever it is must be told. A nice girl who loves me. So beautiful, so disturbing, so upsetting, so sorrowful that you would say she was humanity itself.

The Officer. Here we are! [*He fires a revolver shot into the back of* PANTAGLEIZE's *neck.* PANTAGLEIZE *is still.*]

Pantagleize [*in a voice both gruesome and childish*]. What . . . a . . . lovely . . . day! [*He dies.*]

THE OFFICER *sheathes his revolver. He laughs dully. The lights go out. Twelve strikes from a church.*

And the farce to make you sad is finished.

THE BLIND MEN
(*Les Aveugles*)

A Morality in One Act after Breughel the Elder
(1933)

Translated by GEORGE HAUGER

INTRODUCTORY NOTE

. . . . So, in spite of its small size—but what does that mean?—[Pieter] Breughel's painting entitled "The Parable of the Blind Men" had left me with so intense a recollection that after many years, in 1933, I transposed this touching pictorial anecdote to the theatre, in a few hours and with great ease.

From *The Ostend Interviews*

CHARACTERS

The three men, blind from birth, making their way to Rome as pilgrims:

De Witte	names which	White
De Strop	would have	Gallows Bird
Den Os	as equivalents in English	Bullock

The one-eyed man, king of the ditch country, otherwise the country of the blind, Lamprido

Scene—On a road in old Brabant, not far from the capital city.

THE BLIND MEN

A song is heard. Pilgrims are coming along the road. Their song is rather slow, although howled by men in good health. The pilgrims are, in fact, blind men who proceed by groping with their staffs and holding onto the edge of each other's cloaks. This is their marching song:

Congaudeant catholici
Letentur cives celici
Die ista

The pilgrims halt.

DE WITTE [*singing the last words*]. Die ista . . . [*Speaking.*] Well! Me, I'm stopping. If our pilgrim's song pleases God, it doesn't soften the flints on the road, and my feet are bleeding and my throat is as dry as the crater of a volcano.

De Strop. We've got to stop, because when one of us three stops, all three of us have got to stop, and when one sings, all three have got to sing, and when one walks, all three walk. What a fate!

Den Os. What a fate! Walking a road whose end we can't see, and singing a lament whose Latin we don't understand! Comrades in misery, I propose whining—all three of us, with all our might. Perhaps someone in the clouds or on the earth will hear us. Let us whine!

All Three [*discordantly*]. Miserere! Miserere! Miserere!

A Voice [*in the distance*]. Miserere!

De Witte. Did you hear? [*Silence. They listen.*] Nothing more.

De Strop. I seemed to hear . . . It's hunger and thirst —above all, thirst—that are disturbing our senses.

Den Os. I heard! Do you know what it is? The echo! I'm going to put it to the test. Either it's the devil mocking us and he won't reply, or else it's the completely

227

genuine echo and it will reply, because I'm going to rouse
it religiously.

De Witte. Yes. Sing mass to it.

Den Os [*singing*]. Ky-y-y-y-y-y-y-rie.

All Three. Listen!

The Voice [*in the distance, completing the plain chant*].
Elei-i-son.

De Witte. That's not from a devil! It's an echo, a true
echo, unquestionably an echo from a convent.

Den Os. If this echo would give us alms, or even a pot
of brown ale!

De Strop. No more despair! Our pains, our hunger,
our thirst are going to finish. I know it. Will you hear
the good news? I can see it more clearly than you.

De Witte. Twofold liar! You were born blind like us.

Den Os. Threefold liar! You are the blindest of the
three of us. All the same, tell us this good news.

De Strop. Friends of my sorrow, hear it: we are no
longer far from Rome!

The Other Two. Oh! oh! . . . Oh! oh! oh! . . . Oh!
oh! oh! oh!

De Strop. Haven't you felt the sun getting warmer? We
have been walking for seven weeks. Well, here you are:
we have just heard an echo, an echo that sings mass. In
Flanders, where everything is flat, there is no echo to
speak of. In the mountains, there are echoes. We are in
the mountains! And that painter who painted us not so
long ago and who had been in Italy, didn't he tell us
that we would have to cross the mountains? What was
that painter called, the rum chap who gave us a florin?

De Witte. Breughel, I think.

De Strop. That was his name all right, Breughel. He
maintained that once the mountains were crossed we
wouldn't be far from Rome.

Den Os. He also said that we could go along without
fear or worry, that we would finish up by getting there
in the end, for all roads lead to Rome.

De Strop. Alleluia! We are going to see the dome of
Saint Peter's!

Den Os. Alleluia! We are going to see the Pope in person, and he will work a miracle. He will give us back
our eyes!

De Witte. Alleluia! We are going to see a number of

marvels . . . or we are going to see nothing at all. What is certain is that Rome is the most stunning city in Christendom, and that we shall drink immeasurably there, and eat enormously there, and sleep there, and dance there. I have it on good authority that the Romans are joyful by nature and friends of pleasure. And we shall never go back to Flanders again. I shall settle myself on the steps of the basilica and there I shall finish my days, in the sun.

De Strop. Hey, you wicked parishioner! We shall do what the holy Pope orders us to do.

Den Os. Perhaps he will want us to press on as far as Jerusalem.

De Witte. Or perhaps, when he has seen us, he will advise us to go back to our own country.

De Strop. Quiet! Prick up your ears, quick!

A distant carillon is heard.

Den Os. Well now! Bells in a tower? The bells of Rome!

De Witte. Don't be crazy. It's a carillon: and it's playing a tune I know, a song they sing in the markets at home.

De Strop. I am going to tell you the truth of the matter. It is the famous carillon at Rome. When the Pope heard that three Flemish pilgrims were arriving, he had a tune from Flanders played in our honor. Listen to it, now!

All Three [*singing the tune with the carillon*]. La . . . la . . . la . . . Bing . . . bong . . . La . . . la . . . la . . . Bing . . . bang . . . bong . . . [*Shouting.*] Ring out, holy bells! Ring out for those from Flanders! Here we are! Long live Rome and its thousand churches!

De Strop. How touching it is to hear the songs of our old country in a strange land!

De Witte. You would think you were hearing the carillon at Bruges, where I was born.

Den Os. More likely the one in the proud belfry at Ghent, my noble city.

De Strop. It's exactly the one at Antwerp, that place rolling in money, where I saw daylight.

All three weep discordantly.

The Voice [*laughing heartily, in the distance*]. Ha, ha, ha, ha, ha. ha!

De Witte. Do you hear? Laughter on the skyline! What a marvelous country this Italy is. While we weep, the echoes wear a beatific smile! Then let us laugh!

All Three [*laughing*]. Ha, ha, ha, ha, ha, ha, ha, ha!

De Strop. This humor is not the only wonderful thing. Look at these high snowy summits, now, from which we shall pick out the cupolas and the steeples of the Eternal City.

Den Os. Rather, sniff these strange scents. The flowers smell of incense, I swear it!

De Witte. And I see by a sundial that it is time to set off on the road again. Let us walk and sing. Who's going first? Me! I want to be the first to enter the mystic city.

Den Os. It will be me! I can see better than you.

De Strop. Why not me, the least blind of the three of us?

Den Os. Come on! Let's hold each other by the cloak and tap with our staffs in time with each other.

They walk and sing.

All Three. Plenus pulchris carminibu
Studeat atque cantibus
Die ista

The Voice. Die ista . . .

De Witte. Stop! The echo no longer has the same voice. Which cardinal point is it working from?

De Strop. Haven't we gone back on our tracks instead of going toward Rome?

Den Os. That would be dreadful. I propose to question the echo. Since it knows Latin, it must know geography. I take it upon myself. [*Solemnly.*] Lord Echo, deign to reply to three blind men who are seeking their way. Where are you, subtle Echo?

Voice of Lamprido. In a tree, from which I shall come down to please you. I am a voice mounted on legs, and I shall come to you.

De Strop. I had a presentiment of this: it's a man. So much the better. He will give us alms. I see who is coming. It's a tall man with a round hat.

De Witte. It's a little man with a square hat.

Den Os. Be quiet! It's a tall man who has become little because he's humpbacked like a crane, and his hat is only a cap with badges sewn on it.

Lamprido [*entering*]. Here I am, my good men!

All Three [*taking up the attitudes of beggars and chanting in high-pitched voices*]. Here he is, the sweet Christian! Have pity on poor blind men, renowned sinners; have pity on broken-down pilgrims pilgrimaging in this vale of tears!

Lamprido. Yes, I shall have pity on blind pilgrimaging sinners. [*He laughs.*]

Den Os. Why is he laughing. [*Furious.*] Who are you?

Lamprido. I am Lord Lamprido, king of the ditch country, a wise man who stays perched in a tree instead of stupidly tramping to a Rome which you will never reach. You seek alms? I am going to give you apples, pears, plums, peaches, honey, duck eggs.

De Strop. None of that! We want money!

Lamprido. You won't get that in the slightest; but I can give you advice and my help, which you most certainly have need of.

De Witte. We have no need of your help, nor of your advice. Quite blind as we are, all three of us, we can see clearly enough.

Lamprido. Arrogant man! Do you know what place you are in?

De Witte. We know. We are in the high mountains, on the fringe of the plain of Rome.

Lamprido. Good Lord! Listen to that!

Den Os. Yes, yes. We are blind, not deaf. It was the chimes of Rome.

Lamprido. You simpletons! You are in the ditch country. You have got to believe me because I have the advantage over you of seeing with one eye; for I am one-eyed, but one eye is enough. There are a lot of blind men in the ditch country, where I am king, me, the sharp-sighted with one eye.

All Three [*noisily*]. Ho, ho! He's a cripple! Ha, ha! And he says he's sharp-sighted! Hee, hee! And he maintains that we're not near Rome!

Den Os. Off with you, one-eyed king! We don't want anything to do with you. You are a cheat, and your ditch country doesn't exist. Our long staffs have eyes and describe the appearance of the countryside to us. Get out of here, or we shall beat you!

The Other Two. Yes, beat him. Arrah!

The three of them lash out in all directions.

De Strop. Who's hitting me?

Den Os. You murderer! It's me you're hitting!

De Witte. I'm being beaten! Oh!

Lamprido. What a tragic mistake! They are beating each other and becoming woebegone about it. Hit away with zest, my blind fellows! No? You are stopping? Yes, be peaceable. Now, listen to me: I am going to do you a kindness.

The Three [*whining in chorus*]. Have pity on poor blind men condemned to make pilgrimage for their sins.

Lamprido. Not a stiver, not a brass farthing! Your breaths tell me fairly enough that you are passionately fond of ale. Listen, I want charitably to turn you away from threatening misfortune. [*Pause. The three listen, mouths agape.*] The sun is setting; the purple mist is rising. For weeks now, I have seen you travel backward and forward along the same roads, which do not lead to Rome at all. You haven't left Brabant, and the bells you hear are those in the belfry of Saint Nicholas at Brussels. With my solitary pupil I can pick out from here the city ramparts, the towers of Saint Gudule, and the fabulous warrior Saint Michael, all aflame on his white stone spire.

Den Os. It's disgraceful, making game of three dim-sighted wretches.

De Witte. It's all lies! It's not midday, and it's weeks now since we left the Low Countries.

De Strop. Take care, Lamprido! You are wicked. We shall denounce you to the Pope. Comrades, isn't this a highway robber who's going to injure us?

Lamprido. I tell you for the last time, you are in the ditch country and your path overhangs marshes and flooded meadows. One false step and you vanish. Soon darkness will come down. I am going to take you by the hand and lead you to the shelter of the abbey, where you will pass the night. There is a timely act of charity for you, and the only one I am willing to perform.

De Witte. Let's have done! On our way! And leave this stupid fellow to his rambling.

De Strop. Although we're blind, we have some dignity. See us accept help from someone with one eye! Let's enter Rome this very evening.

Lamprido. Go on! Enter Rome! But take care beforehand to commend your souls and your bodies to Providence. Those who won't take the word of the one-eyed man are blind a hundred times over. [*He gets angry.*] All roads lead to death! [*He laughs derisively.*] Wishing well for one's neighbors is only one more vanity along with the rest! On your way!

The Three. On our way!

De Strop. Good-by, one-eyed man, and thank you for your charity.

Den Os. Good-by, king of ditches, king of frogs and tadpoles!

De Witte. Good-by, driveling echo! Climb back into your tree and preach to the owls. It's time, friends: on our way! And hold my cloak.

Den Os. I'm holding a cloak, hold mine. Who's leading the way?

De Strop. Eastward, straight ahead!

Lamprido. You are going westward, straight into stinking mud, into oblivion. Go on!

The Three. Make way for the glorious pilgrims from Flanders! [*They press on and pass into the distance, and their song rings out.*]

> Haec est dies laudabilis
> Divina luce nobilis . . .

> [*Their song breaks off.*]

Voices of the Three Blind Men. Help! Don't push me! Don't pull me! Lamprido! Help! it's water! Mercy upon us! I'm sinking! I'm drowning! Jesus! Save us! [*More cries are heard, then the last gasps, and the voices are silent.*]

Lamprido. I can do nothing for them. The ditches are so deep. The blind men won't sing any more, and they have come to the end of their road. My brothers, rest in peace, in the old slime from which all men are fashioned. Night is coming on. I am going to get back into my tree where, among the sleeping birds, I shall pray for your souls, blind men, poor blind men. . . . [*He goes.*]

The carillon rings joyfully on the border of twilight.

CHRONICLES OF HELL
(*Fastes d'Enfer*)

A Tragedy *Bouffe* in One Act
(1929)

Translated by GEORGE HAUGER

INTRODUCTORY NOTE

. . . . There is also the bishop in *Chronicles of Hell*—a person raised from the dead who has kicked up a great deal of row, who has upset a great number of people. I am very pleased about it, although I never thought of the possible scandal—so little so that, convinced that it would be long before it was played, I had given this "dangerous" one-act play the form of an oral symphony. It was a kind of dramatic poem of epic inspiration, but all the same (and because I was a man of the theatre) it contained its scenic architecture, equilibrium, and propulsion.

From *The Ostend Interviews*

CHARACTERS

JAN IN EREMO, *Bishop of Lapideopolis*
VENERANDA, *a servant*
SIMON LAQUEDEEM, *auxiliary bishop*
SODOMATI, *the nuncio's secretary*
KRAKENBUS, *vicar-general*
REAL-TREMBLOR, *archdeacon*
DOM PIKKEDONCKER, *pleban (rural dean)*
CARNIBOS, *chaplain*
DUVELHOND, *guardian of the holy relics*
THE MASTER OF THE BUTCHERS
THE BUTCHERS
AN ARQUEBUSIER
FOUR SWISS
THE CROWD

SCENE—A decaying episcopal palace in bygone FLANDERS, around which an invisible and threatening crowd snarls persistently during the whole of this tragedy. At the back, a wide double door, framed between columns that support a pediment, and reached by some steps. There is a Gothic doorway to the left, and farther downstage a low and narrow exit. To the right, a glass bay window looking onto the public square, through which breaks the morbid light of a stormy summer dusk. Tapestries hang in shreds on the walls, to which portraits of prelates are fastened, very high up. Everywhere at the base of the walls there are piles of baroque objects, idols, suns, witches' masks, multicolored devils, totems, stakes, and instruments of torture. But in the foreground stands a heavy table with a crimson velvet cloth, sumptuously laden with silver plate and crystal.

CHRONICLES OF HELL

The chaplain goes around the table shiftily, stealing pieces of meat and swallowing them, while the vicar-general, who has taken up position on the steps at the back, looks through the keyhole.

CARNIBOS. Yum . . . yum . . . I'm nibbling . . . yum . . . I've done nothing! Mutton! Good! Veal! Lovely! Yum, yum, yum. . . . What hunger, what hunger! Nibble here, nibble there, oop! It's the first time so much meat has been seen at the palace. For twenty years, eh, Krakenbus? I've withered. You fed yourself on the fat in your hump, didn't you? Never any meat! I used to cry *Miserere nobis!* each day. Never, while in the town they used to set up altars in the market, bearing tottering sacrifices of rich red meats—used to hang up huge oxen, droves of them . . . Ho! Krakenbus, I saw that, and the skinny people, so skinny they frightened you, like me, murmured yum, yum, yum, before these tantalizing displays! . . . [*He puffs.*] What time are we going to eat, Krakenbus, or is this a show table that will be carried away, load and all? I'm hungry! Say nothing, since you haven't seen what I haven't done. I was setting the cold meats in order! [*He is seized by a violent cough.*] Swallowed the wrong way . . . so . . . Ach! Ouf! [*He spits a piece of meat into his hand.*] Yum! [*And eats it again.*]

Krakenbus [*who has stopped spying, gazes at this scene*]. Heaven has punished you, ravener! This clacking of your jaws is a profanation, Carnibos, a scandal! And the only thing that can be heard of your prayers, Carnibos, is yum, yum, yum. . . . Stop, you devourer! When there's nothing else left, you'll swallow the knives and the cloth. . . . Your sin—

Carnibos. My illness, not my sin! Look, Krakenbus, a chicken. Ho, this leg! [*With his mouth full.*] Those who have a stomach, eat; those who have a hump, glue themselves to keyholes.

Krakenbus [*who has come close to the table*]. It's a pious service that I perform! Take care, my hump contains a second brain, and venom! . . . I am as spiteful as I am humped, as humped as I am spiteful, meat thief! You shall suffer! You shall eat your dirty feet, your knotted guts, your spongy heart! You shall trim yourself to the bone. Put that fowl back in its place and go and wash your hands, your sticky hands. Lick those hands whose marks one finds on sacred cloths that are polluted forevermore. . . .

Carnibos [*humble*]. Yes, reverend hump. My punishment! I once dreamed I was on all fours eating refuse in a charnel house. Yum, yum, yum . . . But tell me, dear doctor of humpology, is what we do in our dreams reckoned against us?

Krakenbus. No, it all depends, chaplain. Yes indeed, when one's head is full of sticky water, greenish pus, like yours. [*He laughs unpleasantly.*] Gnaw your nails, which are too long, as well, chaplain. There are little worms under them. And close your lipless mouth, chaplain. Your breath breeds violet flies. . . . [*He is close to* CARNIBOS.] You will confess these foul dreams to me. I demand it. . . . No? [*With a sudden stamp of his heel, he crushes* CARNIBOS' *foot.*]

Carnibos. Ow!

Krakenbus. Suffer in silence! And let me have your other foot! I'm going to bruise it in its turn; one pain may drive out the other. . . . No? [*In a smooth voice.*] Talking about feet, I have just seen something philosophical. [*Drawing close to* CARNIBOS.] Sorry yet, glutton? [*He lays hold of a slice of meat.*] Open your mouth! [*And he puts the meat in.*] Give thanks, cockroach! Thanks!

Carnibos [*devouring it*]. Thanks, holy hump! . . . Ivory hump! . . . Miraculous hump! . . . [*Having finished, he puffs.*] This spectacle? You must teach me to watch through keyholes. . . . Which eye does one use? Left? Right? They say that in time one's eye becomes shaped like a keyhole. I prefer eavesdropping. There! See my ear, a delicate shell. . . .

*The two priests have gone toward the back and have
stopped on the steps leading to the double door.*

Krakenbus. Bend down, look, and not with half an eye.
Look with all your eyes, for you will never again see
anything like it!

Carnibos [*watching through the keyhole*]. Yum, yum,
yum!

Krakenbus. What do you see?

Carnibos. Meat! Nothing but meat! A hairy bear. No,
it has feet. It's a man. [*Standing upright.*] A dead man!

Krakenbus. Right! And what is a dead man?

Carnibos. Meat.

Krakenbus. No, chaplain. A dead man is two feet! A
human being has to be dead for anyone to notice that
he has feet. I like seeing dead people. And I've seen some!
Men, women too. But never, I swear, was it given to me to
see a dead person like this one! Like this one!

Carnibos. You couldn't say he's naked, hairy as he is.
[*Chuckles.*] A moral in that? When men die, they are
chucked into lime. Beasts? Carved up and eaten. As for
game, it's decently buried, so that it takes on its flavor.
[*He pushes* KRAKENBUS *who has begun spying again.*]

Krakenbus [*standing up, hustles the chaplain*]. The dead
man is still warm. Cross yourself, dipping crumbs!

Carnibos. After you. . . . [*He avoids* KRAKENBUS, *who
is seeking to crush his foot with a stamp of the heel.*] Hi!
My feet are alive. Peace!

Krakenbus. Peace! . . . Let us embrace.

*They go toward each other to embrace, lower their heads,
and bang their foreheads together. Double laughter. The
pleban enters from the left.*

Dom Pikkedoncker. He, he, and I . . .

Carnibos. And the dead man make four.

Krakenbus. A dead man is nobody. Good evening,
pleban.

Dom Pikkedoncker. They told me they were sounding
passing bells, and I couldn't hear them at all, not at all.
. . . Poor, yes. . . . For a bishop—Holy Virgin!—they
should ring royally! Ding-dang-dongs well struck. Not
thin-mouthed bells, great thick-lipped ones that go

[*motion of pulling the rope*] boo-oo-oom! . . . Boo-oo-oom! . . . I'm sweating from it!

Krakenbus. You are an old fool, Dom Pikkedoncker!

Dom Pikkedoncker [*putting a trumpet to his right ear*]. What did you say?

Krakenbus. I pledge my word that a bishop may not be worth a chime of pots and pans! [*Mocking.*] That talks of setting the great bells ringing, and it wouldn't hear the walls of Jericho fall.

Carnibos [*pulling* Krakenbus' *sleeve*]. Take care of the deaf one! . . . He hears nothing of what you shout and overhears everything you whisper.

Dom Pikkedoncker. Exactly. I shall say that display, whose custom is falling into disuse, is necessary. I love ceremony. Even Hell displays such. . . .

Krakenbus. He has been there. . . .

Dom Pikkedoncker [*who has heard*]. Yes. . . . To buy a place there for you, in a noxious dungeon where you will crush slugs, krak, krak, Krakenbus! . . . [*Shaken by laughter.*] And the deceased? . . .

Carnibos. They're rigging it out in priestly fashion. You'll have display! . . . It's the rule. For myself, I'm of the opinion that a sack was enough. . . .

Dom Pikkedoncker [*counting.*] So many candles, so many succentors, so many clerics. . . . A coffin of some size will be needed, you know. . . .

Carnibos. I say a sack would do!

Dom Pikkedoncker. Such a body! What did he weigh? And dead, twice as much as when alive. . . . What were you saying?

Krakenbus. You trickster! Is this trumpet at your ear for listening to thoughts?

Dom Pikkedoncker. A marvelous little horn, my friends, made by a renowned physician, and with which I hear all I want, and even what I don't want. A dead man would be less deaf than me, my friends. Try it. Tell me something!

Krakenbus. How is your rural deanery, dear rural dean?

Dom Pikkedoncker. Not bad, I say. . . .

Carnibos. Do you hear music as well? Listen. . . . [*He sings into the trumpet.*]

That old man Noah one day
Had drunk more than his fill.

I heard his daughter say—
She who liked him ill—

Dom Pikkedoncker [*singing*].

"I'll have the breeches off the fool!
Come, sister dear, and help me pull."

Be quiet! If God had a trumpet like mine! . . . Do you hear bells, at last, bells? [*He lays hold of a knife and strikes the crystal glasses on the table.*] Ting . . . tang . . . Saint Donatus'! Clang, Saint Walburga's! Her name is Maria. . . .

Krakenbus [*who has meanwhile filled several glasses*]. What of it? No. Glasses, I empty them, I do. . . . [*He drinks.*]

Carnibos [*drinking*]. I no longer say yum, yum, but glug, glug. . . .

Dom Pikkedoncker [*drinking*]. Believe me, brethren, I'm in favor of bells and towers, square towers crammed with bells. There are not enough towers being built, there are not enough bells being cast, and that is why religion is losing its allure. When Flanders is bristling all over with towers, Jesus will enter the cities of stone and bronze to the sound of the chimes. And not along the streets, no! He will walk on the towers. . . . [*Senile laugh.*] I'm not drunk, not at all. You will be, today. A great day for the lesser clergy, isn't that so? Wine! Tell me, what did we come here to do?

Krakenbus. To cry! When the shepherd is gone, the sheep go baa-aa! Bleat! Let us bleat! . . .

Carnibos. May the Most High bring it about that the new shepherd does not molest his flock and that he wields a crook rather than a bludgeon! What did we come to do? I know: eat! This light repast is for the vigil. In three days, the triumphal banquet! Then . . . then will be the time for ringing the bells, the great bells. The occasion? Eating in this palace! Starving priests who have come running in packs from all the parishes! Historic day! One used to eat on the sly in this place. I used to go and eat in the privy. . . .

Dom Pikkedoncker. Already? . . . I hear them rumbling, the priests, their innards . . .

Carnibos. It's the crowd gathering.

Dom Pikkedoncker. What does it expect, to eat as well?

Krakenbus. The crowd expects a corpse, a corpse to gaze at. Death, the sight of death, what more gorgeous!

DUVELHOND *has come in and, with hands outstretched, he goes toward the other three.*

Duvelhond. Mi—mi—miserere! D—D—Death is ne—is ne—is never. . . .

Carnibos [*imitating him*]. Who's this? The guar—guar —guardian of the holy relics? [*And as* DUVELHOND *stands with mouth agape, the chaplain thrusts in a piece of meat.*] Swallow it!

Duvelhond [*choking*]. Ah! . . . Ouf! . . . Pfaugh! . . . Ouf! . . . Ah!

Dom Pikkedoncker. Listen to the stammerer! He's giving His Highness' funeral oration! As a deaf man, I find it eloquent.

Krakenbus. That? Already on the way to hew relics from His Highness' remains? They're yours, Duvelhond, yours. . . . His hair, his nails . . .

Carnibos. His last gasp. . . . The last gasp that he belched up. . . .

Dom Pikkedoncker. What?

Carnibos. Oh, worthy of him! One didn't expect less of His Highness in that supreme moment. What was the word? No, I shan't tell it to you, not me!

Krakenbus. Nor me! Why are you growing pale, pleban? Could you have heard this word in your wooden ear?

Dom Pikkedoncker. The thickest walls must have heard it. It's your hump that's growing pale, vicar. And your rat's snout, chaplain. Candle color . . .

Carnibos. I'm pale with hunger, yum!

Duvelhond [*interposing*]. His High—Highness said as he died . . .

Krakenbus [*crushing* DUVELHOND's *foot with a swift stamp of the heel.*] Deo gratias!

Carnibos. Quick! He has two feet!

Duvelhond [*limping and moaning, makes off to the left, shaking his fists*]. Curse you!

He bumps into a newcomer, REAL-TREMBLOR, *whom he almost knocks over.*

Duvelhond. Look out! . . . Your fee—eet! . . . Krak— Krak—

The rest and the newcomer laugh unrestrainedly. Crest-fallen, DUVELHOND *comes back.*

Real-Tremblor. I'm not laughing, you know. . . . [*Hilariously.*] Ho, ho! And in a mortuary! Ho, ho! My feet . . . [*in consternation*] . . . bore me to this place, which is made majestic by the presence . . .

Krakenbus. Of rhetoric? Good evening, archdeacon. Good evening is what is wished.

Real-Tremblor. Good evening, your reverends. . . . A thousand pardons, I was upset. . . . Have you slept these last nights of His Highness' great death agony? The knells that nothing could assuage! . . . The public lamentations! . . . And the august deceased, tell me, have you seen him? . . .

Carnibos. Come here, Real-Tremblor. Why are you quaking?

Real-Tremblor. Strongly affected, you know. . . . Death . . . dead people . . . very frightened, very frightened of them. . . .

Duvelhond. G—go! . . . They are going to . . .

Krakenbus [*barring the way to* REAL-TREMBLOR, *who was attempting to step to the left*]. Stop! You are going to salute His Highness. . . . A terrifying corpse! . . . Eyes still open . . . sagging jaw that will have to be wedged with a breviary. . . . Let's drag him there! Let's shut him up with the dreadful corpse! . . .

Real-Tremblor [*struggling*]. No, no! He was wicked. . . . No! Hated me! Used to say to me, sneak . . . dirty sneak . . . each time!

Krakenbus. How truly he spoke! [*Loosing the archdeacon.*] Is it also true that you were castrated in your young days?

Carnibos. Let's not torment this tormented fellow! . . . What more tormented than a spy? What tale did you come to tell us? Hum, hornet. . . . In return, you won't go to the dead wicked man. . . .

Real-Tremblor. What to tell you? I went in quest of information.

Krakenbus. You have run about the town to take a collection of rumors and remarks. Open your bag!

Carnibos. What is the crowd murmuring?

Krakenbus. The common people . . .

Real-Tremblor. That a saint has just died!

Dom Pikkedoncker [*who has heard*]. That was foreseen! The crowd canonizes! It does in a moment what Rome takes centuries to do! The crowd makes a saint of a mountebank! A saint! . . . What a disgrace sentiment is!

Krakenbus. Come on . . . the bottom of the bag!

Real-Tremblor. Here's the filth. . . . Delight yourselves. . . . [*He waits.*]

Krakenbus [*raising his heel to crush the archdeacon's foot*]. For the sneak, eh?

Real-Tremblor. I was saying . . .

Dom Pikkedoncker. You weren't saying anything. . . .

Real-Tremblor. The common folk were saying, in their jargon, that God had nothing to do with the bishop's passing away. . . . Consequently, they are babbling no longer. They are clenching their teeth and snarling, are the common people. What more do I know? The truth is that at the moment of the passing, the sun's sky suddenly darkened—it's not very light, notice—and grisly storm clouds came and piled up above the town, where they are yet, haunting in their motionlessness. For the crowds, no more is needed. . . .

Krakenbus. Never mind the crowd! But the storm seems to me disturbing. Where is Monsignor tarrying? Does the auxiliary see that the heavens are threatening to fall on our heads?

Real-Tremblor. Monsignor must be in conference with the governor of the Old Town. They are calling out the men under arms. Why? To do the honors—and from other motives. No doubt the governor will order the closing of the city gates as well. . . .

Carnibos. That's the least that can be done, with these masses who know how to read the clouds. Won't they say that the plague will break out, that it's going to rain fiery swords and burning stones? That would be the limit!

Dom Pikkedoncker. The masses are afraid, the masses to whom all occasions for fear are good, like all those for being angry!

Duvelhond. Would you be priests if the ma—masses weren't af—af—raid?

Krakenbus. Let them be afraid. Later, we shall give them festivities, consecration festivities! And if they are

not satisfied with all this blessing, there will be butchery.
There's real politics! Blessing and butchery!

Dom Pikkedoncker. Is yon Krakenbus uttering abuse?

Carnibos. The storm is responsible.

Real-Tremblor. May the storm be without effect on
Monsignor's bowels! Let us ask nothing more!

Krakenbus. Let Monsignor come. It's urgent. Let him
push his belly on the balcony and offer it to the admiration of the crowd! And the nuncio we're expecting! It's
urgent that the crowd have something to look at. . . .
Something other than the canopies of the storm to look at!

Real-Tremblor. In actual fact, the air is heavy, vibrant
with gnats. News from without? Not very reassuring,
and how right you are . . .

Carnibos. Is anyone asking your opinion? It's enough
that the storm's tainting the meat.

Real-Tremblor [*turning his back on the interrupter*].
. . . for nothing augurs well. As soon as the bishop's
death was known, the burgomaster, who knew the crowd
was tired out with three days and three nights of waiting, called upon the brotherhoods to put on their cowls
and to keep moving in an endless procession, very much
reckoning that the crowd would fall into step with the
penitents, as happens with us. A crowd that walks slowly,
intoning psalms, behind crosses and lanterns, becomes the
best, the most good-natured of crowds, doesn't it? Without taking into account that they are, at the time, escorted
by armed men. But what was the reply to the magistrates
from the emissaries of the people? That the people
weren't troubling themselves about the threatening storm,
and that they wouldn't budge, even at the risk of being
struck down on the spot by lightning; that they were
pleased to go in procession in honor of the bishop, but
without priests or sacristans, and only in company with
the carnival giants and dragons, all in silence and with
dignity. This rabble has imagination! . . .

Krakenbus. Enough, weak mouth! You stink of fear.
You are shivering in your shoes and you want your shivers
to spread to the universe. . . . Since you tell your tales
so badly, I resolve that you go and lick the dead man's
nose Bind him! . . .

*The others rush at the archdeacon, who throws himself
flat on his belly on the ground.*

Duvelhond [*shouting*]. Mon—Mon—Monsignor! . . .

Row. They all give a jump. SIMON LAQUEDEEM *enters from the left and swoops down on the group, which immediately breaks up.*

Simon Laquedeem [*tracing blessings*]. Bless you . . . And you, you, you. . . .

Carnibos. He blesses as if he were boxing your ears!

Simon Laquedeem. And that thing? [*He kicks* REAL-TREMBLOR, *who is still lying flat on the ground.*] I have blessed you, drunkard! . . .

Real-Tremblor [*standing up and bowing*]. I have not had anything to drink, Monsignor. . . .

Simon Laquedeem. Are you greeting my stomach? [*He shakes* REAL-TREMBLOR *and pushes him toward the others, who laugh shamelessly. With a sharp gesture,* LAQUEDEEM *stops this courtiers' laughter dead.*] What are you laughing at? [*Sternly.*] Alter your faces! You shall laugh later, and the good last of all. [*Raising his voice.*] For we shall be the last to laugh! [*Smooth-tongued.*] Don't chuckle, don't get excited; assume the bearing of people overwhelmed by an infinite stupor; stick your noses out; let your arms hang down and walk trembling on your feet like Barbary apes after love-making; have your eyes lusterless and full of gray water, and from time to time raise them skyward like blind men counting the stars. You, pleban, with the truffle-nosing snout, try it. Compose your features into this circumstantial mask, which the others will imitate. . . .

Dom Pikkedoncker. Is Monsignor talking to us about his health? In my opinion, nothing is as good as a clyster. . . .

Simon Laquedeem. For the time being, swallow your bowel-washings, you deaf old man! My bowels are my business. For the present, it's the diocese that needs purging of what is obstructing it. The corpse, where is it? Is it prepared?

Krakenbus. Must be. We were waiting for you, Monsignor. And the crowd is waiting. . . .

Simon Laquedeem. I know. . . . The squares will be purged as well. . . . We know our duties. . . . Let the nuncio get here. [*He walks up and down, talking to him-*

self.] I shall purge the palace of these idols. I understand, I do. And I shall drive his shadow away, obliterate him even to the trace of his footsteps! . . . And sweep out these debauched underlings. . . . [*He stops and holds his stomach, his face suddenly drawn.*] Ah!

Real-Tremblor. Poor Monsignor. . . . Monsignor's poor stomach!

Simon Laquedeem [*mumbling*]. My stomach! . . . Calvary of a stomach! . . . The thorns, the nails, and the lance in it. . . . [*Big sigh.*] Ouf . . . it's working loose!

Carnibos. An angel has passed by. . . . The wind from his wing . . .

Simon Laquedeem. Laus Deo! [*He mops his brow. Flashes of silent lightning quiver on the panes of the balcony.*] Who has been in the chamber? None of you? Are they taking hours over embalming him? Are you frightened to go near him dead? He won't bite you any more, my good fellows. . . . [*He goes toward the steps at the back.*] He shan't have the funeral he asked for, in open ground and without a shroud, in the outcasts' enclosure. He will be clad in iron, in lead, and in oak; he will be hidden in the deepest crypt—and the cathedral will press down with all its weight on his bones! [*Having turned toward the archdeacon.*] Go and see if the nuncio is coming to us, Real-Tremblor!

REAL-TREMBLOR *goes out swiftly at the left.* SIMON LAQUEDEEM *is preparing to open the double door at the back when it half-opens. A little black shape comes into view through it.*

Krakenbus. The servant! [*The little shape hugs the walls, seeking to run away. The priests encircle it.*] Catch the crow!

Simon Laquedeem [*apostrophizing the little old woman*]. Have you done your funeral task? [*Pause.*] Oh simplicity! She is weeping! The paradise of the innocent will be yours, old servant: you shall have your wages. . . . Vanish into your garret. Henceforth your master will have no further need of you. Let go of her!

Duvelhond. Impru—pru—dence!

Simon Laquedeem. I say let her make ready her bits of clothes. She has the right to attend the services. Afterward . . .

Carnibos [*shaking the servant*]. What is she muttering in her patois?

Veneranda [*frightened and in a toneless voice*]. *Bid voor de ziel!*

Simon Laquedeem. Pray for the soul? By all means! Go! Let us not see you again! [*Veneranda is pushed, without consideration, to the left, and disappears.*] I am afraid that, although she is unaware of it, this ninety-year-old knows too much. . . . Imprudence, someone said? No. The staircases in this palace are decrepit. . . . One false step. . . . [*Flashes of lightning outside. A silence during which the crowd is heard snarling.*] Darkness is going to fall. . . . And this storm that seems to be holding itself back for the night! . . . And this nuncio! . . . [*Arrogantly.*] Is there no longer any give and take with Heaven?

Noise at the left, from which direction REAL-TREMBLOR *returns, preceding a young priest.*

Simon Laquedeem. Him? Greetings, bambino! And the nuncio? Are you hiding him under your robe? Come, let me embrace you! [*He embraces the new arrival who shields himself.*]

Sodomati. Don't suffocate me! . . . [*Bowing and scraping to all.*] My compliments, Monsignor! And to you, revered, very worthy, learned, and inspired gentlemen. . . . Here we are at last! What den are you drawing me into? The crowd surrounded my carriage. Gallows birds hurled foul words at me. Imagine! They shouted *"Rok af!"* at me. What does that mean?

Carnibos. "Tear off his gown!" . . . nothing else.

Sodomati. Horror!

Simon Laquedeem. No doubt the people thought to see a pretty girl. Never mind that. . . . Have you brought the nuncio to me?

Sodomati. Became unexpectedly ill on learning of the decease of the bishop. Understand? I am acting as his substitute. Have the time to make an appearance, then I'm off, understand? I don't like dramatic ceremonials the way they carry them out in this country. Is this a way of doing things? A bishop dies . . .

Krakenbus. And what a bishop, too!

Sodomati. . . . whom I indeed regret not having known alive! The nuncio became crimson when he was spoken to about this apostle. . . . [*Indicating the wall at the back.*] I can imagine the person, incarnated by these abominations, these idols. . . . Bah! . . . What bad form!

Simon Laquedeem. His friends. . . .

Carnibos. His only friends. . . .

Simon Laquedeem. His court. He was fond of these idols, these monsters, yes, which, he said, consoled him for the hideousness of our human faces. He liked the false gods, his victims, he said, and gazed on them with a culpable pride, like a barbaric warrior counting his trophies. . . .

Krakenbus. We have got to admit that he converted savages, and of a dangerous sort. He had his ways: beating and barking! . . . Poor savages converted in this way to a hard life, and all their gods stolen! Why didn't this formidable zealot stay on the other side of the globe!

Carnibos. More than that! . . . He drew a subtle argument from these idols. "Men of the Church, my savages were nearer to the divine truth in adoring these untrue gods than you, the anointed, who pretend to adore the true god!" he said. . . .

Sodomati. Oh, the shameless creature! He said that?

Simon Laquedeem. Said? No! Shouted . . . bawled . . . howled!

Sodomati. How I pity you, brethren, how I pity you! Free yourselves as quickly as possible from these symbols of Evil. Bury them with your bishop, or, better, burn them. . . . The nuncio spoke to me about them. It is not rash to assert that wooden and metal devils possess baleful powers, and may have been masters of your bishop's mind; not rash to assert that these idols have operated, causing the absurd and foolish actions of your bewitched bishop. . . . The nuncio maintains that this palace is under a spell—and I believe it! Make a colossal pile of faggots. Burn these appurtenances of idolatry. The nuncio even believes that these poisonous powers are spreading, contagiously reaching the town, the country, the whole diocese. And I believe it! . . . Only look at the way the crowd behaves since the death of the wonder-worker, I mean the bishop, the wretch . . . I mean the late Monsignor, whom the Almighty will forgive by reason of his faith and zeal, which were worthy of past ages, but no longer of ours. . . .

Simon Laquedeem. We shall burn them, bambino. . . .

These idols were truly the bishop's mistresses, and they ruled the town and the diocese! Burn? It's the whole poisoned population that should be thrown on the pile, a pile as vast as the diocese . . . [*his voice chokes*] . . . to destroy these packs of wolves—for our pastor's sheep are fierce wolves, believe me!

Sodomati. Calm yourself, auxiliary! . . . If fire can cleanse the diocese, burn, burn. . . . But will the fire change these wolves into lambs? I doubt it. A strange race in this land of marshes, freethinking, subversive, yes, violent, unmanageable! Among you here, heresiarchs spring up like tares! . . . Ungodly race!

Krakenbus. We belong to it, if you don't mind!

Sodomati. You belong to it! I was thinking so as I watched you making faces. And since you admit it . . . It's obvious the idols have taken possession of you as of the others. You make unsightly grimaces like men possessed. You are the suspect priests of a people of possessed souls!

Simon Laquedeem. All that because they wanted to tear off your gown, bambino? Calm yourself, pretty secretary! We shall do our burning. We shall burn the sodomites as well. We know how to behave and how to lead our flocks without the advice of the nuncio, pretty secretary! We shall burn the seed of the heresiarch, and lilies shall sprout in the frog-filled marshes. Our pestilential bogs shall become mystical meadows, ineffable gardens of the nunciature, where little angels with chubby buttocks shall dance. . . .

Sodomati [*superciliously*]. I beg your pardon, Simon Laquedeem! . . . I beg your pardon for having confused you! . . . You are not of this race. . . . I was forgetting. You are indisputably descended from kings and prophets, which I would not have believed had I not read your disclaimer of your ancestors written in Hebrew on a foreskin! . . . Burn the sodomites and the heresiarchs. In addition, burn the Jews, the filthy Jews, since this diocese is overflowing with them, Simon Laquedeem—since it is not known by what operation of unwonted charity this diocese receives them, Simon Laquedeem, to the extent of resembling a huge ghetto. . . .

Simon Laquedeem [*furious, rushes at* SODOMATI]. *Rok af!* Strip him!

Uproar. REAL-TREMBLOR *intervenes and holds the auxiliary bishop back. Outside, flashes of silent lightning.*

Real-Tremblor. The storm . . . oh! . . . Everything is going wrong!

Krakenbus. They will become so excited that they'll draw down a thunderbolt! Instead of calming the crowd! . . . Give me the aspergillum, well soaked. . . .

Simon Laquedeem [*pulling himself up*]. That is right. We are delaying a great deal. Let us show ourselves on the balcony and give blessing. This action may have results. And no doubt the crowd will think we are warding off the storm. Prepare yourselves! Get on my left, Sodomati. The presence of a Roman witness has its importance in these difficult moments.

The group forms up, CARNIBOS *remaining behind, near the table, and* KRAKENBUS *hastening to the right where he goes to open the balcony windows with a crash. At once, the distant murmur outside comes in, amplified, and a harsh though gloomy light floods the room. Slowly, after having drawn themselves up, the priests, with the auxiliary leading, move to the right and disappear on the balcony.* CARNIBOS *does not follow them and sets about stealing pieces of meat which he devours swiftly. Flashes of lightning, nearer and bluish, follow each other in silence. And suddenly a fierce clamor breaks out: booing, whistling, barking, laughter—the violent crowd is insulting the priests. The latter fall back inside in disorder. The balcony windows shut once more; the clamor diminishes. The priests look at one another and, in the chiaroscuro, seem to be counting their number. This confusion does not last long,* SODOMATI *taking the attention of everyone by a disordered gesticulation. Before long, he bursts out.*

Sodomati. We are being booed, do you hear? And for greeting, these sheaves of bare arms, these bundles of fists held out to us! The riffraff of Jerusalem didn't rage more in affronting the Messiah and calling for his execution!

Dom Pikkedoncker. Worthy folk! What riffraff! Alleluia! They cried out, "Alleluia!"

Sodomati. That's what your prestige is capable of, Monsignor! [*Indicating the idols.*] And that is what the prestige of these devils can do! Is it clear enough in this doubtful evening? These devils, unchained by the disappearance of their suzerain, have overcome the vast collection of the crowd, the crowd that will fell you!

Simon Laquedeem. Am I responsible for the civil order? Have I authority to disperse crowds and control storms?

Sodomati. The crowd that will fell you! It will serve you right. And don't reckon on being granted the benefit of martyrdom!

Simon Laquedeem. Go, and may God give you an escort of archangels! Go quickly: this moment is perilous, and those that are coming. For the time being, the crowd will content itself with making water against your coach. Later, you might leap in the air like a puppet and fall down again, impaled through the bottom, on a picket. We are familiar with our people and their humors. . . .

Sodomati. I shall not leave until the obsequies are over, seen by my own eyes. . . .

Simon Laquedeem. Then you will leave without delay, and you will see nothing of the carnival that follows, for the corpse will soon have tumbled down into the vault; go. . . .

Sodomati. Prudence, Monsignor! . . . There have been refractory corpses that would not allow themselves to be interred with ease. As for your carnival, no, I shall not see anything of it; but you are not at all certain of superintending it. . . .

Simon Laquedeem. Will you explain yourself?

Sodomati. The Holy See might become concerned about your bowels. . . . It is acknowledged that this great belly is ill and contains enough stinking breaths to infect all the nearby countries more thoroughly than heresy . . .

Simon Laquedeem [*bursting out laughing*]. Really? Has it been smelled as far as Rome? What a sense of smell, bambino! . . . [*He rubs his belly.*] And if I gave off floral perfumes, wouldn't the cry be, "A miracle"? Tell me, bambino, what is your favorite flower?

Krakenbus. The guard.

FOUR SWISS *carrying halberds have just come in and stand waiting.*

Simon Laquedeem [*going toward the Swiss*]. These, guards? Four vergers rigged out for the occasion. You,

Swiss, will station yourselves at each corner of the funeral couch and will not budge from there. Your vigil will not last long, since the corpse will go to lie in the choir of the cathedral when night falls. Don't look at the jugs. You shall have drink, but later. . . .

Carnibos. Those who keep vigil in a death chamber are sometimes subject to hallucinations.

Real-Tremblor. Let's set our minds at rest: vergers have never been sensitive to the supernatural. Come, Switzers. . . .

Followed by the FOUR SWISS, REAL-TREMBLOR *makes his way to the back and climbs the steps. He opens the double door a little way, makes the men slip through one after the other, and observes the interior. Then, after a moment, he turns toward the company again.*

Real-Tremblor. Facta est! [*He indicates the door.*] Would it not be fitting to gaze in a spirit of Christian sorrow on the mortal remains of Monsignor Jan in Eremo, Bishop of Lapideopolis?

Simon Laquedeem [*after a short pause during which he has questioned his confederates by his gaze*]. Struck by Christian sorrow, we wish to gaze on the mortal remains of Monsignor John of Eremo, Bishop of what you said. . . .

And, with the auxiliary leading, the priests take several steps toward the double door which REAL-TREMBLOR *opens with a calculated slowness. When the door is open, a chamber is revealed, blazingly illuminated by a hundred candles which light up a tilted funeral couch on which, clothed in his canonicals, mitered, and with his crook, lies a man of remarkable height and breadth, with a grayish and shining face, and all angular, like a recumbent figure cut in stone—the mortal remains of Monsignor* JAN IN EREMO, *Bishop of Lapideopolis. The Swiss stand rigid at the corners of the funeral couch. Above the couch, a great crucifix. At the foot of the bed, a coat of arms showing the bearings of the bishop, anchors sable on a field of gold.*

Simon Laquedeem [*with authority*]. *Flectamus genua!* . . . [*At this command, the priests kneel, turned toward the chamber. The auxiliary goes up the steps and stops at the threshold. After a long pause.*] He looks still more formidable dead than living! [*He turns away and comes down the steps and prays aloud.*] *Agnus Dei, qui tollis.* . . . [*He yawns and mumbles the Latin words.*]

The Others [*confusedly making responses*]. *Dona eis requiem* . . .

Simon Laquedeem [*with authority*]. Levate! . . .

On the command, the priests get up. REAL-TREMBLOR *shuts the double door again. Now, after this brief illumination, the gloom has taken on a thickness that the lightning from outside hachures almost continuously.*

Krakenbus. We need lights. . . .

Simon Laquedeem. The servants will bring them when they come for the body. It was my wish that from now until then the windows of the palace should remain dark. Haven't you the most extraordinary illumination dispensed to us from the heavens?

Carnibos. Enough to find one's mouth. I feel weak. . . .

Simon Laquedeem. Sit down! [*The priests take stools from under the table and settle down.* SIMON LAQUEDEEM *remains standing and from time to time walks about.*] Who has played havoc with the food? You, you beast of prey?

Real-Tremblor. The idols. . . . But the jugs are untouched, and the flasks. . . .

Simon Laquedeem. Eat. Drink. In silence, if possible. Silence would be fitting after what we have just seen.

Sodomati. Impressive, what we have just seen! I am unaware of what this man was in life; I know what he is in death, somebody! Tell us about him, Laquedeem. I can't abide silence, particularly in this place, particularly this evening. . . .

Simon Laquedeem. What do you want me to say, since you have said everything? Somebody! There is no other comment. . . .

Sodomati. You seem to be dreaming, Laquedeem. Are you entering into meditation when your clergy are not missing a mouthful? . . .

Simon Laquedeem. I was thinking about the inscrutability of the designs of Providence, the strangeness of certain destinies. . . . Somebody! whose shadow weighs on us, in whose shadow we live crushed down. Somebody. . . .

Krakenbus. He was called Jan Eremo. . . .

Sodomati. Will you tell us his legend?

Simon Laquedeem. No, his true history—the reality is prodigious enough without adding to it. I shall relate it since you dread the silence. It will displease you, as our fogs displease you, and our marshes. . . .

Sodomati. Your storms . . . your gloom . . .

Krakenbus. He was called Jan Eremo. . . .

Simon Laquedeem. Jan in Eremo was his name. . . . John in the desert, in memory of the sand hills where he was found—a child of an unknown mother, a child without a name—by the monks from the monastery of the Dunes, whom his haunting cries had alerted. It is more than seventy years since John was born in the desert, John, son of the sea and the sand, John who used to say, "I am solitude"—which he was!

Real-Tremblor. The people say that he was born of the fornication of a monk and a mermaid!

Simon Laquedeem. And when did that happen? [*He drinks a cup of wine and throws the dregs in the interrupter's face.*] Not much is known of how this accursed being grew up in the monastery, of what his young life was like up to the day of his ordination. He was a rugged pioneer, and a daring fisherman. His brethren looked on him as being attacked by a strange insanity, and were not surprised when, once, they saw him put out to sea on an equinoctial day in a boat he had dug up from the mud, put out to sea and disappear in the foaming tempest. When their brother did not return, they believed he had perished and sang the office for the dead.

Satisfied at his beginning, LAQUEDEEM *gazes on the company. During the short silence, a rumble of thunder, still distant, is heard. All prick up their ears.*

Dom Pikkedoncker. Your belly, Monsignor?

Simon Laquedeem. The bowels of the storm. The sky's grumbling pleases me, for what I am relating to you doesn't call for the song of the nightingale, I assure you, but the heart-rending cry of the sea gulls. How far had I gotten with this man?

Krakenbus. You had just sent him to the bottom, and the monks were singing the office for the dead. . . .

Simon Laquedeem. But it was written that the man whom the tempests and the cannibals did not want would come

back to us some time, after a long, long while, on a day of
calamity, a terrible day when the world and Flanders appeared to be doomed to end. . . . He came into view in
a worm-eaten boat that the ocean shattered on the beach
and whose sides let fall idols. The tides had submerged the
ground inland, and it was by walking on the dykes, as if
he were walking on the waters, that this man reached the
town, this town decimated by the Plague. . . .

Sodomati. In which chronicles are these horrors recorded?

Simon Laquedeem. In my memory. Indeed, I lived
through those baleful days, and I too thought the world
was going to end!

Carnibos. That will happen tonight.

Simon Laquedeem. Eat, Carnibos! At the time I am
calling to mind, you would have done the same as the
wretched inhabitants of this town, you would have devoured purple flesh from the graveyard, fighting with the
rats and the dogs over it, and dying forthwith, to be
devoured in your turn! . . . After the Plague, Famine and
Madness took office in this town shrouded in opaque
yellow mists, our town from which both the count and
the bishop had fled, both the priests and the physicians,
and where I, a young deacon, remained alone to comfort
the dying and drag the blackened corpses to the fire.
[*Pause.*] It was then that he appeared, suddenly looming
out of the mists, bowed beneath a huge cross made from
tarred planks. That was how he appeared! And the plague-
stricken, filled with terror at this apparition, had only one
word . . .

Real-Tremblor. The Antichrist!

Simon Laquedeem. The Antichrist was the word that
sprang from dying lips as this wild processionary passed
by. He certainly had that appearance.

Sodomati. Where was your crucifer going?

Simon Laquedeem. Straight to the market square, where
a huge fire was crackling, in which corpses writhed in
horrible attitudes. Was he going to walk in the flames,
after having walked on the waters? The plague-stricken
followed him, moaning pitifully from hope or fear. . . .
And then what did he do? Threw the huge cross into the
fire. A pillar of flame rose up, a glowing pillar, lifting
the mists. . . . A marvel? Yes! The Plague was vanquished

at once. The yellow mists broke up, the pure sky appeared, and the wind, the great blue wind, drove away the deadly miasmas. A marvel! I can still hear the crackling of the cross, the outcry of that raving crowd, above all the bells, the panic-stricken bells. . . . The survivors had rushed to the churches and had hung themselves in bunches to the ropes, and the bells began ringing, driving other bells crazy—and in the open country, the bells gave as good as they got, rolling the news around the four corners of the horizon, the astounding news of the end of the Scourge. . . .

Sodomati. And the author of the marvel?

Simon Laquedeem. Priest John worked another miracle. Not content with having bound the Plague in chains, he ran the Famine to earth. This inspired, or simply astute, man had discovered the siege stores in the town vaults, casks of wine and beer, salt meats, dried fish, flour, all of which was thrown to the hungry. At night, the moribund were drunk and sang and danced as at fair time. At dawn, the women were pregnant. Life was carrying on. The town had a master, Priest John! The corpses buried, the streets cleaned, the craftsmen at work, life carried on. . . . [*Pause.*] And when, after some weeks, the count came back, the bishop, the clergy, the physicians, the notables, and all those who had fled the Plague, they ran up against the master of the town and didn't know what to do. The bishop and the clergy wanted to recover this palace from which they had fled, and ran up against Priest John—what am I saying?—against Bishop John, Bishop Jan in Eremo, sent by the tempest. . . .

Sodomati. He was, certainly! He was!

Simon Laquedeem. He was! This priest in his madness had rigged himself out in the miter, had laid hold of the crook, the crook with which he dealt out blows like a hardened trooper to the old bishop and his runaway priests, uttering the most abominable abuse that clerical ears have ever heard. And Bishop John remained in the palace, a triumphant impostor protected against all justice by the vicious adoration of the butchers and the fullers, until the day that Rome, this Rome with designs more inscrutable than those of Providence, consecrated the imposture . . .

Sodomati. The History is written, don't amend it!

Simon Laquedeem [*forcefully*]. . . . consecrated the imposture! . . . You know the rest.

Sodomati. Not at all! I know the beginning, from your so striking evocation, which must leave you tired. Tell me the end, how he died. . . .

Simon Laquedeem. By God! Are you unaware of that, seeing that you are writing the History? He died a godly death, that's all. . . .

Krakenbus. When does an ecclesiastic die otherwise, even if he gives up the ghost calling on Beelzebub? . . .

Simon Laquedeem. He died a godly death, but in an unusual way; and could it be otherwise? This man who had his life, had to have his death. He had it! And the end was worthy of the beginning. . . .

Sodomati. The end which he foretold, it seems?

Simon Laquedeem. Such premonitions are not rare. He foretold it, exactly. . . .

Sodomati. Weren't the physicians forbidden to come near him?

Simon Laquedeem. He refused their aid, thrust them aside, and treated them as jackals. Since you are making investigations, learn that his distrust was intense. His strength was obviously declining. From day to day the skeleton's grin shaped itself in the mummified flesh of his face.

Sodomati. You describe with talent, but what disorder . . .

Real-Tremblor. Hadn't he passed the seventy years mark? Long ago. . . .

Simon Laquedeem. Since he loved the prophetic manner, he gave up his stubborn silence to utter some phrases that can be considered heavy with meaning, or as childish as the ramblings of comatose old men usually are. What did he say that may be worth anything?

Carnibos [*raising a finger*]. "The hour I am aware of is coming, forestalling the one God appointed, and I accept it, since He allows it to be forestalled. . . ." Explain that to me!

Sodomati. That could be explained. . . . But what disorder?

Simon Laquedeem [*who pretends not to hear the question*]. Yes, it was a touching moment when I administered the last sacrament. Although overcome by a deep torpor, prefiguring the last sleep, Monsignor watched what we were doing with a half-open eye, the eye of a scraggy old eagle. . . .

Sodomati. Well?

Simon Laquedeem. This eye, laden with an unspeakable hatred, missed nothing of my actions, followed my hands. And as I was holding out the host, the eye shot a flash of steel at me, the lips welded themselves together. But as I solemnly adjured him to receive the body and the blood of the living God, the eye grew dim and the lips unsealed. He communicated.

A fairly long silence. Stillness. The rumbling of the storm is heard, greater than before.

Sodomati. He communicated. . . .

Simon Laquedeem. Then? [*Speaking quickly, having become nervous.*] Suddenly erect, the dying man entered into a brief and harsh contest against invisible aggressors— angels or demons—of which we were the terrified witnesses. But the wrestler, seized around the waist and flung full length on his couch, fell broken. Death was winning! Then? The confirmation, the melted wax in the mouth, the red-hot iron on the feet—for we were still in doubt. . . . [*Pause.*] Do you know enough?

Sodomati [*getting up*]. No! I ask you a last time, what disorder . . .

Simon Laquedeem [*bursting out*]. How do I know? [*He seizes the secretary by the shoulders and speaks into his face.*] These questions! Have you an inquisitor's commission, little priest? There should have been previous notice. There is a right way of replying to such examinations. . . .

Sodomati. Isn't it the current question I'm asking, just as all the town is asking it, all the diocese? [*He frees himself.*] Pardon the little priest. . . . He's a nasty noser, isn't he? You understand? He's amazed that his question upsets you to this extent. . . .

Simon Laquedeem *indulges in gesticulation unaccompanied by any words. During this silence filled with gestures, a long flash of lightning makes a pale false daylight. The auxiliary finds his voice again and speaks violently.*

Simon Laquedeem. On my conscience! I swear . . . I swear I had no part in the death of His Highness! . . .

Thus I reply to the perfidious. And may a thunderbolt—
if I am lying—fall in at once on our heads, may the
thunder, if I am lying . . .

*Another blinding flash of lightning. And a thunderbolt
falls and strikes quite close. Everything makes a cracking
sound. For a brief moment the room seems to be crackling
in an outbreak of bluish fire as it is filled with a violent
astral light that all at once goes out. The priests have risen
at the shock and make defensive gestures. Outside, the
crowd answers the thunderbolt by a tremendous outcry.
A brief confusion reigns around the table. Voices are
confused. Only* LAQUEDEEM *has not stirred. He dominates
the uproar.*

 Simon Laquedeem. Sit down! What's the matter with
you?
 Carnibos. The thunder . . . fell on us . . . on the
palace . . .
 Simon Laquedeem [*roaring*]. I heard nothing! [*Turning
suddenly.*] What's happening to make your teeth chatter?
 Sodomati. What's happening? Why the thunder is talking, a voice from on high!
 Simon Laquedeem [*roaring*]. And what if I tell you
that nothing is happening? [*The priests have drawn close
to the auxiliary and stand around him.*] Frightened? Of
what, my children? [*He does his utmost to laugh.*] A
farce, a macabre farce! [*But the double door opens a little
way, and one after the other the* SWISS *escape through the
narrow gap. They seem incoherent and as though distracted. Without seeing anything, they make for the left.
The auxiliary springs toward them and bars their exit.*]
And you, vergers? Is the chamber on fire? Frightened as
well? Frightened? [*The four utter inaudible words and,
hustling the auxiliary, go out like madmen. The auxiliary
runs to the double door.*] A farce, I say! Don't move!
Frightened? Not me, ha, not me! Frightened of what?

SIMON LAQUEDEEM *pushes the halves of the double door
wide open, and the mortuary chamber is revealed, blazing
with its thousand lights. Six toneless cries, the six cries
of terror of the six priests, who are congregating at the
left, ready to flee, and the ominous laugh of the auxiliary,
rumbling above the bleatings. At the foot of the couch and*

turned toward the room stands Jan Eremo, *crook in hand, made taller still by his high miter, a dark and heavy mass hieratically sculpted and as though vibrating in the light.*

Krakenbus. Help! . . . An evil spell!

Sodomati. Exorcize it!

Simon Laquedeem [*who retires backward from the chamber toward the priests*]. A farce, a macabre farce! . . . Who has planted this dummy on its feet? Or what power is dwelling in this corpse? Answer, Eremo! Dead or alive. . . .

The bishop has stirred at his name, and takes a step forward like a block that is going to tumble down.

Carnibos. Alive!

Simon Laquedeem [*drawing farther back*]. Not a genuine corpse! An impostor even in your death! What do you want? Prayers? Have you seen Hell? [*The priests are leaving. The auxiliary keeps on drawing back.*] Have you come back to disclose that you are damned? [*To the priests, who are in flight.*] Shut the doors! [*Addressing the bishop who comes forward very slowly and who has raised his right hand to his throat.*] What? Have you swallowed your tongue? What? Are toads going to shoot out of your mouth? Expect nothing from me, you automaton or ghost, nothing. . . . [*He goes out.*]

Noise of the door being bolted—noise of running around in the corridors, and calling. The hubbub dies away. And there is silence. A solemn silence which is aggravated by the growling of the crowd, like the rumbling of the ceaseless thunder, and on which is superimposed the deep pedal of the storm that seems vocal and growls in unison with the crowd.

The bishop has clumsily come down the steps. With empty gaze, he comes forward in the room, his crook wielded spasmodically like a blind man's staff. At each lightning flash, his face shines like metal; the gold embroidery that covers him lights up. He bumps against the banquet table. At each lightning flash, the crystal glass and the silver plate flare up. The bishop has seized a knife with which he pokes in his mouth, flicking out the wax that was obstructing it. He spits out the pieces of wax, throws the knife down, takes hold of a goblet, and drinks with head flung back. He throws the goblet away and, like a gargoyle, spews out in a jet the wine he was trying to swallow. Then he becomes transformed. A permanent rattle, like the grating of a rusty pump, comes from his freed mouth, and nothing other than this rattle will come from it. He breathes in the air and seems to expand. He becomes animated; his empty gaze is filled with phosphorescent lights. The septuagenarian becomes a kind of jerkily moving athlete, the prey of a powerful oppression. Without respite, his right hand tries to loosen invisible bonds around his throat. From time to time he thrusts his hand in his mouth, as though he were trying to pull out some plug that was choking him. Unutterable torture! Is he an old man still in the death agony, who asks to die? Is he a deceased person come back again, thrust aside by Death, who asks to live once more? Now he is in action. His gaze has sought for exits. He walks to the right where the lightning leaps about—the balcony. He is heard shaking the windows—but the windows fly into pieces. Outside, the crowd is throwing stones and bellowing. The bishop retraces his steps and hugs the back wall. Painfully mute, he turns to the terrorized or hilarious idols, as though he were asking their help, and touches them pitiably, strokes them. Since the idols remain unchanging in their grimaces, their master turns away from them and begins to turn around on the spot where he is standing when, at the left, the bolts work and, the door opening, light marks the exit. The bishop immediately goes toward this light, while voices call him in the walls: "Monsignor! . . . Monsignor! . . ." *Monsignor dashes forward and disappears. The room stays empty for a while. The noise of running around resounds in the walls. And the gang of priests rushes into the mortuary chamber from the back. The auxiliary runs nimbly around the couch, leaps the steps leading to the room, and, pursuing his course around the table, moves obliquely to the left and precipitately shuts the door through which the bishop went. Then he goes back to the center of the room where the others, breathless, have parked themselves. Only* REAL-TREMBLOR *insists on locking the double door at the back, which he has closed behind him, and he returns brandishing the key.*

Real-Tremblor. He's in his cage, the evil one!

Simon Laquedeem. Locked up, eh? He won't come out of there except to the sepulcher! And if it's necessary that this dead man should die, he shall die! That's my business. You, keep cool and collected! Press your buttocks together, but do what you are told, otherwise there will be slaughter!

Sodomati. The scandal! . . . We are lost!

Simon Laquedeem. You are, if I wish it. Pitch yourself into the water. I am staying on deck. Who will help me?

Duvelhond. Ky—Kyrie . . .

Simon Laquedeem [*lays hold of* DUVELHOND *and pulls him away from the group*]. I'll Kyrie you! Go down and fetch one of the arquebusiers of the guard. [DUVELHOND *goes out by the front left exit.*] You, Real, go and make sure the militia are still holding the approaches to the palace! And you, Carnibos, look for some lanterns! [*The archdeacon and the chaplain go out by the same exit.*] Let me know if the people's pot is still boiling. We must make haste, or we shall furnish the bones for the soup. . . .

Sodomati. Not die . . . not like that. . . .

Simon Laquedeem. Flayed, grilled, like pigs! [*Fat laugh.*] The nuncio scented it. What a surprise, eh? Another marvel from down there! Write quickly to Rome. Can you smell the sulphur? I'm not troubled by it. . . .

CARNIBOS *comes back carrying two lanterns which he hangs on the wall.*

Simon Laquedeem. Light? That? then we are really in the abyss. Let the lightning illuminate my deeds. The worst has come to pass. . . .

REAL-TREMBLOR *comes back.*

Simon Laquedeem. What have you to say?

Real-Tremblor. That the worst is to come, Monsignor. The rabble are surging forth under the lash of the storm. The militia are holding out with great difficulty. . . . But the butchers are mustering. With them, it will soon be all up. The rabble want their bishop!

Simon Laquedeem. We shall give him to them.

Real-Tremblor. They will come and take him. The militia are still holding out, I said; but on the inside. And the rabble are piling up barrels of powder. We are going to be blown up. . . .

Simon Laquedeem. The ascension of the clergy. Splendid! [*Furious.*] Blow up! . . . For how are you helping me? Who is sacrificing himself?

Krakenbus. First, let us know is this ghost threatening us or beseeching us?

Carnibos. And then, his throat. . . . What does it mean?

Simon Laquedeem. The ghost is choking. The host, which he received in hate and not in love, is throttling him, this host which can neither come up again nor go down and burns the dying man whom Heaven and Hell fling back by reason of this unachieved communion. No, this living man is no longer alive, and this dead man is not so! He is suspended in Time as the host is in his body. Come, let a Christian, let a priest tear out the host—or thrust it in. . . .

Sodomati. You are a priest and a Christian: do it!

Simon Laquedeem. He would cut through my wrist with a bite of his teeth! But you, with your woman's hands . . . [*To* REAL-TREMBLOR, *who is going toward the exit.*] Where are you going? To save your skin?

Real-Tremblor [*going*]. My idea. . . . Save you all!

Simon Laquedeem [*made furious by this flight*]. Get out! Leave me alone. . . . Save yourselves, every one of you! . . . And your souls! . . . Get out! [*He hurls himself into the group of priests and drives them to the exit with blows from his fists.*] Up there . . . on the roof . . . and higher . . . a charge of powder in your backsides!

Short scuffle before the exit, through which the hustled priests are lost to sight. Alone, the auxiliary wipes his brow and comes back, listens to the crowd and the storm growling, then, catching sight of the idols, walks over to them.

Simon Laquedeem. And you, evil spirits, you, his faithful, are you going to help your master? Will you defend him in misfortune, you grotesque dolls? Will you escort him in the outer darkness? Have I got to struggle with you as well? You don't stir, in your immemorial ugliness? Don't expect anything more. Your master is caught in the trap. You are afraid of me? Rightly so! No living person would ever dare what I am daring. . . . [*He goes to the back and stops on the steps. Pause. Challenging.*] Eremo! [*After a pause.*] Jan Eremo! [*After a pause.*] Jan in

Eremo, Bishop of Lapideopolis! [*Short pause.*] By the
Archdemon who rules you . . . [*Short pause.*] Are you
still wandering in this world? . . . [*A violent impact
shakes the door, which makes a cracking sound and continues violently shaking for a moment. The auxiliary has
taken a spring backward.*] I have my answer!

And SIMON LAQUEDEEM *is making his way to the exit when*
DUVELHOND *looms through it, preceding an* ARQUEBUSIER.

Duvelhond. The arque—que—buus—buus—buus. . . .
Simon Laquedeem. Booze? Wine for you, you villain!
Set up your arquebus!
The Arquebusier. Yes, Monsignor!
Simon Laquedeem. And hurl your grapeshot into this
door, this great door. . . . [*The door is shaken again.*
THE ARQUEBUSIER *bustles about.*] You understand?
The Arquebusier. No, Monsignor. . . .
Simon Laquedeem. Why?
The Arquebusier. Is there a man behind it?
Simon Laquedeem. No.
The Arquebusier. A beast?
Simon Laquedeem. Yes, a mad one! Go away! [*He
snatches the weapon from* THE ARQUEBUSIER, *who runs
off. To* DUVELHOND.] And you, get out! [*He sets up the
arquebus and turns its wheel lock.*]
Duvelhond [*fleeing, his hands over his ears*]. Jhesus!
Simon Laquedeem. Your Jhesus had better not be across
my path. I'll . . . [*The shot fires, in a cloud of smoke.
Some of door's boards are shattered. The face of* JOHN
EREMO *appears, open-mouthed, in the hole, which is lit
up. And the rattle resounds. The auxiliary rushes to the
back, yelling.*] You, still? What do you want? Black
sacraments? Gall for your thirst of the damned? I shall
fill this dead mouth with lead! This mitered skull shall
fly to pieces! [*He pushes the arquebus into the hole in
the door. The bishop's face has disappeared, but the
weapon is seized from the other side, and a struggle for
possession of it begins. Panels smash; the hole grows
bigger. Finally,* LAQUEDEEM *lets go of the weapon, which
disappears inside. Taken aback, the auxiliary returns to the
center of the room, puts his hands to his head, staggers.
. . . A tremendous explosion shakes the palace and is
followed by the applause and hurrahs of the crowd.*

LAQUEDEEM *has pulled himself together.*] Petards? Wait, my people. . . . You shall have your joint of meat. And you will commend the knacker! [*He rushes to the front left exit and disappears.*]

The room stands empty. But a hand, then an arm come through the hole in the door and seek the latch. Then a processional cross comes out, shaft first. This cross also feels about, digs itself under the cover molding and becomes a lever worked from inside. The double door groans under the pressure and takes the strain. The cross jerks more hurriedly and the cover molding splits away. The vanquished door gives completely. The bishop looms in the opening. He has neither crook nor miter, his gaze is mad, his neck is craned, and his hands are held forward ready for the attack. He comes down the steps and stops, as though amazed to be alone. A noise on the left. Alerted, the old man goes and stands close to the back wall, among the idols, where he remains stock-still, merged with the monstrosities. A second explosion shakes the palace and is answered by the storm, which is just now unleashed, and the crowd, crazy with lightning and gunpowder. At this juncture, SIMON LAQUEDEEM, carrying an ax, enters by the mortuary chamber. Having gone around the couch, he appears on the threshold of the room, ready for the attack.

Simon Laquedeem. Eremo! . . . [*He comes down.*] Eremo! . . . [*He goes about the room in every direction.*] Eremo! . . . [*Endlessly turning about.*] Eremo! . . . Eremo! . . . [*Having stopped, dumbfounded, in a childish voice.*] Jan! . . . [*Then, with tiny steps, he retreats toward the idols without suspecting the danger he is approaching, the bishop having held back his rattle. The auxiliary repeats a last time.*] Eremo! [*And roars.*] Murderer!

The idols tumble down. LAQUEDEEM, *attacked by* EREMO, *lets his ax fall. Merciless standing struggle. The two of them rattle in their throats. The pair roll on the ground, then struggle kneeling, without letting go of each other. Hubbub and shouts in the corridors. Someone comes running. The door on the left is shaken. Voices hoot, "Monsignor! Monsignor!"* CARNIBOS *comes in through the exit, discovers the fight, shouts, "Murder," and disappears.*

The fight goes on, the pair struggling like stevedores. For a second they disentangle themselves, then, head down, they rush toward each other. LAQUEDEEM *collapses under the impact but escapes on all fours.* EREMO *has picked up the ax. The door on the left has given, and the priests have come in. Flattened against the walls, they stand paralyzed with terror at what they see.* LAQUEDEEM, *who has half raised himself, bellows woefully. And the bishop, his rattle transformed into a kind of fiendish laugh, comes toward him fiercely, brandishing the ax.*

But while the last stage of the fight has been going on, REAL-TREMBLOR *has come back through the exit, violently dragging along* VENERANDA, *the old servant. Pushing her by the shoulders, he catapults her into the middle of the drama. And all of a sudden, the drama stands still in space, just as the justiciary ax stands still in the air. Silence has fallen in the same way the thunderbolt fell—very fatefully. And in the silence, the emptiness rather, in which nothing breathes—even the crowd and the storm holding their peace—the old woman is seen hopping toward the bishop and yelping in his face.*

Veneranda. What are you doing? [*The bishop lowers his arm and the ax, which* VENERANDA *snatches from him and lays down. Then.*] Why have you come back from the dead? [*The bishop, who has lost his stiffness and some of his height, has bent humbly toward the old woman, and he speaks. Nothing comes from his mouth, but he speaks, like a dumb man swollen up with burning words. He points to the back of his throat.*] Kneel down! [*The bishop slips to his knees, his head thrown back. The servant thrusts her fingers into his mouth, then takes them out.*] Spit out what was tormenting you! . . . [*The bishop has a spasm and spits out something, at which he gazes in amazement for a moment, on the floor.* VENERANDA *is already helping him to get up.*] Come along, John! . . . [*The bishop is on his feet.*] Come and die! . . . [*And the bishop is no more than a tottering old man whom* VENERANDA *pushes to the mortuary chamber. When he gets to the steps, a renewal of strength draws the bishop up again, and he turns toward the priests and* LAQUEDEEM, *who is still on his knees as though felled. The old woman has anticipated this undertow of hatred and commands.*]

Forgive them [*the bishop stiffens*] . . . if you want your forgiveness! . . . [*Shrunken and with his face suddenly changed, the bishop raises his right hand, with fist clenched, in a last pugnacious gesture. The old woman insists, hissing.*] Absolve them! . . . [*And as the gesture persists, she slaps the bishop full in his face.*] Your mother is ordering you to do it! . . . [*The fist opens at last, and becomes a hand. With his eyes closed, the bishop blesses the bowed heads, very slowly, and as though reluctantly. His arm falls again. And, turning his back on the assembly, supported by* VENERANDA, *he goes into the mortuary chamber. It seems that he hides his face before disappearing.* VENERANDA *is still heard speaking as she closes the double door again.*] Stretch yourself out, my child! And die amid your tears!

Silence hovers. LAQUEDEEM *has gotten up and goes and stands calmly at the gap in the double door. He gazes on the interior. As though crushed by the blessing received, none of the priests moves, except that* SODOMATI *slips hypocritically to the place where the bishop knelt and picks up what he spat on the ground. He stands examining "it" in the hollow of his hand. The auxiliary has turned around and comes back.*

Simon Laquedeem. The dead man is dead! [*Pause.*] Jan in Eremo, Bishop of Lapideopolis, is dead by his true and violent death, dead, twice dead, thoroughly dead! [*An immense flash of lightning, like a dawn—and there is no more thunder and lightning. The crowd has begun muttering again, but without anger, and sorrowfully. Knells come from nearby towers.* LAQUEDEEM *has gone up to the nuncio's secretary and seizes him by the wrist.*] The host?

Sodomati. Take it: you consecrated it. . . .

The other priests have begun to talk confusedly. LAQUE-DEEM *addresses them.*

Simon Laquedeem. Who wants to take communion?

REAL-TREMBLOR *indicates* VENERANDA, *who is slipping through the slightly open door and moving off to the left.*

Real-Tremblor. She does!

Simon Laquedeem [*who in three strides has seized the old servant, and grips her left arm*]. You! Rejoin in eternity him to whom you gave birth. . . .

Veneranda. Och God!

Simon Laquedeem [who has pushed the host into the old woman's mouth. He murmurs the consecratory words, of which the only ones heard are:—] Corpus . . . custodat . . . [And he releases VENERANDA. *The servant takes one or two steps toward the exit, slides down the wall, and dies.]*

Sodomati. Amen. This man will go a long way. . . .

Simon Laquedeem. To the grave, dearest! . . . Listen to that! The rabble are in the building! *[They listen. An uproar in the corridors. Shouting.]* The butchers! *[The priests fall back toward the right.* LAQUEDEEM, *in the center of the room, does not retreat.]* Rely on me, clericity!

The uproar has stopped. A great blow on the door at the left. A red light floods the room. And a colossus, bald, torso bare, with sheathed cutlasses at his leather breeches, comes forward. Nine other giants enter in his wake, some of them carrying torches. They form a group on the left and wait. They are THE BUTCHERS *with their* MASTER, *who goes gravely toward the auxiliary.*

The Master of the Butchers. Waar ligt Jan-men-Kloote?

LAQUEDEEM *does not answer, pretending not to understand the language of the people, and looking* THE MASTER *firmly in the eye.* THE MASTER *appears to ponder, then unhurriedly lays hold of one end of the table, says, "Hop!" and turns it over, with all it bears. During the crash, several priests have cried out. Then,* THE MASTER *comes back to the auxiliary and unsheathes one of his cutlasses, passing it under his nose and repeating.*

The Master of the Butchers. Waar ligt Jan-men-Kloote?

This time, LAQUEDEEM *points his forefinger toward the mortuary chamber. At a signal from* THE MASTER, *four butchers separate from the rest and go into the chamber. The light of the candles floods the room. After a moment, the four return, carrying the couch on which lie the bishop's remains, dressed in priestly adornments. The four stop near* THE MASTER *with their burden. The auxiliary has begun to pray in a low voice.*

*Simon Laquedeem. Chorus angelorum te suscipiat et
eum Lazara quondam. . . .*

*The Master of the Butchers [interrupting him]. Bakkes
toe! [And he gives another signal.]*

The convoy goes out. THE BUTCHERS *follow the corpse,
but moving backward, with their* MASTER, *who does not
cease to watch the auxiliary, last.*

No one stirs when THE BUTCHERS *have gone. One guesses
that the convoy is leaving the palace, for the crowd gives
a final howl—of triumph—that is prolonged and becomes
a kind of endless lamentation that will continue to get
more distant. And the great bells, countless in number,
will start ringing in the towers. Night has finally fallen.
Alone in the middle of the room,* SIMON LAQUEDEEM *has
put his hands on his stomach. He laughs derisively.*

Simon Laquedeem. These obsequies. . . . Ho, ho! . . .
You'll see! . . . When they invest the cathedral, they will
quickly come seeking us! . . . Only the Church can bury.
. . . [*Pause. Suddenly the auxiliary bends at the knees and
staggers.*] Aah . . . aah!

Real-Tremblor [rushing to hold LAQUEDEEM *up*]. Monsignor! . . . Your bowels?

Simon Laquedeem [pushing REAL-TREMBLOR *away*].
Damnation! . . . [*The priests have come forward and
make a circle—the auxiliary writhes on the spot.*] Aah
. . . aah! . . . [*A long shudder shakes him.*]

Krakenbus. Is he going to die?

Sodomati. In that case, I believe in God!

But LAQUEDEEM, *who had just lost his balance, draws himself up again to his full height.*

Simon Laquedeem. Deliverance!

Krakenbus. Deliverance! The corpse is outside. . . .

Carnibos. The smell remains. Ugh! [*He holds his nose.*]

Simon Laquedeem. The odor of Death!

Sodomati. Do you think so?

CARNIBOS *disappears at the back.*

Simon Laquedeem. True, it doesn't smell nice! . . . The
odor of Death, I say! The dead stink.

Real-Tremblor. The living too.

Simon Laquedeem. True, true . . . they stink! . . .
[*He gives a fat laugh.*]

CARNIBOS *comes back swinging a smoking censer.*

Simon Laquedeem. Fine! Incense! . . . Some incense!
. . . A lot of incense!
Carnibos [*swinging the censer majestically*]. I'm censing!
Simon Laquedeem. Open the balcony! What d'you say,
Pikkedoncker?
Dom Pikkedoncker. Dung!

Laughter cascades. The priests sniff each other like dogs.

Simon Laquedeem. Dung? Who?
Dom Pikkedoncker. Not me! Him! . . . And you, Monsignor! . . . Dung!

*Panic laughter breaks out, and this hilarity is accompanied
by digs in the ribs and monkeylike gesticulations. Seized
by frantic joy, the priests jump about comically in the
clouds of incense, repeating all the time, "Dung! . . .
Dung!"*

Simon Laquedeem [*thundering*]. The pigs! . . .
They've filled their cassocks with dung!

*He crouches—gown tucked up—his rabbinical face ex-
pressing demoniac bliss—while the curtain comes slowly
down on these chronicles of Hell.*

LORD HALEWYN
(*Sire Halewijn*)

A Play in Fourteen Scenes
(1934)

Translated by GERARD HOPKINS

INTRODUCTORY NOTE

[Halewyn] is a medieval character whose "geste" could have Frankish or perhaps even Eastern origins: it could equally well have been brought back from Syria by the Crusaders; but in any case it constitutes the oldest known Flemish Song—the most dramatic as well.

[The moral of *Lord Halewyn*] For you, that Virtue is rewarded. For me, that the most obvious lever of heroism is funk.

From *The Ostend Interviews*

CHARACTERS

LORD HALEWYN

EDWIGGHA, *Halewyn's mother*

GRIFFONS
HYLEJOCK
ULFORD
WOLVENTAND
} *Halewyn's men-at-arms*

PURMELENDE, *Countess of Ostrelande*

BARBARA, *her waiting maid*

THE DUKE OF OSTRELANDE

THE DUCHESS OF OSTRELANDE

KAROLE, *Count of Ostrelande*
GODFRUND, *captain of the Castle of Ostrelande*
IWYN, *a soldier*

THE FORESTER

HIS WIFE

THE WATCHMAN

THE VASSALS OF OSTRELANDE

SCENE—In the Flanders plain, not far from the German Ocean. The season is Winter; the time, the Middle Ages.

LORD HALEWYN

Scene I—*On the walls of the Castle of Ostrelande.*

A Shrill Voice. Halt! Who goes there!
A Deep Voice. Who holds the watch?
A Shrill Voice. Flanders of the Black Lion!
A Deep Voice. God and the Lion defend us!
A Shrill Voice. And the free realm of Ostrelande!

Silence. Captain Godfrund *enters from the left, the
      soldier* Iwyn *from the right.*

Godfrund. Come hither, soldier; are you cold?
Iwyn. No, Captain. The wind has dropped. Look at the
tower: the flag no longer flaps.
Godfrund. The air is mild; there's snow on the way.
The light is failing, and the plain grows dark. Raise your
trumpet, take a breath, and blow.
Iwyn. That I will, Captain.
Godfrund. To the west. [*The soldier sounds a plaintive
note.*] No one is listening; no one hears your trumpet
sounding toward the dusk. But sound it must. Useless to
blow your summons, north and south, and east and west.
Who should take notice of it here, on this plain, where
no men close their eyes except in death. Still, that's how
things have been done here, since time immemorial. . . .
[*He laughs as with a familiar.*] Well, young soldier, this
sentry duty's tough, eh, here on the ramparts?
Iwyn. Tougher for the spirit, Captain, than the body—
this silence and the sturdy castle keep where nothing stirs.
'Tis like keeping guard over a sepulcher! And all the
stretch of plain where nothing moves, and the great sweep
of sky. Though, come to think of it, the sky's not still—
clouds driving in from the sea . . . and the birds screech-
ing. . . . But apart from clouds and birds, there's nothing
moving. The silence here is heavier than my armor.
Godfrund. One gets used to it. When you are old, and
the winds have worn you thin, you will have lost your
tongue and any wish to speak. You'll have come to the

279

end of speech. But what's the odds? You've got your brazen trumpet. They say we Flanders folk are taciturn, Iwyn, but that's because there's nothing much to talk about, living the way we do. [*He laughs.*] . . . You're ordered to sound your trumpet, lest you fall asleep at your post.

Iwyn. No, Captain, no! I blew, and look—those yellow lights!

Godfrund. A few lamps in the village.

Iwyn. And in the castle yard a window blazing!

Godfrund. That is the old Duke's room, the Duke of Ostrelande, our master.

Iwyn. See, there's another!

Godfrund. And that, his lady's, our pious Duchess.

Iwyn. And there, a third. . . .

Godfrund. That is Count Karol's, heir to Ostrelande.

Iwyn. And there, in the keep, that glow of colored glass?

Godfrund. The room of Purmelende, our young Countess. [*Silence.*] . . . Dreaming, soldier? That keep, those colored panes, have set you dreaming, eh? [*Silence.*] Have you ever yet had sight of her, of our young Countess of Ostrelande? [*Silence.*] She is white of skin and golden-haired, slim as a lily, as a stalk of golden wheat. But violent, too! A young savage. . . . If ever you hear upon the bridge the thundering hooves of a high-mettled horse, lean over the battlements and watch the road. You'll see her then, our young Countess, hair in the wind, and riding like one possessed. [*Silence.*] Her age is sixteen years, her eyes are violet-hued . . . [*Silence.*] But I was forgetting . . . As soon as the first flakes of snow begin to fall—if snow it does—then raise your trumpet and blow three times, but quietly.

Iwyn. I will blow.

Godfrund. That is the wish of our young mistress.

Iwyn. A strange wish!

Godfrund. A strange girl! [*Silence.*]

Iwyn. Out there, Captain, look! Low down toward the north, that emerald gleam?

Godfrund. I know.

Iwyn. Is it a tower above the sea, bearing a beacon light for sailors?

Godfrund. It is a castle light.

Iwyn. What castle?

Godfrund. Are you a native of this country? No? Well, you will learn quite soon enough what that castle is, and what lord lives in it!

Iwyn. An old soldier like you must have seen many things.

Godfrund. Many, indeed—and from them has come much sorrow. [*Silence.*] Soldier? Why are you staring at that flame which flickers, northward . . . [*A long silence.*] Soldier? Why are you looking at the glowing window in the keep?

Iwyn. I ask your pardon, Captain. I was thinking that the green light far away, and this yellow one nearby, are looking at one another across the plain.

Godfrund. No, they can see each other, but they are not looking. [*Silence.*] Loneliness is playing tricks with you. Soon, you too will have no eyelids left! So, shake yourself! It has begun to snow. Sound your trumpet greeting to the snow. Those are the orders!

The trumpet sounds quietly, three times.

SCENE II—*A cellar in* HALEWYN'S *castle.*

HALEWYN [*singing*].
> White snow and scarlet blood,
> Maidens' blood and Angels' snow,
> At my singing, snow, drip blood.
> Love and die—you maids of snow. . . .

Voice of Edwiggha. Halewyn!

Halewyn. Cry, Mother mine, cry to your son, for he can hear you. Find him, if your instinct leads you truly. Holla! . . . Do you know the way to this deep cavern paved with bones? You will see that in this buried spot there is a splendor in the darkness! . . . Holla, good Mother! . . . Could you but see what work my hands are at, you'd dash your brains out on the steps! . . . [*He sings.*]
> Come from the woods, my darling wolves . . .

[*He speaks.*] O mirror, magic mirror, no light gleams in you. Now seven times have I commanded you to show the image that obsesses me. Mirror, give it me. In the name of the blighted archangels, I command you! Show me the image! Show it to me!

Voice of Edwiggha. Halewyn! . . . Halewyn!

Halewyn [*singing*].

Little maidens come to me . . .

[*He speaks.*] The gulfs of darkness open! The mirror is obedient to my voice! Now it is growing clearer. . . . It has the color of ashes! . . . Satan, be praised! . . . I see a country stretching to infinity, infinity. . . . It is snowing in the mirror, in the mirror's infinite depths. . . . It is a country of innocence, pure, so pure. . . . I will leap into this lying mirror and eat the snow. . . . Ho! . . . Mirror I will break you like a baleful star if you do not show her to me, show her coming to me over the snowbound plain!

Voice of Edwiggha. Halewyn! . . . Halewyn! . . . Halewyn!

Halewyn. May your belly burst asunder and your bowels gush out and knot themselves about your throat, old screech owl! What need have men like me of mothers? Come on, come on, tear a way through this door of iron with teeth and nails. . . . Come, and you shall see your son in ecstasy unspeakable. . . . [*He sings.*]

There is no more frost nor cold. . . .

[*He speaks.*] O magic mirror, you grow pale, pale as a swan at sight of a nymph! Your snows are troubled. Two lamps draw close, or are they wandering stars? No, two violet eyes that lay a sheet of blue across the snow. It is she, it is you, your gaze caught in a snare. . . . Come nearer, eyes, drawn by my finger to the mirror's surface. Let me plunge into your violet depths! [*He raves.*] Get ye gone, good spirits! She of the violet eyes, she of the spellbound eyes will come to me through snow. . . . Aid her, Satan. . . . She will come [*with a sob*] and she will love me. . . . [*He sings harshly.*]

Ecstasy I give, and with it, terror. . . .

Voice of Edwiggha. Halewyn . . . where are you hiding?

Halewyn. I am here, old fool. You will not enter, for he whom you seek is not he who answers you. My face glows with the phosphorescent light of rotting wood!

Voice of Edwiggha. Open the door! I know that you are at some evil work. . . .

Halewyn. Evil, in truth, and yet, despairingly, since evil's not, as good is, limitless. Since you have smelled me out, I'll open to you. Old nettle eater, you shall know all. [*The hinges creak.*] . . . Welcome to this place of darkness!

Enter EDWIGGHA.

Edwiggha. Halewyn, what are you about, here in this crypt, that needs such darkness? No, do not speak, for what you do is evil. What seek you in that mirror? No, do not speak! I can no longer recognize you!—your face is livid and your hands are claws that clutch and clutch at nothing. Your eyes are the eyes of the damned. I can see that you are in torment. What man alive could hope for happiness in such a place of darkness. Do not Christ's five wounds bleed for you?

Halewyn. I want no pity from you, nor good counsel! —nor yet to hear, in this place, the name of Christ! What do you want?

Edwiggha. To tell you of my dread. You are setting out again. The horses are all saddled; the men-at-arms have had their wine. You will go again as you have gone before. Halewyn, do not go. This time there will be no return for you.

Halewyn. Go I will.

Edwiggha. Alas! Not iron doors nor walls of stone will keep you back, nor death nor damnation will stay your feet. For days now you have been singing. Your mouth is swelled with song.

Halewyn. Who was it put that song into my mouth?

Edwiggha. Whom go you out to seek in this harsh plain—to seek and not to find?

Halewyn. Love, my dear dam!

Edwiggha. Do not blaspheme!

Halewyn. Lechery, then—in which you once conceived me! . . . [*He laughs.*] Better by far, dear Mother, to have tossed me in the privy when I was born!

Edwiggha. Could I have known to what I was giving life?

Halewyn. Give me what you have never given yet— your blessing.

Edwiggha. I cannot!

Halewyn. Then die! [*He strikes her: she falls.*] Lie there you broken puppet, old witch without a broomstick! . . . Weep your briny tears. . . . I am going now. . . . Born of hatred, I will track down love!

Edwiggha. You will not come back!

Halewyn. I shall not come back if I find love. Now for this one last time I go, and as I go, I sing. As for this

mirror here, I shatter it. [*He breaks the mirror.*] Good-by,
Mother. Curse me since you know not how to bless. Let
go of my knees! Listen to me. When I was a child you
did not teach me God. Now that I am a man I have found
the devil. I am the devil's bondslave. Holla! bodyguard!
[*He goes out singing.*]

> White snow and scarlet blood
> Maidens' blood and Angels' snow . . .

Edwiggha. Halewyn!—murderer!

Voice of Halewyn.

> At my singing, snow, drip blood. . . .
> [*His voice dies away in the distance.*]
> Love and die, you maids of snow. . . .

A horn sounds.

SCENE III—*On the walls of the Castle of Ostrelande.*

A SHRILL VOICE. Halt! Who goes there!
A Deep Voice. Who holds the watch?
A Shrill Voice. Flanders of the Black Lion!
A Deep Voice. God and the Lion defend us!
A Shrill Voice. And the free realm of Ostrelande!

*Silence. The captain enters from the left, the soldier from
the right.*

Godfrund. How did you spend your hour, soldier?
Iwyn. I lit the lanterns.
Godfrund. Did you notice nothing?
Iwyn. The slow falling of the snow.
Godfrund. And nothing else?
Iwyn. I heard the mournful barking of the mastiffs.
Godfrund. And then?
Iwyn. A concert of cawing crows.
Godfrund. And was that all?
Iwyn. No, there was hunting in the plain. I heard the
wailing of the horns.
Godfrund. From which direction?
Iwyn. Northward from here.
Godfrund [*bellowing*]. By the Cross and the Lance, by
the Nails and the Sponge!
Iwyn. Should I sound the alarm, Captain?
Godfrund. Sound for the snow, sound for the coming
on of night, sound for storms, and sound for comets,
sound when you are bored, but now do not sound. Sound

not for misfortune, since misfortune sounds its own alarm: misfortune sounds upon the hunting horn.

A horn is heard in the distance.

Iwyn. Captain, you're shaking. Is it war?

Godfrund. If only it meant dying for our master! Soldier, I have been a fighting man for many years, and my heart is colder than these rampart stones. But when I hear a horn toward the north, then my heart splits. . . . You do not understand? . . . If you could hear what's whispered in the peasant huts when the horn sounds from the north; if only you could . . .

A distant call of trumpets.

SCENE IV—*The interior of* THE FORESTER's *hut. A dog growls.*

THE FORESTER's WIFE. Stop it, you brute! Lie down, you snarling beast! It's only your master, and my man, coming from the forest. Bark, old russet-pate, for the big woodman, there at the door with his load of snow.

Enter THE FORESTER

The Forester. A fair load, and all sizable logs. Evening, old lady. Snowing, it is, till naught's to see but white. A hard winter sets dry wood burning. Dry, hard weather suits me proper. Down, lad, down!—what, snarling?

His Wife. Yes, husband, and won't give over, neither. He can hear . . .

The Forester. And so can I. . . . Ever since the snow set in, there's been a running and a leaping of the horns. The gentry at their sport, but Od's blood—what game can they be after?

His Wife. When the horns stop there'll be a sound of singing. . . . God does naught to bring that fiend to justice. . . .

The Forester. God, say you! Why God's afeared of that there devil. Why don't the Count of Flanders, who's not perched near so high, come out and round up this unruly vassal. . . . I've known men sawed in two with a notched plank for less. Yet this singer out of Hell . . .

His Wife. First, Magdaléna, then black-haired Godeliva, then Sabine of curly head . . . four, five, six, seven . . . all of 'em buxom, gentle, modest lasses. . . .

The Forester. And mad to boot. . . . What can we do, save pray for their souls, seven times over!

His Wife. Pray? . . . What good does praying do their mothers! Why don't you men . . .

The Forester. We men's done what we could with scythes and hatchets. What use be they against the devil? There was but a hundred of us fit to carry arms in all the realm of Ostrelande. As to the castle garrison—a few old men and varlets gray atop. One Easter Day our Duke's own son set out alone to fight this murderer of our girls. He warn't laid out dead, to be sure, but ever since, he's been stretched in his room—a poor broken thing. . . . Listen! [*Silence. The dog growls.*] . . . There's the old watchman with his beetle crushers, making his rounds. . . . Hark!

Voice of the Watchman [*singing*].

> If you have girls of age to love,
> Then double-lock them in their rooms.

The Forester. Well cried! . . . But there baint no girls here, old friend, nor under all the roofs of Ostrelande. None of them left. There's been a mort too much singing here for all of us. . . . He may well sing, that roisterer. . . . I've seen them girls in the forest, adangling from the branches like a row of birds with their necks wrung. . . . What! Crying, old lady?

His Wife. 'Tis a song of death and misery, and woe to her as hears it. . . . Dear God! Make young maids deaf!

The Forester. But I've just told 'ee that there baint no maidens left, not of that young and silly age.

His Wife. Yes, one there be—and she is fair and golden.

The Forester. Purmelende of Ostrelande? . . . Ho! ho! Thee must be raving!

His Wife. Hark, husband! The horns are drawing near.

The sound of a horn.

SCENE V—*In* PURMELENDE's *bedchamber.*

BARBARA. And down came the snow in a hundred thousand little pieces which all knew one another. And when they reached the ground, they joined together and the snow was nothing but a great spread of woven stuff. And all the land of Flanders was wrapped in a white winding sheet. Is it the snow you long for, Countess? I used to have a sinful longing for those heavy-headed roses which

set the senses swooning with their scent—but that was
when longings were proper to my age. . . . The snow
smells of nothing. I know that the cravings of a young
and lovely daughter of the manor are different from those
of an old serving-woman such as I have become. But I
was once sixteen, as you are now. . . .

Purmelende. Spin your wool, and leave the talking to
your wheel.

Barbara. Have I said something that I should not say?
Then I'll stay mum, though that's not easy. How you do
love the silence—it makes your large eyes larger. Well, if
I may not talk, I'll sing. [*She sings.*]

> Oh, he is gone into the East
> All with his cross and banner-o
> For to fight his fill in the Holy Land
> With a broken heart behind him-o!

[*She cries.*] Ouf! Why do you clap your hand upon my
mouth?

Purmelende. To keep that stupid nonsense in. Do you
not know some song of love?

Barbara. Of love? Such songs are sinful. How all your
face does crinkle when you speak that word! Do you
know what love is?

Purmelende. Those who know can never put their
knowledge into words, and have, as I have, smooth or
tortured faces. I know that it is fatal and all-powerful,
that it is mighty as the sea which cannot tell its thoughts
but drags you down or casts you up. [*She laughs.*] You
know nothing, old though you are. What answer will you
make if I ask why I long so fiercely for the snow—why
body and soul are so closely locked in battle that I am all
exhausted? Why it is that I pass from frantic joy to
leadenlike despair. Why I am hungry for the grass and
thirsty for the rain. Why I faint at sight of a knife's edge,
yet long to see the beaded blood— Answer the girl who
asks you. . . .

Barbara. You are sick, and should see a priest.

Purmelende. Prayers and philters are of no avail! Where
—if sick I am—shall I find a cure? In the air, were I light
as a bird, in the depths of the earth if I could burrow; in
water which makes the body swell, or in fire that turns
it into ashes. . . . Am I evilly bewitched? No, for I feel
that demons are as far from me as angels. . . .

Barbara. Some spell is on you, that's for sure.

Purmelende. Then it is on creation, too, but the secrets of the spell are all forgot. . . . [*Silence.*] I hoped that the quiet snow would bring me peace, but its touch is fire! I have hung a relic round my neck, but all in vain.

Barbara. You are no longer beautiful, you have grown ugly! You must restrain yourself!

Purmelende [*raving*]. And so . . . and so . . . Rather than stamp my foot upon the flags, rather than tear my sheets or break my crucifix, I think it would be better far to throw all to the winds, and flee, to change into a beast and run about the world, stark mad, howling with pleasure and with fear, a beast forspent, whose throat, when it can run no longer, the hunter's knife will cut and let out the warm blood. . . .

Barbara. She is turning mad!

Purmelende. Yes, mad . . . and well I know it! Put out the torch. You will forget the words my lips let fall.

Barbara. What was it that you spoke?

Purmelende. Words. . . . See, I am calm again. We must be silent now, and listen. Do not fear, old dame. This morning I was still a girl. At dusk I saw the falling snow; it had the look of blood. And now, tonight, I am a woman. [*Silence.*] I hear the signal!

Barbara. The horn?

Purmelende. It was sounding for me!

Barbara. Oh, heavenly Saviour! Do you know who blows it?

Purmelende. What do I care! This is the stars' doing! I think that he is drawing near the castle. But, maybe, it is his wish that I shall go to him.

Barbara. Jesus! Bar the doors!

Purmelende. See, I grasp your wrists. Moan if you will, or pray. The moon is up, and gazing down on me. Do you hear nothing?

Barbara. The beating of a heart, of *yours!*

Purmelende. Nothing but my heart?

The horn sounds again.

Barbara. Nothing—I swear it!

Purmelende [*laughing*]. Nothing? The moon's puffed out his cheeks and red-faced blows upon the horn. . . . [*Peremptorily.*] Go to the great chest and bring my gown of wool, my copper girdle, and my diadem. Also the flask of perfume.

Barbara. Now, in this dead of night?

Purmelende. How should I know that it is night? I can see the plain to where it meets the ocean.

Barbara. But why these festal clothes?

Purmelende. Who knows? I may be going to a feast. But first I must see my father, my mother, and my brother. Give me the key that hangs there at your side.

Barbara. Not that one, no!

Purmelende. Then I will take it! [*The horn sounds a rapid call.*] I hear. [*In a low voice.*] I can no longer laugh or cry, but move forward like a sleepwalker on a tight-rope. Useless now trying to find, within the mirror, what I am, for it is filled with snow.

Barbara. If you be Purmelende, signed with the cross, then pray to Heaven: there is yet time.

Purmelende. I am fast bound in the moon's rays. She draws me to her. She is the goddess who sways us women.

SCENE VI—*In the nightbound plain. A sound of horns and galloping horses.*

HALEWYN. Halt! Dismount. You, Griffons, hold the bridles. Gather round, the four of you, and answer. Who is your master?

All. You, Halewyn!

Halewyn. What dangers would you face for Halewyn?

Hylejock. The most bitter death!

Ulford. The most savage god!

Wolventand. The foulest fiend!

Halewyn. My thanks. And you, Griffons?

Griffons. Sir, a sharp sword is better than big words!

Halewyn. Spoken like soldiers! . . . In truth, you make two fine pairs of cutthroats. Now listen. Here we are at the limits of my land. The snow lies deep, and up above there shines a huge and evil moon. Look up in wonder at that skyey beacon whose dead radiance sets a halo round your murderers' jowls. It will be midnight in the moon if I read its dial aright. . . . One can see a great distance. I see . . . Ulford, can you see too, and if so, what?

Ulford. Northward, your castle, sir, all bristles like a porcupine.

Halewyn. And you, Wolventand—even though your eyes are at mutual war.

Wolventand. Sir, to the left, the marshy forest land,

where there's nothing but thin woodland grass and rotting birds.

Halewyn. And you, Hylejock of the festering, fly-bitten eyes?

Hylejock. Stap me! The topmost towers of Ostrelande!

Halewyn. And you, Griffons, with your screech owl's beak—what do *you* see, old hairy ruffian?

Griffons. Wonders, fine sir! First, Halewyn in person, dry enough to set a high branch creaking. Damme! If I were a Christian I'd not care to meet with him at midnight, in a churchyard! [*The others laugh.*] Next, the moon with scabs upon her face—a nose and a mouth, and holes for eyes. But she hangs moonstruck in the sky, dazed beyond measure—a battered planet. From where she is she can see all that happens, and does not understand a damn thing! Listen, moon! Here's Halewyn's bodyguard will use you as a butt for arrows! . . . I'll take a shot . . .

Halewyn. Stop!

Griffons. Ach! And last, a pretty sight enough—a sturdy tree with rosy rounded fruit, all ripening in the moonshine: fruit overripe and juicy. I'd like a sniff at them! I can count seven fleshy medlars.

Halewyn [*laughing*]. Say clearly what you mean!

Griffons. That wondrous tree is called Lord Halewyn's instrument of justice—in vulgar parlance, a gibbet. Best keep away from it, for all them danglers are coldly virtuous, cold as their feet. Have I said enough?

Halewyn. See, hear, and say nothing, is a profitable maxim. . . . Now listen to what Halewyn has to say. I am about to leave you, my tough old war dogs. You will wait behind this hillock here for my return. When you hear me singing, you will know that I am off toward the south, alone. . . . Later my song will come back, but I shall not be alone. Whom I shall bring beneath the gibbet, and what I shall do in that place of my delight, is not for you to know. Be blind, but not deaf! If, in my moonlight ride, singing and blowing on my horn, I sound three notes of summons, that will mean trouble, or peril from the plain. Then, to horse, and in a dozen bounds. . . .

Griffons. You've said enough, my master. Ours to jump to it at the rallying signal, ours to know nothing of your pleasures!

Halewyn. My pleasures? Have you ever seen me joyous when I come from my solitary hunting? [*Raising his*

voice.] You have your ration of hot wine, all of you.
Drink it down. . . . Where is my horse? . . . Midnight
approaches. . . . Raise your trumpets to your lips, lads,
and, turning your backs, sound, through all the spaces of
the dark, the solemn call of all true followers when their
master rides abroad. . . . Holla! [*The four ruffians turn
their backs and sound.*] . . . And what your parting
words?

All. Holla! . . . Chantaigle! . . . Holla! Halewyn of
the three eagles!

HALEWYN *rides off. His horn sounds.*

Griffons. What is he singing?
Voice of Halewyn [*singing*].
          My gibbet is a sturdy tree
          And rattling chains its burden:
          A tight and choking guerdon
          For her who comes my way. . . .
                    [*The song dies away.*]
          For Halewyn loves only once
          And loves none but the maid.
                    [*Silence.*]

SCENE VII—*In the passages of the Castle of Ostrelande.*

BARBARA. Do not go farther, Countess. The stairs are
treacherous. This castle is a labyrinth. You will meet
nothing but walls, and only one way out. Where is it that
you wish to go? Yes, this is the way down: steps and more
steps, steps without end. Let us pause. Countess, do you
know me? What is happening to us? Sometimes you fall,
and lie more rigid than a statue. Are you sleeping? Now
you move forward like a ghost. Do you know where you
are going? Let us climb again to your chamber.

Purmelende. Raise your lamp. Why has he stopped
singing? Why, having come so close, has he withdrawn?
Do you hear singing, Barbara?

Barbara. Dear God! Who should be singing? . . . Never
have I known so deep a silence. . . .

Voice of Halewyn [*singing in the distance*].
          None have been who could resist
          The magic of my voice. . . .

Purmelende. O joy! He is singing!
Barbara. This silence?
Purmelende. What matter the name you call it by! Lift

up your lamp and chase away our following shadows. Once upon a time there were three doors just here.

Barbara. There still are three.

Purmelende. Behind those doors lived three whom once I loved.

Barbara. They still live on behind those doors, and you still love them, do you not? Your father, your mother, and your brother.

Purmelende. Maybe I love them still; but I cannot now recall their faces. Strike on this first door with the golden knocker.

BARBARA *strikes.*

Voice of the Duke of Ostrelande. Who knocks?

Purmelende. My lord, it is your daughter, Purmelende. She dreams, and in her dream someone is singing in the plain. The song is an imperious summons. What must your daughter do within her dream?

Voice of the Duke. Go to her bed and dream that she is sleeping. I never dream. Good night.

Purmelende. I dream that I do not obey. Much is permitted when the reason slumbers. But is the singer singing as I hear him in my dream?

Voice of Halewyn [*singing*].

You who know not love as yet.
Listen to the sounds afar. . . .

Barbara. Why do you tremble?

Purmelende. That was his voice!

Barbara. It was the sputtering of the lamp. This is a night of terrors. Will you soon wake up?

Purmelende. Move on, and at the second door strike with the silver knocker.

BARBARA *strikes.*

Voice of the Duchess of Ostrelande. Who is it there?

Purmelende. Mother, it is your daughter. She is dreaming, and in her dream she has knocked upon your door. A heart is carved upon your door, and she has struck it. Answer me, Mother. What does one do when one is dreaming as I dream, and hears divinest singing?

Voice of the Duchess. Kneel, join your hands in prayer, for only the song of angels is divine. Sleep, my child, and may the angels fill your dreams with fragrance. . . .

Purmelende. O Mother! Has life taught you no more than that?

Barbara. You are unsteady on your feet. Come, come away to bed.

Purmelende. Be silent! Hold your lamp close to my ear and it will sing.

Voice of Halewyn [*singing*].

> Let your heart be struck with wonder,
> Deck yourself in fine adornments. . . .

Purmelende. Am I beautiful tonight?

Barbara. Your face is drawn and pale.

Purmelende. Strike once again, here at the third door, with the knocker of iron.

BARBARA *strikes.*

Voice of Karol. Is that you, Captain?

Purmelende. My brother, I am deep in dreams. If only you could know how deep. Someone is singing. Shall I hearken to him?

Voice of Karol. Get you to bed! . . . And plunge your heated face in icy water. Go to the devil, if 'tis the devil charming you!

Purmelende. Brother. [*Silence.*] Only I am left to answer my own questions. To each and all their sleep. The dreams they dream are wandering through this castle. Their dreams turn and twist within these passages, and strike against the vaults. My dream seeks a way out. Stop praying, Barbara!

Voice of Halewyn [*singing*].

> Love is what I'll give to you,
> Love, and more besides.
> You shall escape from Time's strong tide—
> Death is what I'll give to you.

Purmelende. So be it: I have understood, I come! It is a cruel song, but I can hearken to no other! Barbara, give me the lamp! [*She takes the lamp and runs away.*]

Barbara [*in the darkness*]. How dark it is, Countess; you should not act like this. Come back! This is ill done! She will fall, she will not come back! Dear God! She has stolen the lamp! Give her Your light, O God! . . . a little of Your light! [*She utters a deep moan.*]

SCENE VIII—*On the walls of the Castle of Ostrelande.*

A SHRILL VOICE. Halt! Who goes there!

A Deep Voice. Who holds the watch?

A Shrill Voice. Flanders . . .

Silence. The captain enters.

Godfrund. Who holds the watch, soldier?

The soldier runs up.

Iwyn. Is that you, Captain? I was on lookout. . . . Suddenly I saw lights in the plain. One of them broke from the others and came leaping nearer, nearer.

Godfrund. Torches?

Iwyn. Yes, at our very feet, there, in the stables. . . .

Godfrund. So? Who would groom horses at this hour? . . . Take your trumpet. . . . [*A dull sound is heard.*] What is that din?

Iwyn. The bridge has been let down across the moat.

A noise of galloping.

Godfrund. Who's that?—that figure all in white? Sound the alarm! Call up the Duke! [*The soldier blows a rapid call, then the ducal summons.*] What are we to do? What answer give? Were we keen-eyed enough? Cease your blowing. If someone's fleeing, let him go. Here is the Duke.

THE DUKE OF OSTRELANDE *enters.*

The Duke. Who holds the watch?

Godfrund. Flanders, my lord. There was a mysterious stillness. Suddenly the bridge was lowered. Someone has fled.

The Duke. Northward, is it not so? Then, let her go, to the world's end! She has betrayed her honor. There shall be no pursuit. . . . Let her go. . . . If your father's voice can reach you still, hear what it says. . . . Flee to the world's end, and beyond! May your horse come back riderless, or bearing only your outraged body!

Godfrund. My lord, is that your final order?

The Duke. Half-mast the flags. There is one soul the less within these walls. [*He moves away.*]

SCENE IX—*The plain. The horn sounds. There is a noise of galloping.*

PURMELENDE. I flee, I flee as though all whom I have loved had driven me with violence from my home. On, Sorrel, on, my horse! The sea is near, and you all flecked with foam, like it. The moon laughs at us. Why do you rear your neck? On, on still farther, on to that flame which frightens you on the horizon there; that furnace into which the two of us shall leap. Fear nothing: hurry! What if the light goes out? What if the horn goes dumb. . . . My guardian angel does not ride with us. On, on to the north, to the singing voices, to the north which is all flame! . . . Should any bar your way, be it my father, an archangel, or God Himself—ride him down! Nothing now exists but that bright fire, which sings. Listen. . . .

Voice of Halewyn [*singing*].
> I will drink up all your blood;
> I will eat your tender heart.
> Hang about my neck, nor start—
> I have love to give for blood. . . .

Purmelende. Where are you hiding, who have love to give? Under the lifeless snow, or in the tattered clouds? Ah! Sing again!

Voice of Halewyn [*singing*].
> White snow and scarlet blood,
> Maidens, answer to my song. . . .

Purmelende. I come to you, a virgin white, but flushed with crimson blood: I answer to your magic song . . . and when I am beside you—what?

Voice of Halewyn [*singing*].
> Love is what you'll seek of me . . .

Purmelende. Love is what I seek . . .

Voice of Halewyn [*singing*].
> And death shall be your portion. . . .

Purmelende. O voice! I make my answer. Love is not what I want, but only to love: it is not death I want, but only to die of loving. I ask for nothing, and I give you all. Come to me, be you man or blazing fire! No, I must go to you! . . . Bravely, dear Sorrel, on . . . on to the fire! . . . May I be burned to ashes and scattered to the four winds, so I be only fire, like you, and like you consumed in one living pyre. . . . Hurry! The flames are leaping. . . . A living body stands within the blaze, and, living, burns. . . . It is he! . . . On, on! [*She rides off at a gallop.* HALEWYN's *horn sounds a note of triumph.*]

SCENE X—*A room in the Castle of Ostrelande.*

A VOICE FROM OUTSIDE. Halt!
Another Voice. Who holds the watch?

The First Voice. Flanders of the Black Lion. . . .
The Second Voice. God and the Lion defend us!
The First Voice. And the free realm of Ostrelande. . . .

Silence.

The Duchess. God be our shield, and our poor daughter's, too!
The Duke. I forbid you to speak of her—even to think of her. She has gone to meet her fate. Not a tear will I shed: so are we all who bear the name of Ostrelande.
The Duchess. I am a mother; that is my only name.
The Duke. The women of our house do not complain nor weep.
The Duchess. Oh! Hard of heart!
The Duke. That hardness made our Flanders great and glorious!
The Duchess. What have I left if I may neither weep nor make complaint?
The Duke. Pray for the soul of her who is dead.
The Duchess. My daughter is not dead; instinct tells me so.
The Duke. I bid you all the same, recite the Office of the Dead.

Silence.

A Voice from Outside. . . . and the Lion defend us.
Another Voice. . . . the free realm of Ostrelande.
The Duke. Time has blunted the claws and broken the back of that symbolic lion we brought back out of the Holy Land. His mane is turning white. We are but ancient lions and can do nothing now but roar at the hovering hawk.
The Duchess. Dear husband, I can see the tears running from your eyes.
The Duke. That is most false!
The Duchess. Forgive me, but I thought I saw . . .
The Duke. I say I am not weeping. Those of Ostrelande never weep. [THE DUKE *turns away*.]

Silence.

A Voice from Outside. Halt!
Another Voice. Who holds the watch?
The First Voice. Flanders of the Black Lion.

SCENE XI—*In the plain.*

GRIFFONS. Croak! . . . Croak! Up, mates, and leave your beds of snow. Come listen, here's good luck. . . . Croak!

Ulford. I heard the crows.

Griffons. Up with you all, that crow was me. . . . Jump to it, mates. The moon is setting—'tis a scurvy sight. No heavier gloom will hang above this plain—not even on the day of Antichrist!

Hylejock. And what of Halewyn? Are we to wait for him much longer?

Griffons. I am a crow and not a soothsayer! But this I tell you—the snow's not dimmed my sight, and you can take my word, our master's not yet started on his fun, or else he hasn't finished. By my billet in Hell I swear there's no new trophy on the gibbet, or, more strictly speaking, lads, there's no fresh joint on our lord the butcher's hook!

Wolventand. Wait! . . . Them was the orders. No flourish on the horn?

Griffons. Nothing! Since midnight there has been no music but your drone of snores, and they gave me a proper fright! Croak! Croak!

Ulford. Hey! Stop it, you! We must find Halewyn. Over to the gibbet, fast as you can. If our master is not there, where in the world can he be?

Griffons. I'll go—old crow will bring you news. [*He goes out.*]

Silence.

Wolventand. Don't seem the night'll ever end—what a job!

Ulford. All jobs are good as bring good money.

Hylejock. I'd plump for war—there's better pickings!

Ulford. Better pickings, but not a better prince.

A cry in the distance.

Wolventand. Listen, boys! Old crow's acroaking!

Another cry, closer at hand.

Ulford. Sounds bad. . . . Saddle and mount!

GRIFFONS *enters.*

Griffons. Back to the castle. . . . Halewyn . . .

Ulford. Seen him?
Wolventand. What'd he say?
Griffons. Nothing. . . .
Hylejock. He coming?
Griffons. No.
Ulford. What's up?
Griffons. To the castle, quick! There's danger here. God's hand has struck!

They leap on their horses and make off.

SCENE XII—*In the plain.*

VOICE OF EDWIGGHA. Halewyn! . . . Halewyn!
Echo. Halewyn? . . . Halewyn?
Voice of Edwiggha. Halewyn! . . . Halewyn! . . . Halewyn!
Echo. Halewyn? . . . Halewyn? . . . Halewyn?

EDWIGGHA *enters and wanders aimlessly.*

Edwiggha. My son, my son, where are you? I am alone here in the plain, and the fog is getting thicker. Your mother is lost, and is looking everywhere for you, her lost child. . . . Answer me! . . . Where are you, Halewyn?
Echo. Halewyn?
Edwiggha. I would call on God for help, but there is no cross to be found on Halewyn's land. . . . Must I wander like an old stray bitch? . . . The bitter night has hold of me. . . . Where have you been? . . . What have you been doing? . . . I no longer have a son. . . . For the last time I will call your name. . . . Halewyn! . . . Halewyn!

A trumpet blast sounds close at hand.

Echo. Halewyn? Halewyn?

PURMELENDE *enters, riding hard.*

Purmelende. Out of my way!
Edwiggha [*flinging herself at the horse and stopping it*]. I cry you mercy! Tell me, you on horseback, have you seen my son?
Purmelende. Who is your son?
Edwiggha. Halewyn is my son.
Purmelende. Yes, I have seen your son.

Edwiggha. Where is my son?

Purmelende. Your son is here! . . . He is looking at you from my outstretched arm!

Edwiggha [*shrieking*]. Your head! . . . Halewyn! [*She dies.*]

Purmelende [*with a savage laugh*]. Halewyn!

Echo [*laughing*]. Halewyn!

Purmelende. Call him, but he will not hear: his race is ended. On, Sorrel, on! The dawn is breaking. I'll sound the news of our return, and may my trumpet give to the free realm of Ostrelande a joyful waking! [*She sounds her trumpet and rides off.*]

SCENE XIII—*On the walls of the Castle of Ostrelande.*

IWYN. Halt!

Voice of Godfrund. Who holds the watch?

Silence. The captain enters.

Godfrund. We are alert and wakeful. Not a soul this night has closed an eye, and now the winter sun is show-ing in the east. Far better it should never rise again, and this, our realm of Ostrelande, be forever buried in the fog!

Iwyn. Should I sound the dawn call?

Godfrund. Sound, since it is the custom; but stuff something in your trumpet's mouth. . . . [*The soldier blows a muted blast.*] Faith, now! A perfect lamentation! Nothing else, henceforth, shall be heard through all the length and breadth of Ostrelande. . . . [*A horn sounds briskly.*] . . . Ah! Heaven gives me the lie direct! . . . Did you hear that? . . . It came from northward, from the road. . . . Who comes?

Iwyn. A horseman with raised arm, blowing his trum-pet. . . .

Godfrund. Summon up the Duke! [*The soldier sounds a call.*] Who is it rides so early?

Iwyn. A woman!

Godfrund. Sound yet again! . . . She has crossed the castle ditch. The bridge is down. Now can the sun rise and start his daily course! Sound the dawn call!

Iwyn. That I will, Captain. . . . But look there, to the north . . . what is that?

Godfrund. A castle burning . . . but what matter? . . . Sound!

The soldier sounds a gay blast.

SCENE XIV—*The great hall in the Castle of Ostrelande.*
A crowd of vassals.

THE DUKE OF OSTRELANDE *enters, followed by his wife and*
son. A fanfare. The vassals shout a welcome.

THE DUKE. Good my liegemen, I have called you hither
to celebrate a deed which adds one more to the glories
of my house. You, my old comrades in arms, and all you
others, good and faithful dwellers in the realm of Ostrelande, shall be partners in my joy. Great jars of wine
shall pass from hand to hand, but listen first, and give
your thanks to God, our mighty Suzerain. Sing then the
psalm appointed from of old for Saints' days.
   All [*singing*].

> Now laud and honor to our God
> Here and in every place.
>
> A better life on earth we crave
> And honor in the grave
> In Heaven's high Hall
> For God, His love.

   The Duke. O God, our Master: I pray Thee hearken
unto us who once were in Jerusalem for to deliver Thy
Holy Sepulcher. Hear, yet once again, the singing of the
fierce warriors of Flanders, and look down on this our
house and all the Flemish land. Sing, faithful liegemen—
and raise your hunting spears!

All sing.

The First Chorus.	What is the noblest beast?
The Second Chorus.	The Rampant Lion!
The First Chorus.	What does the Lion at the Feast?
The Second Chorus.	Drinks till his headpiece swims!
All.	The deepest drinker's he of the noble mane!

   The Duke. Drink then, in the Lion's name!
   All. Long life to Ostrelande and the Rampant Lion!

All drink. THE DUKE *empties his cup, and calls for silence.*

   The Duke. Time was, my friends, when I was that
valiant lion, but now I am old. Hear now that in my
vaults I housed a young she-lion, not knowing that she

was of the race of famous hunters. You shall see the prey
she has brought home to me. Make way for my daughter!

PURMELENDE *enters.*

The Duke. Purmelende, draw near. In what dream are
you walking? Can you see us? I can see you. You hold
yourself stiff and upright for all you bear a heavy sword,
and something round enveloped in a cloth. Lay down
your burden on this granite slab, and stand here in the
midst, that we may wonder at your beauty which still
shines bright, though you be mortal pale.

The Duchess. My daughter!

The Duke. Be silent, wife!

Karol. My sister!

The Duke. Be silent, son! Keep all of you the most
respectful silence, for a dead man has just been brought
within these walls. Sound, trumpets, welcome for a
funeral! [*The trumpets sound a dirge.*] Will no one ask
whose coming here we celebrate?

Godfrund. In the name of all your vassals, good my
lord, who may this dead man be?

The Duke. I tear away this cloth, this winding sheet. I
take this dead man by the hair and hold him up for all
to see—this dead man dangling from my hand, this head-
piece drained of blood!

All [*shouting*]. Halewyn!

The Duke. Halewyn—the noble killer of young maids!
Heap no insults on this dead man's head. I here declare
this serpent is no more, who had not the heart of a man,
nor the soul of a man, nor a man's spirit. He sought his
happiness in crime, and did not find it. He perished
miserably by this sword, the sword he meant to use,
how dolefully we all can see by the despairing grin upon
his livid lips. Never again will they sing the fatal song.
Answer me, Halewyn, do you repent your crimes?
[*Silence.*] Will you ask pardon of your God and of your
fellow men? [*Silence.*] He does not answer. But you, my
daughter, you will speak and tell us how this singing head
has fallen dumb.

Purmelende. I will speak, Father, yes, I will speak, if you
will give me back the head.

The Duke. No, my child! Your hands are trembling
still. . . .

Purmelende. Give the head, for it is mine since it was I who took it from his body.

The Duke. That is truly said. Take it, and speak of what you did.

Purmelende [*snatching the head and hugging it to her*]. I heard the magic song and fell into a very lucid sleep, where all my feelings were awake and only my will was fast bound in slumber. Like all my sinning sisters I obeyed his voice, and went to him as the bird flies to the trapper's lure. I moved as light as air in a new world where snow shone bright as crystal under the stars. Souls after death must all most surely pass through that winter land. I doubted all creation, and myself. Words and thoughts no longer had a meaning. I passed on, far from the beaten paths, beyond Good and Evil.

The Duke. This is a tangled tale.

Purmelende. He was waiting for me, all ice and fire, and in his face shone a most baleful beauty, like that of a fallen archangel still glowing with the light of Heaven, sweet with its odors, and yet already eloquent of Hell. I knew that I was lost and ran to him, the while his golden-circled mouth sang songs of lust. His face shone with the light of rotting wood, and the sight of it brought tears into my eyes. I saw that he, for all his talk of bliss, was misery incarnate. I sought for tender words of consolation, but none would come. I took his hands, meaning to kiss them humbly.

The Duke. Be brief!

Purmelende. Then my dream was filled with movement. Halewyn, without a word, but breathing hard, drew me beneath the gibbet. I did not struggle; I felt no fear, only a delicious apprehension. I even led the way, and smiled at the bodies of the seven maids, feeling no jealousy. I breathed in the smell of rotting flesh. The moon was slobbering with pleasure.

The Duke. Will you never have done!

Purmelende. I am near the end. . . . Halewyn set his sword upright in the snow, the sword that you see here. He threw aside his cloak, and, with his eyes fast fixed upon me, began to draw his coat of mail over his head. Again and again he spoke through his clenched teeth, saying: "Purmelende of Ostrelande! Purmelende of Ostrelande! . . ."—and I repeated it like a refrain: "Pur-

melende of Ostrelande! Purmelende of Ostrelande." . . .
I had heard that name in my waking life and wondered
to whom it could belong. I could not find an answer: none
of the seven there was called by it. Then, suddenly, I
remembered! That name, my name, sounded in my head,
in the darkness, like a clanging tocsin. I knew then that I
was Purmelende of Ostrelande and broke from my dream,
stung by the cold and borne up by my terror. What
happened then was the mad, the relentless act of Purmelende of Ostrelande. She saw a man bent double, his head
caught in a coat of mail, his arms imprisoned. She saw the
dangling corpses and their hideous grimace. She saw the
sword. Upward it whirled with a hissing sound, and I
saw—for it was I who did the deed—a shrieking head
bounding across the snow. I ran after it and caught it in
mid-air. I wedged it between my knees and filled the
gaping mouth with snow to stifle its blasphemies. And I
said: "Pray to God now, my lord, since you are dying.
. . ." The head still tried to sing, though very quietly.
And, since the snow could not stifle it, I pressed my mouth
to its mouth, and finally they died, both head and song,
together.

The Duke. Enough! The rest we know. Are you still
sleeping? Throw far away that rotting head. Drink up
your wine, heroic girl, you Judith of our day. . . . Cease
looking at that head and look at us, your parents and your
vassals. What else is there you wish to say, now at the
end?

Purmelende [with a terrible shriek]. Halewyn! [*She
falls. There is a wild movement of panic in the hall.*]

The Duchess. My child!

The Duke. Stay where you are, all of you. So young a
heart could ill endure all that. That she should swoon is
natural.

The Duchess. Her heart is shattered!

The Duke. Dead? Is my girl dead? [*Silence.*] . . . Here,
Halewyn, lies your last victim. . . . [*Silence.*] So be it,
then, since she is dead with honor still intact. My friends,
no need to hold me up, leave moaning to the women. I
shall not reel beneath the blow. Turn from that corpse
which holds a severed head clutched to its breast. What's
happened here will be forever unexplained. My friends,
restrain your feelings. . . . I am the Duke of Ostrelande.

Our arms have never known dishonor. Shed no tears, but let the feast proceed. Fill up the goblets. Heralds, sound your trumpets: let all the world know that Death is of our company. On your feet! Drink the toast, and sing! . . . So does the Duke of Ostrelande command!

There is a sound of trumpet blasts and singing.

DRAMABOOKS
(Plays)

When ordering, please use the Standard Book Number consisting of the publisher's prefix, 8090-, plus the five digits following each title. (Note that the numbers given in this list are for paperback editions only. Many of the books are also available in cloth.)

Mermaid Dramabooks

Christopher Marlowe (Tamburlaine the Great, Parts I & II, Doctor Faustus, The Jew of Malta, Edward the Second) (0701–0)

William Congreve (Complete Plays) (0702–9)

Webster and Tourneur (The White Devil, The Duchess of Malfi, The Atheist's Tragedy, The Revenger's Tragedy) (0703–7)

John Ford (The Lover's Melancholy, 'Tis Pity She's a Whore, The Broken Heart, Love's Sacrifice, Perkin Warbeck) (0704–5)

Richard Brinsley Sheridan (The Rivals, St. Patrick's Day, The Duenna, A Trip to Scarborough, The School for Scandal, The Critic) (0705–3)

Camille and Other Plays (Scribe: A Peculiar Position, The Glass of Water; Sardou: A Scrap of Paper; Dumas: Camille; Augier: Olympe's Marriage) (0706–1)

John Dryden (The Conquest of Granada, Parts I & II, Marriage à la Mode, Aureng-Zebe) (0707–X)

Ben Jonson Vol. 1 (Volpone, Epicoene, The Alchemist) (0708–8)

Oliver Goldsmith (The Good Natur'd Man, She Stoops to Conquer, An Essay on the Theatre, A Register of Scotch Marriages) (0709–6)

Jean Anouilh Vol. 1 (Antigone, Eurydice, The Rehearsal, Romeo and Jeannette, The Ermine) (0710–X)

Let's Get a Divorce! and Other Plays (Labiche: A Trip Abroad, and Célimare; Sardou: Let's Get a Divorce!; Courteline: These Cornfields; Feydeau: Keep an Eye on Amélie; Prévert: A United Family; Achard: Essays on Feydeau) (0711–8)

Jean Giraudoux Vol. 1 (Ondine, The Enchanted, The Madwoman of Chaillot, The Apollo of Bellac) (0712–6)

Jean Anouilh Vol. 2 (Restless Heart, Time Remembered, Ardèle, Mademoiselle Colombe, The Lark) (0713–4)

Henrik Ibsen: The Last Plays (Little Eyolf, John Gabriel Borkman, When We Dead Awaken) (0714–2)

Ivan Turgenev (A Month in the Country, A Provincial Lady, A Poor Gentleman) (0715–0)

Jean Racine (Andromache, Britannicus, Berenice, Phaedra, Athaliah) (0717–7)

The Storm and Other Russian Plays (The Storm, The Government Inspector, The Power of Darkness, Uncle Vanya, The Lower Depths) (0718–5)

Michel de Ghelderode: Seven Plays Vol. 1 (The Ostend Interviews, Chronicles of Hell, Barabbas, The Women at the Tomb, Pantagleize, The Blind Men, Three Players and a Play, Lord Halewyn) (0719–3)

Lope de Vega: Five Plays (Peribáñez, Fuenteovejuna, The Dog in the Manger, The Knight from Olmedo, Justice Without Revenge) (0720–7)

Calderón: Four Plays (Secret Vengeance for Secret Insult, Devotion to the Cross, The Mayor of Zalamea, The Phantom Lady) (0721–5)

Jean Cocteau: Five Plays (Orphée, Antigone, Intimate Relations, The Holy Terrors, The Eagle with Two Heads) (0722–3)

Ben Jonson Vol. 2 (Every Man in His Humour, Sejanus, Bartholomew Fair) (0723–1)

Port-Royal and Other Plays (Claudel: Tobias and Sara; Mauriac: Asmodée; Copeau: The Poor Little Man; Montherlant: Port-Royal) (0724–X)

Edwardian Plays (Maugham: Loaves and Fishes; Hankin: The Return of the Prodigal; Shaw: Getting Married; Pinero: Mid-Channel; Granville-Barker: The Madras House) (0725–8)

Georg Büchner: Complete Plays and Prose (0727–4)

Paul Green: Five Plays (Johnny Johnson, In Abraham's Bosom, Hymn to the Rising Sun, The House of Connelly, White Dresses) (0728–2)

François Billetdoux: Two Plays (Tchin-Tchin, Chez Torpe) (0729–0)

Michel de Ghelderode: Seven Plays Vol. 2 (Red Magic, Hop, Signor!, The Death of Doctor Faust, Christopher Columbus, A Night of Pity, Piet Bouteille, Miss Jairus) (0730–4)

Jean Giraudoux Vol. 2 (Siegfried, Amphitryon 38, Electra) (0731–2)

Kelly's Eye and Other Plays by Henry Livings (Kelly's Eye, Big Soft Nellie, There's No Room for You Here for a Start) (0732–0)

Gabriel Marcel: Three Plays (Man of God, Ariadne, Votive Candle) (0733–9)

New American Plays Vol. 1 ed. by Robert W. Corrigan (0734–7)

Elmer Rice: Three Plays (Adding Machine, Street Scene, Dream Girl) (0735-5)
The Day the Whores Came Out to Play Tennis . . . by Arthur Kopit (0736-3)
Platonov by Anton Chekhov (0737-1)
Ugo Betti: Three Plays (The Inquiry, Goat Island, The Gambler) (0738-X)
Jean Anouilh Vol. 3 (Thieves' Carnival, Medea, Cécile, Traveler Without Luggage, Orchestra, Episode in the Life of an Author, Catch As Catch Can) (0739-8)
Max Frisch: Three Plays (Don Juan, The Great Rage of Philip Hotz, When the War Was Over) (0740-1)
New American Plays Vol. 2 ed. by William M. Hoffman (0741-X)
Plays from Black Africa ed. by Fredric M. Litto (0742-8)
Anton Chekhov: Four Plays (The Seagull, Uncle Vanya, The Cherry Orchard, The Three Sisters) (0743-6)
The Silver Foxes Are Dead and Other Plays by Jakov Lind (The Silver Foxes Are Dead, Anna Laub, Hunger, Fear) (0744-4)
New American Plays Vol. 3 ed. by William M. Hoffman (0745-2)
The Modern Spanish Stage: Four Plays, ed. by Marion Holt (The Concert at Saint Ovide, Condemned Squad, The Blindfold, The Boat Without a Fisherman) (0746-0)
Life Is a Dream by Calderón (0747-9)
New American Plays Vol. 4 ed. by William M. Hoffman (0748-7)

THE NEW MERMAIDS

Bussy D'Ambois by George Chapman (1101-8)
The Broken Heart by John Ford (1102-6)
The Duchess of Malfi by John Webster (1103-4)
Doctor Faustus by Christopher Marlowe (1104-2)
The Alchemist by Ben Jonson (1105-0)
The Jew of Malta by Christopher Marlowe (1106-9)
The Revenger's Tragedy by Cyril Tourneur (1107-7)
A Game at Chess by Thomas Middleton (1108-5)
Every Man in His Humour by Ben Jonson (1109-3)
The White Devil by John Webster (1110-7)
Edward the Second by Christopher Marlowe (1111-5)
The Malcontent by John Marston (1112-3)
'Tis Pity She's a Whore by John Ford (1113-1)
Sejanus His Fall by Ben Jonson (1114-X)
Volpone by Ben Jonson (1115-8)
Women Beware Women by Thomas Middleton (1116-6)
Love for Love by William Congreve (1117-4)
The Spanish Tragedy by Thomas Kyd (1118-2)

SPOTLIGHT DRAMABOOKS

The Last Days of Lincoln by Mark Van Doren (1201-4)
Oh Dad, Poor Dad . . . by Arthur Kopit (1202-2)
The Chinese Wall by Max Frisch (1203-0)
Billy Budd by Louis O. Coxe and Robert Chapman (1204-9)
The Firebugs by Max Frisch (1206-5)
Andorra by Max Frisch (1207-3)
Balm in Gilead and Other Plays by Lanford Wilson (1208-1)
Matty and the Moron and Madonna by Herbert Lieberman (1209-X)
The Brig by Kenneth H. Brown (1210-3)
The Cavern by Jean Anouilh (1211-1)
Saved by Edward Bond (1212-X)
Eh? by Henry Livings (1213-8)
The Rimers of Eldritch and Other Plays by Lanford Wilson (1214-6)
In the Matter of J. Robert Oppenheimer by Heinar Kipphardt (1215-4)
Ergo by Jakov Lind (1216-2)
Biography: A Game by Max Frisch (1217-0)
Indians by Arthur Kopit (1218-9)
Narrow Road to the Deep North by Edward Bond (1219-7)
Ornifle by Jean Anouilh (1220-0)
Inquest by Donald Freed (1221-9)
Lemon Sky by Lanford Wilson (1222-7)
The Night Thoreau Spent in Jail by Jerome Laurence and Robert E. Lee (1223-5)

For a complete list of books of criticism and history of the drama, please write to Hill and Wang, 72 Fifth Avenue, New York, New York 10011.